From the Abortion Holocaust . . .

IN 1971 U.S. SUPREME COURT JUSTICE WILLIAM O. DOUGLAS PROPOSED THAT LEGAL PERSONHOOD BE CONFERRED ON A "VALLEY, AN ALPINE MEADOW, A RIVER OR A LAKE" JUST AS IT HAS BEEN BESTOWED ON SHIPS AND CORPORATIONS. *(p. 96)*

In 1936 the **Supreme Court of Germany "refused to recognize Jews** living in Germany as **'persons'** in the **legal sense."** *(p. 95)*

* * * * *

In 1973 the **U.S. Supreme Court** declared that "the word **'person,'** as used in the Fourteenth Amendment, does **not include the unborn."** *(p. 95)*

THE SANCTITY-OF-LIFE ETHIC EMBODIED IN THE HIPPOCRATIC OATH WAS DROPPED FROM USE IN MEDICAL SCHOOLS ONLY TWICE IN MODERN HISTORY: TODAY AND DURING THE TWELVE YEARS OF THE THIRD REICH. *(p. 140)*

At the Hadamar euthanasia hospital patients killed with injections were told that they were for "**treatment** of their **lung disease."** *(p. 126)*

* * * * *

In 1976 Dr. Willard Cates called abortion the **"preferred treatment"** for **"unwanted pregnancy:** the number two **sexually transmitted disease."** *(p. 127)*

"I FEEL SORRY FOR A STARVING CAT . . . A FETUS THAT NOBODY WANTS—THAT'S NOT SAD." *(p. 99)*

—Dr. Howard I. Diamond, 1977

"What should we do with this garbage." *(p. 101)*
—Christian Wirth on the problem of body disposal at Treblinka, 1942

* * * * *

"An aborted baby is just garbage." *(p. 102)*

—Fetal researcher Dr. Martti Kekomaki, 1980

THE UNBORN ARE THE MOST ABSOLUTELY OPPRESSED MINORITY IN HISTORY. *(p. 198)*

Heads severed from **inmates exterminated** in the gas chambers were utilized as **"paperweights"** in the offices of camp commandants. *(p. 77)*

* * * * *

The **brains, organs and bodies of aborted babies** encased in a **"paperweight"** type of plastic block were sold by a Chicago biological supply firm. *(p. 78)*

SOME FOUR HUNDRED LAWS AND DECREES WERE ENACTED AGAINST THE JEWS LEADING UP TO THE "FINAL SOLUTION." *(p. 180)*

At the Nuremberg Doctors' Trial in 1947 witness Walter E. Schmidt defended the Nazi holocaust with the statement: "The **jurists** in Berlin **told us** this was a **legal matter . . . quite legal.**" *(p. 43)*

* * * * *

In 1980 abortionist Dr. Michael Jackson furnished an identical rationalization in support of today's abortion holocaust: "I just go by what the **courts say** . . . I only do **what's legal.**" *(p. 43)*

CONTEMPORARY ABORTION PROPONENTS DISPUTE THE HUMANITY OF THE UNBORN AS VOCIFEROUSLY AS THE NAZIS QUESTIONED THE HUMANITY OF THE JEWS. *(p. 94)*

In the **Nazi death camps** annihilation as an **assembly-line enterprise** came of age: "A man would step off a train in the morning, and in the evening his corpse was burned and his clothes packed away for shipment to Germany." *(p. 38)*

* * * * *

A woman can enter an **abortion chamber** on her lunch hour and, by the time she is due to return to work, all the remains of her unborn baby's body are obliterated by an **assembly-line process** which would make even the most avid Nazi technician gasp in awe."*(p. 38)*

FINANCIALLY, AFTER YEARS OF STRUGGLE, I CAN'T HELP FEELING A LITTLE LIKE THE TEXAN WHO DRILLED FOR WATER AND STRUCK OIL." *(p. 75)*

—Abortion convert Dr. Mark Julienne, 1970

The **I.G. Farben Chemical Corporation's dividends** on its investments in Degesch, manufacturer of Zyklon B gas **doubled** from 1942-1944, a period when millions were being gassed to death in concentration camps. *(p. 76)*

* * * * *

The **Upjohn Pharmaceutical Company's** announcement of plans for the development of a vaginal suppository for abortion was accompanied by a **spectacular rise** in its common **stock** from a low of $32 a share to a high of $56. *(p. 77)*

THE UNWANTED OF THE PAST AND THE PRESENT HAVE HAD MUCH MORE TO FEAR FROM EDUCATED ELITES THAN FROM EITHER MOBS IN THE STREETS OR BACK-ALLEY BUTCHERS. *(p. 198)*

Auschwitz commandant Rudolf Hoess bragged that he "knew of **not a single case where anyone came out of the chambers alive.**" *(P. 64)*

* * * * *

A physician abortionist boasted that dismemberment of the unborn in D & E abortion "**never ever results in live births.**" *(p. 65)*

"NO NEWBORN INFANT SHOULD BE DECLARED HUMAN UNTIL IT HAS PASSED CERTAIN TESTS REGARDING ITS GENETIC ENDOWMENT . . . IF IT FAILS THESE TESTS IT FORFEITS THE RIGHT TO LIVE." *(p. 80)*

—Nobel laureate Dr. Francis H. Crick, 1978

In 1925 in *Mein Kampf,* Adolf Hitler referred to **Jews** as "**a parasite in the body of other peoples.**" *(p. 100)*

* * * * *

In 1973 a radical feminist group characterized the **unborn** as "**a parasite within the mother's body.**" *(p. 100)*

WHEN HITLER CAME TO POWER THE WORLD'S LEADING AND MOST INDEPENDENT PRESS WAS REDUCED TO AN AGENT OF THE MINISTRY OF PROPAGANDA. *(p. 145)*

The subjects were forced to undergo death-dealing experiments "**without receiving anesthetics.**" *(p. 65)*

—Freezing experiments, Dachau concentration camp, 1942

* * * * *

"The fetuses are fully alive when we cut their heads off, but **anesthetics are definitely unnecessary.**" *(p. 66)*

—Fetal researcher Dr. Martti Kekomaki, 1980

"WE FED A LINE OF DECEIT, OF DISHONESTY, OF FABRICATION OF STATISTICS AND FIGURES. WE CODDLED AND CARESSED AND STROKED THE PRESS. WE, IN ONE SHORT YEAR, SUCCEEDED IN STRIKING DOWN THE ABORTION LAWS OF NEW YORK STATE." *(p. 146)*

—Former abortion clinic director Dr. Bernard N. Nathanson, 1980

"**Charitable Foundation for Institutional Care.**" *(p. 128)*
(Organization responsible for implementing Nazi euthanasia program)

* * * * *

"**Charitable Organizations**" **engaged in** "**Promoting Health.**" *(p. 128)*
(Tax exempt designation granted to abortion clinics by Internal Revenue Service)

The Abortion Holocaust

The Abortion Holocaust

Today's Final Solution

William Brennan

LANDMARK PRESS

St. Louis
1983

Landmark Press
Box 13547
1461 Dunn Road
St. Louis, Missouri 63138

Library of Congress Catalog Card Number: 82-83960
ISBN 0-911439-01-3

Printed in the United States of America by
Gateway Press, Inc., St. Louis, Missouri

First Printing — June 1983
Second Printing — September 1984

This book is dedicated to the proposition that a knowledge of the kinship between past and current atrocities represents an indispensable step toward halting the modern resurrection of one of history's most monstrous chapters.

Contents

List of Charts

Illustrations

Chapter 1

The Abortion-Holocaust Connection

The wholesale annihilation of European Jews and other victims by the Nazis represents one of the darkest chapters in the history of man's inhumanity to man. Millions of human beings were brutally exterminated: shot to death, asphyxiated by gas, or burned alive.

What is being done to scores of unwanted unborn human beings on a daily basis in contemporary America and throughout the world is every bit as cruel and inhuman. Fetal research proponents Drs. Willard Gaylin and Marc Lappe have provided an unusually candid portrayal of abortion procedures as "unimaginable acts of violence" which "subject the fetus to dismemberment, salt-osmotic shock, or surgical extirpation."[1]

Atrocities Past and Present

In the Eastern territories special killing units, *Einsatzgruppen,* followed upon the heels of the German Army in a systematic search-and-destroy mission bent on eradicating Jews, Gypsies, the insane, and the handicapped. The victims were shot in cold blood in front of huge ditches. Their bodies toppled into the gaping holes of massive graves. Many expired from their wounds. Others were buried alive and suffocated to death.[2]

Vacuum aspiration abortion, the most common method of destroying unborn children in the first trimester of pregnancy, is an especially brutal procedure. The child's tiny body—including arms, legs, head, and torso—is torn away from the walls of the uterus, ripped apart, and reduced to smithereens by the force of a suction machine many times more powerful than a vacuum cleaner. Little wonder that some nurses have referred to the aspirator as "the murder machine."[3] The obliterated remains are sucked out of the womb through a transparent tube into a collecting bottle. They are examined and then incinerated or flushed into the sewer. The entire destruction-disintegration process usually takes no more than several minutes.

Destruction inside the gas chambers of concentration camps was a painful and extended process in which the victims desperately gasped for breath and life. The hardiest inmates sometimes trampled upon women, children, and the elderly in their futile efforts to escape the deadly fumes. Body-disposal squads developed "special hook-tipped poles," thrust deep into the flesh of the newly exterminated, to facilitate the task of removing entangled, bloated, and deformed corpses with blood oozing from their noses and mouths.[4]

A prime example of contemporary scientific butchery, D & E (dilatation and extraction) abortion, involves the use of curettes to mutilate victims beyond the first trimester of pregnancy, and forceps to extract their slaughtered remains from the womb piece by piece. "The sensations of dismemberment," according to veteran D & E abortionist Dr. Warren M. Hern, "flow through the forceps like an electric current."[5] The solid, well-formed heads of the victims must frequently be crushed before removal. Then the butchered body parts are assembled to ensure that the uterus has been completely emptied.

During the height of the killing season at Auschwitz living children were tossed directly into the fires of crematorium furnaces or flaming pits. Their screams could be heard throughout the camp compound. The purpose underlying this particular atrocity was two-fold: either "to economize on gas" or "because there was not enough room in the gas chambers."[6]

The injection of concentrated salt solutions into the amniotic fluid surrounding the unborn child is another example of the sheer barbarism with which human lives are done away with in the mid-trimester of gestation. The corrosive saline often burns away the outer layer of skin, exposing the raw, red under-surface. The effect is similar to that of napalm on innocent war victims. For the victims the dying process is agonizing and prolonged, lasting from one to several hours.[7] Columbia University surgeons compared saline killing to "acute salt poisoning of infants" accompanied by "widespread vasodilatation, edema, congestion, hemorrhage, shock and death."[8] Experienced saline abortionist Dr. William B. Waddill acknowledged that saline produces "such a caustic and tremendously bad and hostile environment for the baby that it just creates an enormous destructive process."[9]

During the 12 years of the Third Reich the holocaust consumed some 6 million Jews, 5 million non-Jews, 275,000 handicapped Germans in euthanasia hospitals, a quarter of a million Gypsies, and countless numbers of unborn expendables.

Since the 1973 Supreme Court decision which sanctified abortion on demand, well over 10 million unborn lives have been extinguished by heinous acts of medical extermination not even legally permitted against animals, birds, or fish. The uterus, which once had been a private sanctuary exquisitely suited for growth and development, has been transformed into a deadly environment polluted beyond belief by the invasion of lethal instruments and poisonous substances that defy the most fundamental laws of ecology and humanity!

Crucial Questions

Given such deplorable acts of violence perpetrated on a massive scale against past and present victims, some vexing questions need to be examined: How have incomprehensible horrors become routine realities? Why do they continue unabated? Why the silence, the apathy, the indifference on the part of so many bystanders? Why haven't more people insisted on halting the contemporary bloodbath? What can be done to stop today's massive slaughter of the unborn?

It is these crucial questions which this book will attempt to address and answer.

The prevailing view of abortion in contemporary society is that of a minor surgical procedure carried out by upstanding physicians in the antiseptic settings of clinics and hospitals. It is this highly positive image—concocted by members of the medical establishment, legitimized by the legal structure, buttressed by linguistic technicians, implemented by advanced technologies, and disseminated by a media elite—which helps sustain the assembly-line massacre of over one and one-half million unborn children annually in America alone.

The present-day carnage directed against the unwanted unborn will not begin to cease until a much larger segment of the public becomes aware of an entirely different perception of abortion as a horrendous holocaust comparable to the enormous destruction perpetrated on the unwanted of the Third Reich.

The Framework for Analysis

This book will show that the abortion-holocaust connection is a perfectly valid one to make at two levels.

First, abortion in America, both before and after the 1973 Supreme Court abortion decision, will be compared to abortion in Germany and parts of Europe, both before and during the Third Reich. Additional information will be provided on Hitler's role in abortion expansion.

Second, the largest part of this study is given over to a comparison of abortion in contemporary American society with the killing of postnatal discards by the Nazis. The emphasis here is on the universality of the victimization process in which Jews and others of the Third Reich and the unborn of today's society have been subjected to bureaucratic annihilation, experimental atrocities, monetary exploitation, distorted linguistics, and a massive media coverup.

Underlying the numerous parallels between past and present barbarities are some pervasive themes which will be analyzed extensively: 1) The power of technology to conceal the victims and reduce mass killing to the trivial level of a technical procedure. 2) The power of terminology to relegate the victims to a less-than-human level and obscure their extermination under a blanket of semantic camouflage. 3) Physicians as credentialed executioners of the unwanted, a role diametrically opposed to the physician-as-healer ethic embodied in the Hippocratic Oath and its modern counterpart, the Declaration of Geneva.

Each chapter of this book is intended to convey a maximum amount of information in a concise manner. A question-answer format is employed to enhance readability and furnish immediate comprehension of the parallels examined. A special feature designed to highlight the striking similarities between the holocaust perpetrated against the Jews and the modern medical war on the unborn is the inclusion of twenty charts in which many of the most important comparisons are placed side-by-side on the same page where they can be consulted at a glance.

All of the parallels selected for analysis are fully documented from many primary sources, including correspondence, memoranda, and conference notes compiled by the perpetrators; war crimes trials testimony; medical and legal journals; concentration camp survivors' accounts; medical policy statements; historical records and documents; and books on various facets of past and present destructive activites. Even the most skeptical reader will find that the copious notes at the end of the book support only one possible conclusion: the associations drawn between previous and current monstrosities are neither fabricated nor exaggerated, but alarmingly authentic.

The Holocaust Perspective and Contemporary Barbarities

The final chapter of this book, "Counteracting the Repetition of Historical Atrocities," emphasizes the importance of becoming knowledgeable about the findings uncovered and offers suggestions for communicating this information to members of the medical profession, legislators, the media, and the public at large. As long as abortion remains at the psychologically-remote and abstract level of removing insignificant tissue or contents from the womb, not that many people are likely to get upset. The holocaust perspective, on the other hand, possesses a tremendous potential for breaking through this facade and revealing the harsh realities of large-scale killing, whatever the historical period of their perpetration, and whether the victims be born or unborn. Only when people are allowed access to the concrete, emotionally repugnant facts of unborn baby killing will they be filled with outrage and motivated to demand an end to the destruction.

To point out that today's medical abortionists are doing the same thing to the unwanted unborn as the Nazis did to their victims does not have the remotest connection to anti-Semitism. There is nothing inherently anti-Semitic about emphasizing how other victims, in addition to Jews, have undergone persecution, degradation, and annihilation. To invoke the specter of anti-Semitism against anyone who dares attempt to draw parallels between the killing of Europe's Jews and the destruction of America's unborn amounts to a diversionary device meant to prevent the exploration and disclosure of information containing horrendous ramifications. Such a tactic flies in the face of the indispensable message expressed by almost every survivor who has ever written about the Nazi holocaust: a warning to the world that what happened to the Jews during the Nazi era was not so unique that it could not or would not happen again. Forging links between prior and present brutalities is decidedly pro rather than anti-Semitic, and in perfect accord with the priceless legacy left to civilization by the death camp survivors.

Although every holocaust ever perpetrated is a unique event in its own right, this should not detract from what all holocausts share in common. The central horror of any holocaust—whether it involves the extermination of Jews by the Nazis, the massacre of Russians by the Soviet regime, the eradication of Cambodians by the Khmer Rouge, or the slaughter of unborn children by medical doctors—is the systematic destruction of millions looked upon as indiscriminate masses of subhuman expendables. The basic ingredients for a holocaust exist whenever any society can be misled into defining individuals as less than human and therefore devoid of value and respect. Once any group of individuals, born or unborn, is not deemed worthy of the designation human, the precedent is established for defining ever growing numbers of people out of the human race, therefore rendering them stateless and bereft of human rights, including the most basic right, that of life itself. When the rights of some are extinguished, the rights of all are placed in dire jeopardy.

It is this broad notion of a holocaust that constitutes the foundation upon which the comparisons in this book are based. The evidence compiled is bound to force the reader into a confrontation with many disquieting revelations, especially the alarming extent to which abortion comprises the contemporary repetition of one of history's darkest chapters. Awareness of the links between past and present atrocities represents an essential step toward halting the current appalling state of affairs, and thus putting an end to a situation so aptly captured in the famous admonition of philosopher George Santayana: "Those who do not remember the past are condemned to relive it."

Chapter 2

The Campaign to Legalize Abortion in Pre-Nazi Germany and Pre-Roe v. Wade America

The Legal Status of Abortion Prior to Nazi Germany and Roe v. Wade America

Wasn't the abortion law in Germany highly permissive before Hitler came to power and highly restrictive afterward?

The truth is just the other way around. Abortions were actually far more prohibitive in pre-Hitler Germany than they ever were during the 12-year Reich. For the 60-year period leading up to the Nazi takeover, Germany had what was probably the strongest abortion law in the world. Section 218 of the German penal code, enacted in 1871, contained the following provision pertaining to abortion:

> A pregnant woman who shall purposely cause herself to abort or who shall kill her child in utero shall be subject to a penitentiary sentence . . . The same punishment shall be imposed on any person who, with the consent of the pregnant woman, applied or administered the means to induce the abortion or to cause the death of the child.[1]

Significantly, the reason for the passage of this law can be readily ascertained from the wording employed. The main thrust of the law was on protecting "the child in utero" from the onslaught of abortion perceived as an act designed to "cause the death of the child." Many years later, in 1926, prominent Berlin gynecologist Dr. Max Hirsch pointed to the reason for not legalizing abortion as a form of therapeutic treatment: "it violates the legal rights of the unborn child."[2]

The abortion law of 1871 recognized the existence of the unborn child as a bona fide human being in need of legal protection from the assaults of medical and non-medical perpetrators alike. It is completely devoid of such misleading euphemisms as "interruption of pregnancy." Consignment to the penitentiary as a punishment for those who violated its provisions demonstrates the gravity with which the framers of the law viewed the matter of induced abortion.

Up until Hitler came to power, Germany's strong law against

abortion remained basically intact. However, during the 1920's and early 1930s a rash of proposals for modification of this law were put forth in the *reichstag* (legislature). The one making the greatest headway involved allowing more leeway for physicians to perform abortions when the mother's life or health was jeopardized. This indication, nevertheless, only reached the draft stage and did not yet possess the full force of law until after the Nazis assumed control of the government. Then, dubious medical factors along with many radical proposals for changing Germany's abortion law were finally granted legitimacy through the Nazi legal machinery.

How were America's abortion laws prior to 1973 related to the abortion law in pre-Nazi Germany?

The events preceding the legalization of abortion by the U.S. Supreme Court in 1973 closely parallel what happened in Germany in the decades before abortion was legalized by the government of Adolf Hitler. The campaign for enactment of stringent abortion laws in the United States between the 1860s and 1880 produced what historian James C. Mohr characterized as "the most important burst of anti-abortion legislation in the nation's history. At least 40 anti-abortion statutes of various kinds were placed upon state and territorial lawbooks during that period."[3] The Virginia abortion statute of 1873, typical of many passed during that era, contained some features strikingly similar to Germany's anti-abortion law of 1871:

> If any person administer to, or cause to be taken by a woman, any drug or other thing, or use means, with intent to destroy her unborn child, or to produce abortion or miscarriage, and thereby destroy such child or produce such abortion or miscarriage, he shall be confined in the penitentiary . . . No person, by reason of any act mentioned in this section, shall be punishable when such act is done in good faith, with the intention of saving the life of such woman or child.[4]

Virginia's abortion law was not as strict as Germany's since it allowed abortion when either the mother's or child's life was at stake. On all other counts—including intention, language employed, and punishment for violation—it just about duplicated its German counterpart. This was especially evident in its portrayal of the individual in the womb as an "unborn child" and abortion as an act designed "to destroy such child."

Almost all the restrictive abortion statutes stayed on the books, some of them for over a hundred years, until the late 1960s when the assaults against laws protective of human life before birth began to take their toll. By the end of 1972 only 19 states changed their abortion laws despite a relentless avalanche of pro-abortion propaganda that inundated state legislatures throughout the land. While all 19 states permitted abortions to preserve the health of the pregnant woman, just four of them required no reason whatsoever for destroying the unborn child. One state, New York, actually reversed its abortion-on-demand law, only to have it overturned by Governor Nelson Rockefeller's veto. Thirty-one states had withstood the enormous pressures exerted and retained the strong anti-abortion laws enacted, for the most part, during the latter half of the nineteenth century.[5]

The Campaign to Legalize The Destruction of the Unborn

What were some of the most common devices employed to legalize the killing of unborn children in pre-Nazi Germany and pre-Roe v. Wade America?

The staging of mass demonstrations in support of abortion law abolition, an emphasis placed on the dangers of abortions attributed to quacks and butchers, and grossly inflated maternal death rates attributed to illegal abortions.

Mass Demonstrations

According to a Berlin correspondent, by the late 1920s and early in 1930 the campaign to abolish the German abortion law had become highly politicized, including within its ranks, besides the usual assortment of radicals, "medical circles whose political sympathies are with the Left." A major strategy used to create sentiment in favor of abortion law abolition consisted of "theatrical performances (which, in some instances, had degenerated into mere mass meetings)."[6]

The mounting of mass demonstrations in the late 1960s and early 1970s served as a highly successful tactic in the American pro-abortion movement for doing away with laws protective of unborn human lives. Former abortion luminary Dr. Bernard N. Nathanson recounted that one such march, staged with considerable "theatrical flair," featured a corps of young mothers wheeling baby carriages and chanting slogans in front of the state capital in Trenton, New Jersey.[7]

The Dangers of Illegal Abortions Attributed to Quacks and Butchers

Isn't it true that most of the illegal abortions done in pre-Hitler Germany and pre-Roe v. Wade America were performed by quacks or backstreet butchers, therefore causing needless deaths among thousands?

The contention that huge numbers of abortions resulted in thousands of women losing their lives at the hands of inept, unsavory operators constituted a powerful propaganda weapon intended to elicit public and professional support for loosening the abortion laws of both countries. What better way to demonstrate the unenforceability of "rigid" abortion statutes and pave the way for acceptance of legalized abortion implemented by credentialed executioners in the respectable atmospheres of safe and sanitary settings!

Give some examples to show how the purported dangers of illicit abortions at the hands of so-called quacks served as a pretext for discrediting Germany's abortion law.

At a session of the League of German Medical Societies in September 1925 Dr. Vollmann characterized induced abortion as having reached "the extent of an epidemic." Although acknowledging the unavailability of "exact statistics" on the matter, he claimed that as many as 400,000 induced abortions were performed in 1921, and listed chronic abdominal disease and high maternal mortality as the most dangerous complications. This provided him with the justification to recommend legalizing the "interruption of pregnancy" for "certain distressing circumstances or impelling motives."[8]

Early in 1926 the Prussian Council on Public Health expressed alarm about the "deaths of mothers" caused by the increase in abortions during the previous 20 years. The approach offered for resolving this problem included spreading among the people "information concerning the danger to life from induced interruption of pregnancy," and replacement of the law on abortion then in effect with a much milder version.[9]

Two noteworthy arguments put forth at a 1926 meeting of the *reichstag* in support of abolishing penalties for abortion when carried out by a licensed physician focused on the frequently invoked themes of unenforceable laws and non-skilled, non-medical abortionists:

> The punishment as a means of preventing abortion has been shown to be noneffective, for the number of abortions

is increasing at an alarming rate.

As a consequence of the punishment imposed, abortions are performed in an unprofessional manner, which causes great harm to health and great loss of life.[10]

The physician's refusal to perform abortions, declared the Berlin Chamber of Physicians in 1929, "has often led the petitioner to engage an unskilled person with the consequent death of the mother." The Chamber thereupon called for a change in the law to permit an expansion of indications for medical-induced abortions.[11] In 1931 Dr. Julius Wolf referred to Germany's abortion law as "a survival of barbarism" and identified "charlatans" as a prime source of the great suffering caused by abortion.[12] After a retrospective look at Germany's past history of illegal abortions, the official publication of the medical federations, *Deutsches Aerzeblatt,* claimed that most abortions were done by "underhanded quacks," resulting in an annual toll of 16,000 maternal deaths. In addition, "300,000 women are said to have become ill because of the intervention, half to two thirds of whom fail to recover their health."[13]

Provide some instances of how the perils attributed to illegal abortions performed by butchers and quacks have been used as a propaganda device to subvert America's abortion laws.

In a manner closely resembling that of Dr. Vollmann in Germany of the mid 1920s, American obstetrics professor Dr. Frederick J. Taussig in 1936 etched a comparably grim portrait of "disease and death that follow in the wake of this plague of abortion." He also embellished this portrayal with such highly inflated figures as 681,600 induced abortions per year resulting in an annual maternal death rate of 8,000 to 10,000. This served as a backdrop for attacking the abortion laws which he dubbed "unjust, unenforceable . . . harsh . . . antiquated." Taussig then proposed legalizing abortions for such indications as "preserving the mother's life or health," "cases of physical depletion," or "moral irresponsibility of the mother."[14]

In the early 1940s the journal *Southern Medicine and Surgery* blamed "these statutes now in force" for producing "the whole underground movement of abortion with its butchering quacks."[15] A 1955 conference sponsored by the Planned Parenthood Federation of America and the New York Academy of Medicine provided Dr. Alan F. Guttmacher and others with a forum for declaring abortion laws "inoperable," and emphasizing "the harm that accrues therefrom."[16] This thrust prompted the conference participants to support modification of abortion statutes for a greatly expanded range of indications.

During the 1960s misleading statistics in the service of assaults against laws protective of human life before birth continued to escalate. Dr. Jerome Kummer asserted that several studies showed "a total of more than one million abortions for 1960, with a possibility of more than 5,000 deaths resulting therefrom." From this, he identified a fundamental requirement of reform: "modification of the present unenforceable laws."[17] A 1964 sociological study of criminal abortions sounded the alarm about the huge numbers of illegal abortions performed annually and the disastrous outcome. "Out of this number," proclaimed authors Jerome Bates and Edward Zawadzki, "at least five thousand women die each year."[18] An influential pro-abortion tract penned by Lawrence Lader in 1966 attributed the "abnormally high percentage of abortion deaths" to the "pitifully small number" of legal abortions allowed. Women are then forced, he declared, into an underground of abortion largely inhabited by "hacks and butchers" and "quack doctors."[19] In the same year the California Committee on Therapeutic Abortion reinforced the grim numerical claim of widespread destruction from illegal abortions in a brochure entitled "The Truth About Abortion: Must 10,000 Women Die This Year?"[20]

Inflated Death Rates and Illegal Abortions

How do you know that the annual maternal death rates attributed to illegal abortions in pre-Nazi Germany were highly inflated fabrications?

It strains credibility to the breaking point to believe that the number of women dying from illegal abortions annually (16,000 in pre-Nazi Germany) was more than double that of a country at least twice as large (5,000 to 10,000 in pre-Roe v. Wade America). The population of Germany in the decades preceding Hitler's ascent to power remained at approximately 66 million. The population of the United States in the decades before the 1973 Supreme Court abortion decision increased from over 151 million in 1950 to over 203 million in 1970.

Another reason the 16,000 abortion-induced-deaths assertion constituted a wildly exaggerated figure relates to the position of German medicine long before Hitler came on the scene. From the first half of the nineteenth century through a little beyond the first quarter of the twentieth century, German medicine was preeminent throughout the world: a citadel of learning, far-reaching scientific discoveries, and success in alleviating diseases which had plagued humanity for decades. Even the disaster of World War I proved to be only a temporary setback. In 1924 the German medical universities were, according to an assessment by Abraham Flexner, "still as a group the best organized, the best equipped, and the most solidly conceived that exist. Neither teaching nor research has stopped."[21] It is inconceivable that an annual maternal death rate from illegal abortions of 16,000 would have been permitted to happen in a country so renowned for its medical achievements. This is particularly the case when one considers the fact that many of these abortions were performed by medical doctors!

What about the illegal abortion maternal death rates in pre-Roe v. Wade America? How do you know they were also grossly inflated?

The same reasons that cast a long shadow of disbelief over the authenticity of the German figures do likewise to the American figures. During a period when American medicine had attained a position of world leadership similar to that enjoyed by German medicine of the past, it is hard to believe that American doctors would have tolerated a situation where up to 10,000 women lost their lives from an orgy of abortions in violation of the law. All the more incredible since the large majority of abortions were perpetrated by licensed physicians!

Another source for disproving the high maternal death rates attributed to underworld abortions is census data. While pro-abortion propagandists were terrorizing the public with endless horror stories about thousands of women being butchered in the wake of an epidemic of illicit abortions, a few individuals tried to counter the climate of near hysteria by referring to statistics obtained from census material. Even stalwart abortion defender and former Planned Parenthood medical director Dr. Mary S. Calderone acknowledged that in 1957 "there were only 260 deaths in the whole country attributed to abortions of any kind."[22] Former Oak Park (Illinois) public health director, Dr. Herbert Ratner, employed census information to point out that only 114 deaths in 1963 "were due to abortions that were criminal, self-induced, or without legal indications."[23] The truth of the matter, however, failed to prevail and the pro-abortion scare tactics helped push abortion on demand to the ultimate heights of respectability as the law of the land in 1973.

Dr. Bernard N. Nathanson, former pro-abortion pioneer and former abortion clinic director, has furnished an insider's view on the 5,000 to 10,000 maternal deaths a year attributed to illegal abortions and the motivation underlying the distortion of death statistics. "I confess that I knew the figures were totally false," he revealed. "But in the 'morality' of our revolution, it was a *useful* figure, widely accepted, so why go out of our way to correct it with honest statistics."[24]

Medical Outlaws

You said that medical doctors performed most of the illegal abortions in Germany before the Nazi government assumed power. Do you have any evidence to support this?

Most German doctors were not prone to acknowledge or publicize the heavy involvement of licensed physicians in the illicit destruction of unborn lives. Their strategy was to place most of the blame on quacks and unscrupulous individuals. Once in a while, however, it became apparent that a large number of abortions against the law were performed by skilled doctors in prestigious medical settings.

A study of abortions performed at the Berlin University Women's Hospital in 1916 revealed that "89 percent of miscarriages were purposely induced."[25] This represents one of the first attempts to confront the large-scale killing of the unborn, a reality so often concealed under the label of "miscarriages."

Another rare disclosure of the extent to which German physicans violated the law against killing the unborn came to light in a book published in 1931 containing the case records of 426 artificially induced abortions done by a "small town practitioner." In a large percentage of these cases, women were aborted "on very slight pretext, and in some instances as often as two or three times a year on the same patient."[26]

Do you have information to show that American physicians performed most of the illegal abortions predating the 1973 Supreme Court abortion decision?

Although the quacks and unsavory characters of American society have been saddled with the lion's share of responsibility for performing criminal abortions, a fairly sizeable number of American doctors have admitted that credentialed physicians in good standing, rather than backalley butchers, were the main perpetrators.

In 1933 Dr. Abraham J. Rongy, a fellow of the American College of Surgeons, described the physician as "the chief agent of abortion," the one who "flouts the law."[27] Several years later Washington University obstetrics professor Dr. Frederick J. Taussig characterized anti-abortion statutes as the most universally disregarded laws in history, and medical doctors "the official 'bootleggers' of abortion."[28] (This latter phrase was intended to evoke the days of prohibition when many people were breaking the laws against sale of alcoholic beverages). "Although the performing of abortions has been forbidden to physicians since the time of Hippocrates," observed Dr. Harold C. Taylor at an abortion conference in 1942, "nevertheless the abortionist is drawn principally from the ranks of this profession."[29]

By the late 1950s Dr. Alan F. Guttmacher reported that 85 percent of the abortion operations done at New York's Mount Sinai Hospital from 1952 to 1956 "at least *bent* the law, if they did not fracture it."[30] In another study under the revealing title, "The Law That Doctors Often Break," Guttmacher disclosed that the percentage of illegal abortions at the same hospital rose to "more than 90 percent."[31] The close resemblance this bears to the illicit abortion activities carried out in 1916 at the Berlin University Women's Hospital is remarkable.

A large majority of 180 obstetricians surveyed regarding their attitudes toward North Carolina's permissive abortion act of 1967 acknowledged that the new law had little effect other than "to have simply legalized something that we had been doing for many years."[32]

Briefly review the propaganda devices used by German and American doctors in their campaigns to legalize abortion.

A summary of the legal status of abortion in pre-Hitler Germany and pre-Roe v. Wade America and the tactics created to discredit laws protective of human life before birth is contained in Chart 1 on page 16.

Chart 1

Agitation for Legalizing the Killing of the Unborn

Pre-Nazi Germany	Pre-Roe v. Wade America
The Legal Status of Abortion	
"A pregnant woman who shall purposely cause herself to abort" or "any person" who "shall kill her child in utero shall be subject to a penitentiary sentence." (Section 218, German penal code, 1871)	"If any person administer to, or cause to be taken by a woman, any drug or other thing" with "intent to destroy her unborn child . . . he shall be confined to the penitentiary." (Virginia abortion statute, 1873)
Mass Demonstrations	
In the late 1920s doctors helped stage demonstrations resembling "theatrical performances" in order to create public sentiment against Germany's abortion law. *(American Medical Association Journal,* July 19, 1930)	In the late 1960s doctors helped stage demonstrations conducted with "theatrical flair" in order to galvanize public opinion against state abortion laws. (Former abortionist Dr. Bernard N. Nathanson, 1979)
Abortion Law Assaults	
The abortion law represents "a survival of barbarism." (Dr. Julius Wolf, 1931)	Abortion laws are "harsh" and "antiquated." (Dr. Frederick J. Taussig, 1936)
Perpetration of Illegal Abortions	
Blamed on "underhanded quacks." (Assessment of medical publication *Deutsches Aerzeblatt)*	Blamed on "butchering quacks." (Assessment of medical journal *Southern Medicine and Surgery*)
Maternal Deaths Attributed to Illegal Abortions	
16,000 women die each year. (Greatly inflated figures manufactured by pro-abortion doctors in their campaign to legalize the destruction of the unborn)	Up to 10,000 women die each year. ("I confess that I knew the figures were totally false. But in the 'morality' of our revolution, it was a useful figure." Dr. Bernard N. Nathanson)
Medical Outlaws	
In 1916, 89 percent of the abortions "purposely induced" at the Berlin University Women's Hospital were in violation of the law.	"More than 90 percent" of the abortions performed at Mount Sinai Hospital in the 1950s were illegal.

Chapter 3

The Expansion of Abortion In the Third Reich and Roe v. Wade America

Why do you equate the Third Reich with Roe v. Wade America?

The Nazi regime ushered in an era of unprecedented legalized destruction. The unborn comprised the first category of victims earmarked for killing under legal auspices. Next came the German handicapped and mentally disabled, and then the Jews, Gypsies, asocials, and others.

The U.S. Supreme Court in its Roe v. Wade abortion decision has opened up another unparalled age of lawful annihilation. The unborn have experienced the greatest brunt of the killing. The legacy of legalized extermination bequeathed to contemporary society by Roe v. Wade threatens ever more vehemently growing numbers of postnatal discards, particularly underpar infants and the seriously afflicted aged.

Are you aware that some prominent people claim that the Nazi government strongly opposed abortion and enacted restrictive abortion laws?

Yes. The following statements reflect a sampling of their comments:

"The Nazis themselves prohibited abortion, imposing on its practitioners draconic punishments." (Professor Henry Friedlander, *Teachers College Record,* February 1979).[1]

The Nazi Germans tightened the abortion laws, and the logic that set up the concentration camps was "ferociously anti-abortion." (Dr. Malcolm Potts, *Newsweek,* January 28, 1980).[2]

The anti-abortion movement's "most vicious bit of rhetoric" is "its continual assertion that legal abortion has murdered more people than Hitler." Actually, "under the Nazis, abortion was a serious crime." (Ellen Willis, *Village Voice,* February 4, 1980).[3]

"Hitler himself, and the Nazi doctrine he created, were unequivocably opposed to any individual right to abortion." (Gloria Steinem, *Ms,* October 1980).[4]

Aren't they right? Didn't the Nazis enact a highly restrictive abortion law?

The abortion law during the Nazi era was far more open-ended than generally acknowledged. Abortion legalization on an expanded scale did not come about in Germany until 1933 when the Nazis assumed power. Although intense agitation for legalizing the destruction of the unborn led by physicians and medical organizations had already taken hold, the law protective of human life before birth remained basically intact. The host of proposals introduced into the *reichstag* during the 1920s and early 1930s for "liberalizing" or abolishing Germany's abortion law stayed in the draft stages until the Nazi takeover.[5] The government of Adolf Hitler transformed abortion from the tentative phase of bills and proposals to the conclusive stage of full-fledged legality.

Aren't the abortion laws of contemporary American society fairly restrictive?

The legal status of abortion in today's America is considerably more extensive than many people are aware of or are willing to admit. The U.S. Supreme Court in 1973, like the Nazi government in 1933, endowed abortion with incomparable legitimation. Even though the propaganda campaign against the unborn directed by doctors, medical associations, and likeminded elitists inundated all the states in the 1960s and early 1970s, only a few actually changed their laws to permit abortion for an extended list of indications. Within a large majority of states, laws protective of unborn human life were retained, while bills promoting its destruction went down to defeat.[6] On January 22, 1973, this all came apart. The Supreme Court reduced the strong wall of legal protection erected on behalf of the unborn to rubble. Bills and proposals in support of unborn baby killing were suddenly elevated to a position of matchless prominence as the law of the land in all 50 states.

Specific Legal Provisions for Abortion

You say that the Hitler government and the U.S. Supreme Court handed down rulings responsible for mass extermination directed against unborn expendables. Would you identify more fully and specifically the legal provisions you are referring to?

The struggle for legal recognition of abortion expansion did not meet with success until 1933, when Hitler became chancellor of Germany. Building upon intense medical-induced agitation for legalized destruction of the unborn, the Nazi government approved of lawful abortion in line with the guidelines established by the Berlin Chamber of Physicians. This leading promoter of permissive abortion under the guise of health laid down the following criteria for governing legal abortion in Nazi Germany:

> (a) For each district of Berlin a staff of consultants in the various specialities is appointed, who reviews the cases in which abortion is asked.
> (b) Reliable evidence that a danger threatens the life or health of the mother must be presented.
> (c) The abortion can only be done in public hospitals or private clinics approved by the chamber of physicians.
> (d) Decision on eugenic indications must be left to the so-called "hereditary health" courts created by the new sterilization law.
> (e) The execution of the abortion must be entrusted to a specialist.
> (f) Illegal abortions undertaken by nonmedical persons will be punished.[7]

Decades of medical propaganda aimed against laws protective of unborn human life served as an indispensable backdrop for the U.S. Supreme Court, in its Roe v. Wade decision of January 22, 1973, to decree abortion on request as the law of the land. In a deplorable display of raw judicial power, the Court granted physicians a degree of raw medical power beyond the wildest expectations of even the most vociferous proponents of abortion. The key provisions of what may well be one of the most sweeping documents of destruction ever enacted include the following:

> (a) For the stage prior to approximately the end of the first trimester, the abortion decision and its effectuation must be left to the medical judgment of the pregnant woman's attending physician.
> (b) For the stage subsequent to approximately the end of the first trimester, the State, in promoting its interest in the health of the mother, may, if it chooses, regulate the abortion procedure in ways that are reasonably related to maternal health.
> (c) For the stage subsequent to viability, the State in promoting its interest in the potentiality of human life may, if it chooses, regulate, and even proscribe, abortion except where it is necessary, in appropriate medical judgment, for the preservation of the life or health of the mother.
> The State may define the term "physician," . . . to mean only a physician currently licensed by the State, and may proscribe any abortion by a person who is not a physician as so defined . . .
> Examples of permissible state regulation in this area are requirements as to the qualifications of the person who is to

perform the abortion; as to the licensure of that person; as to the facility in which the procedure is to be performed, that is, whether it must be a hospital or may be a clinic or some other place of less-than-hospital status; as to the licensing of the facility; and the like.[8]

How would you compare the legal provisions for abortion in Nazi Germany and contemporary America?

The following parallels are strikingly evident:

1) Medical autonomy in all facets of abortion.

2) Health of the mother as a wedge for mass abortion.

3) Physicians as legal executioners of the unborn.

4) Hospitals and clinics as the major killing centers.

5) Transformation of destructive activities into valid medical procedures when carried out by credentialed medical personnel in approved medical settings.

6) A total disregard for the existence, let alone rights, of the unwanted unborn child.

Weren't those who performed abortions in Nazi Germany severely punished?

Only when they departed from the criteria established by the Berlin Chamber of Physicians in 1933. Few doctors found it necessary to violate the new abortion law since the criteria were broad enough to encompass a wide range of rationalizations for destruction of the unborn.

The Maternal Health Rationalization

A prime criterion formulated by the Berlin Chamber of Physicians in 1933 for performing abortions required the presentation of reliable evidence that "a danger threatens the life or health of the mother." Doesn't this prove that abortion laws under the Hitler regime were restrictive instead of permissive?

Not at all. The restrictiveness or permissiveness of legal abortion hinges in great part on how the concept of health is interpreted. Long before Hitler came to power, physicians and medical organizations employed the mother's health as a global term to justify abortion for a wide range of indications, including both social and economic factors. In 1929 the Berlin Chamber of Physicians, reflecting a rapidly developing medical consensus, passed a resolution recommending the inclusion of "social and economic conditions" in deciding whether pregnancy constituted a "danger to the health of the mother.''[9] Significantly, it was this same Berlin Chamber of Physicians that was responsible for incorporating the ''health of the mother'' as a valid indication for legalized abortion during the Third Reich.

Another preview of how broadly the health justification for abortion was to be construed in Nazi Germany was revealed in 1929 by Federal Health Services Director Dr. Hamel in his testimony before the *reichstag.* ''The health of the woman—considered from all angles,'' he explained, ''is the decisive factor.''[10]

The mother's health thus served as an umbrella that covered abortion for an almost limitless range of excuses. In many instances, this amounted to nothing less than abortion on demand. The decisive category, health, was open-ended enough to permit abortion for almost any possible justification.

Didn't the U.S. Supreme Court in 1973 highlight the mother's health as one of its main considerations for justifying legalized abortion? Doesn't this demonstrate that the Court did not favor abortion on demand, but abortion only for those pregnancies that actually threatened the mother's life or health?

The Court's employment of such terms as ''health of the mother'' and ''maternal health'' in actuality created the legal monstrosity of abortion on request for all nine months of pregnancy. Like the Berlin Chamber of Physicians in 1933, the U.S. Supreme Court of 1973 interpreted the concept of health very loosely to encompass a broad spectrum of rationalizations.

This particular distortion of meaning did not develop out of a void. One of the many available wide-open definitions of health was supplied by the American College of Obstetricians and Gynecologists which, in 1968, approved of abortion in cases where the pregnancy ''may threaten the life of the woman or seriously impair her health.'' This highly influential medical group also furnished the following interpretation: ''In determining whether or not there is such risk to health, account may be taken of the patient's total environment, actual or reasonably forseeable.''[11]

Thus, drawing upon decades of medical propaganda for permissive abortion under the guise of health and buttressed by the World Health Organization's definition of health as ''a state of complete physical, mental and social well-being,'' Justice Harry Blackmun identified what the Court considered legitimate health-related reasons for abortion. The ''medical judgment'' pertaining to abortion, he wrote, ''may be exercised in the light of all factors —physical, emotional, pyschological, familial, and the woman's age—relevant to the well-being of the patient. All these factors may relate to health."[12]

How strikingly similar is the above definition, both in style and substance, to the way health was defined to legitimize abortion in Germany during the Third Reich: "the health of the woman—considered from all angles—is the decisive factor."[13]

The Eugenic Imperative

Did eugenics comprise an important rationalization for legalized abortion in the Third Reich and Roe v. Wade America?

In the decades before the Nazis took over control of the German government, eugenics constituted one of the prime justifications put forth for legalizing the killing of unborn children. Agitation for public support of eugenic abortion, manifested around the beginning of the twentieth century, grew out of a strongly entrenched eugenics movement preoccupied with the degeneration of the German race attributed to an overabundance of inferior people, the institutionalized insane, and criminals.[14] The eugenicists were determined to rid Germany of its unfit elements. Advocacy of abortion as a method of "artificial selection" of the subpar for oblivion did not get off the ground until euthanasia proponents had established a racist-imbued pattern of propaganda against postnatal expendables. Then eugenic abortion and euthanasia proposals proceeded alongside one another throughout the 1920s and into the 1930s.

Eugenics was one of the major indications used to justify legalizing abortion during the decades preceding the U.S. Supreme Court's decision supportive of abortion on request. The promotion of eugenic abortion in America, beginning in the 1930s, did not appear out of nowhere, but followed upon several decades of dire warnings about the contamination of the American populace from genetically inferior stock spearheaded by eugenicists operating out of prestigious Eastern universities.[15] During the 1930s euthanasia joined abortion as part of a eugenic-inspired campaign to legalize the elimination of defectives and potential defectives. This two-pronged thrust came to an abrupt halt in the 1940s as the horrendous consequences of eugenics under the Nazi regime were communicated to a shocked world. Eugenic thinking in the form of proposals for aborting the defective unborn made a comeback in the mid 1950s and increased in the 1960s and 1970s.

What were some of the specific eugenic-based proposals developed in generating support for legal abortion expansion before the Hitler government and the U.S. Supreme Court came up with their final solutions?

A fundamental strategy underlying the campaign to elicit public acceptance of eugenic abortion was unveiled by Dr. H. Poll at a meeting of the Berlin Society of Public Health Culture in 1921. "If physicians should be able to fix in the public mind that it is a crime to bring sick children into the world," he explained, "then, eugenic ordinances and laws that today are looked on as baleful interferences with personal freedom would come to be accepted as a matter of course."[16]

Dr. Poll's approach toward gaining public support of eugenic abortion did not cease with the fall of the Third Reich. If anything, it may have become indelibly rooted in the medical and social fabric of America. According to an assessment made by Dr. T. Ferguson Rodger in a 1968 issue of the *American Journal of Psychiatry,* a majority of people today are likely to consider it an "injustice" to "bring into the world a physically or mentally handicapped child or even to run the risk of doing so."[17]

By 1931 a number of eminent German practitioners, gynecologists and others agreed that a revision of the abortion law should allow for "eugenic considerations."[18]

At an American abortion conference held in 1955, the participants incorporated "eugenic indications" in one of their resolutions calling for modification of abortion statutes.[19]

When were eugenic indications for abortion endowed with full-fledged legal respectibility in Germany of the past and contemporary America?

It was not until after the Nazi government came to power that eugenic justifications for abortion became legally recognized. Special hereditary health courts were established to facilitate the destruction of unborn children suspected of being afflicted with some type of defect or abnormality. In 1934 the Hamburg Eugenics Court cited a "racial emergency" as the basis for embarking on a program of eugenic abortions. "A pregnancy may be interrupted," it pronounced, "in case either parent has been legally declared to present hereditary and transmissible defects."[20]

The 1973 U.S. Supreme Court abortion decision, which declared that abortions could be performed for any reason whatsoever as long as the doctor is willing to do them, furnished the logical foundation for the dramatic increase of eugenic abortions in today's America. The Court's allowance of abortion throughout all phases of pregnancy has proven to be a powerful stimulant for the rapid spread of amniocentesis and other prenatal diagnostic techniques intended to identify with increasing scientific certitude those intra-uterine victims considered not up to par with contemporary eugenic standards.

What kinds of procedures were developed to implement eugenic abortions in the Third Reich? What are the main approaches used to carry out eugenic abortions in contemporary America?

In Nazi Germany and the countries under Nazi domination pregnant women and the fathers of their children were subjected to racial examinations to determine the probability of carrying a child with genetic abnormalities. This examination consisted of a medical, social, and psychiatric history conducted by experts from the Race and Settlement Main Office.[21] The medical associations of Germany had previously agitated for acceptance of a broad range of conditions to justify legal destruction of the unborn. The eugenic grounds for abortion included such illnesses as Huntington's chorea, epilepsy, dimentia praecox, asocial psychopathy, manic-depressive insanity, mental retardation, amaurotic idiocy, and other anomalies.[22]

According to the decree which established the procedure for carrying out eugenic abortions on female Eastern workers, "if on the basis of the racial examination the offspring is expected not to be racially valuable, the consent for abortion is granted."[23] The sick bays and sick wards of the death camps served as the locales where unborn children who failed to measure up were destroyed.

Eugenic abortions in contemporary America are performed in university-based eugenics centers where medical experts employ the most sophisticated techniques to detect and destroy unborn children beset with some type of defect or genetic-related illness. At one such "model" genetic screening and "treatment" facility, the Wisconsin Clinical Eugenics Center of the University of Wisconsin (Madison), ultrasound and amniocentesis are utilized to determine the presence of such afflictions as Down's Syndrome, spina bifida, hydrocephalus, inherited metabolic disorders, anencephaly, congenital nephrosis, fetal liver dysfunction, atresia within the digestive tract, and various sex-linked disorders. In those cases where the finding is affirmative, 75 percent of the parents decide to have their handicapped child aborted.[24]

A team of experts consisting of physician-geneticists, genetics associates, obstetricians, high-risk nurse clinicians, cytogeneticists, biochemists, and fetal pathologists is called upon to ensure that every facet of the destructive decision is carried out in the most efficient and "humane" manner possible. After the abortion, according to acting director Dr. Renata Laxova, "the fetus is carefully investigated for external characteristics of the condition suspected, photographed, X-rayed, karyotyped, and a detailed autopsy is performed."[25]

The psychological trauma associated with participation in a lethal enterprise is dealt with through the provision of counseling sessions and by offering the parents the opportunity to view and fondle the victim, and take home the autopsy report and photographs of their destroyed offspring. In the words of Dr. Laxova:

> Parents are asked if they wish to see, hold the fetus (frequently they do), and whether they wish to receive photographs as well as copies of the autopsy report. After discharge, communication is maintained with the couple and their physician. An attempt is made to provide and ensure support during the grieving process.[26]

Compared with the American system of searching out and doing away with the afflicted before birth, the Nazi approach was exceedingly primitive. The Nazi racial supremists depended upon scientifically dubious information collected from parents suspected of possessing tainted genetic backgrounds. The American genetic elitists, in contrast, rely on the deadly precise data yielded by the most scientifically advanced methods of prenatal diagnosis.

Even the most dedicated Nazis, with their much vaunted reputation for technological know-how in the service of annihilation, could not begin to match the efficiency and comprehensiveness of operations at the Wisconsin Clinical Eugenics Center! Even the most desensitized Nazis would most likely experience extreme discomfort if confronted with the macabre details of how the deaths and defects of the victims at this institution are documented!

Number of Abortions Under Nazi Rule

How many abortions were actually performed in Germany during Hitler's reign?

Exact figures are hard to come by. Nevertheless, according to an article which appeared in a 1935 issue of the *Deutsches Aerzeblatt,* the official journal of the medical federations, a half-million abortions were performed annually in Germany.[27] If this is anywhere near an accurate barometer of the actual incidence of abortion, it represents an enormous number of unborn human lives destroyed. For a country comprising some 65 to 67 million people at that time, one-half million abortions annually hardly qualifies as the manifestation of a restrictive abortion policy in operation. The excessive extent to which the concept of health was abused can be gleaned by the fact that a large majority of abortions were done under the pretext of "the mother's health." Furthermore, the figure of one-half million may well be an underestimate because many abortions were officially classified as miscarriages.

What about Dr. Malcolm Potts' characterization of the Nazi logic that set up the concentration camps as "ferociously anti-abortion"?

This is even more absurd than saying that abortion in Nazi Germany was severely restricted.

The Nazi government, unfortunately, was not confined within the borders of Germany, but also dominated the huge territories of the East, including such countries as Poland, Hungary, Rumania, Czechoslovakia, Yugoslavia, and parts of Russia. It was here the Nazi government's pro-abortion policies became far more blatant and extensive. The killing of the unborn was considered a high priority item in the overall program of genocide. Abortion, along with gassing, shooting, imposed starvation, and sterilization, functioned as potent weapons for reducing the so-called "surplus" population perceived as genetically or socially useless.

Abortion constituted a prime method of extermination employed in the death camps against female Eastern workers.

How many abortions were performed in the nations under Nazi occupation?

Again, there are no precise figures available. It will never be known for sure how many human lives, either born or unborn, were snuffed out under the yoke of Nazi oppression. There is consensus on one point: the numbers stagger the imagination. The number of abortions performed "in the name of the purity of German blood" was so massive that Clarissa Henry and Marc Hillel, in their book *Of Pure Blood,* characterized it as "incalculable."[28]

Abortion Decrees for the Eastern Territories

What were some of the key decisions pertaining to abortions in countries under Nazi domination?

In addition to the outright extermination of Jews in Nazi-occupied territories, the Nazis developed a plan for eliminating other groups residing in these same areas. One of the earliest indications of this can be gleaned from an interministerial conference held on May 27, 1941 at the Ministry of the Interior of the Reich. Prominent among the measures considered essential for reducing the surplus populations was the following: "Official authorization for abortion at the mother's request."[29]

A decree of October 19, 1941 provided the basis for introducing abortion and other genocidal measures into countries under Nazi rule. They were directed mainly against the Polish people.[30]

On July 23, 1942, Martin Bormann sent instructions to Alfred Rosenberg for carrying out a new order which expanded abortions beyond Polish women to engulf all non-German females. "When girls and women in the occupied territories of the East have abortions," wrote Bormann to Rosenberg, "we can only be in favor of it; in any case, German jurists should not oppose it."[31]

I understand there were also a series of abortion decrees related to Eastern female workers. Could you specify some of the major ones?

An order of March 11, 1943 issued by the Reich Health Leader Dr. Leonardo Conti directed that "in the case of Eastern female workers pregnancy may be interrupted if the pregnant woman so desires."[32]

A circular signed by Dr. Ernst Kaltenbrunner on June 9, 1943 contained information on the procedural aspects of implementing the "Interruption of Pregnancy of Eastern Female Workers" decree.[33]

Several months later, on August 1, 1943, another circular letter from Dr. Kaltenbrunner indicated that abortions were also meant to encompass Eastern female workers of Polish descent.[34]

Who were these Eastern female workers?

Women who were exploited as slave laborers for the Nazi war effort. If they happened to become pregnant, they were aborted at Auschwitz and other locales so their services could continue to be used by the I.G. Farben Corporation and other industrial firms responsible for keeping the Nazi war machinery operating. One of the many documents submitted in testimony at the Nuremberg trials features a list of female workers who, between April and June 1944, "were admitted to the sick ward of the I.G. Farben Industry A.G., Auschwitz, at the request of the Association of German Health Insurance Physicians, district branch Katowice, for pregnancy interruption."[35]

A Method of Population Control

To what extent has propaganda highlighting the dangers of overpopulation played an important role in legalizing and sustaining the legality of unborn baby killing in the Third Reich and Roe v. Wade America?

By the early 1930s, concern about the escalating birth rates, particularly among those with hereditary defects, reached a level of near hysteria in Germany. In an address to the Prussian Council on Health on July 2, 1932, Dr. Schopohl warned that "the biological heritage of the German people is menaced" because families with "an unsound heritage are increasing unchecked."[36]

It is this type of ominous language which helped facilitate the legal destruction of not only the German handicapped, but also the unwanted unborn of captive European countries. A report issued in 1943 pointed out that the Reich decree pertaining to "interruptions of pregnancy of female Eastern workers and female Poles" was considered "a safety measure for the German people" because "the high birth rate of female Eastern workers and female Poles represented a biological weapon against the German people."[37] Accord ing to a letter addressed to the Reich Commissioner for the Strengthening of Germanism, the designation "undesirable population increase" provided the basis for aborting female Eastern workers at Auschwitz.[38]

Grim warnings of impending doom resulting from a runaway population have played a significant role in developing and perpetuating today's abortion culture. Many a pro-abortion physician has capitalized on population explosion terminology to justify the expansion of legal abortion. In the March 1970 issue of *Obstetrics and Gynecology,* two medical advocates of abortion contended that "man is threatening to annihilate himself by the very mass of his numbers" and "at our present growth rate, man will be forced either to starve himself or kill his neighbors."[39]

Such wildly gruesome accounts, although thoroughly refuted by responsible scientists and demographers, have proven to be dramatic and compelling enough to enhance the acceptability of killing off the unborn as a legitimate method of averting the disaster associated with overpopulation run amuck. Dr. Paul R. Ehrlich, popularizer of the "population bomb" metaphor, has characterized abortion as "a highly effective weapon in the armory of population control."[40] This view has even filtered down to the high school level where a large majority of students in an "ecography" class in Massachusetts agreed with a student who stated that if abortion is murder, "it's murder in context—it's self defense. We've simply got to defend ourselves against an increasing population."[41]

Enforced Abortions

According to the wording of many decrees pertaining to Eastern female workers (ie., "abortion at the mother's request" and "pregnancy may be interrupted if the pregnant woman so desires"), it seems they simply granted women the right to choose abortion.

If one accepts the wording at face value then the portrayal of abortion as a purely voluntary matter (on the part of the woman, but not the unborn child) is unmistakable. Like so many other things in the Third Reich, however, a huge gap existed between the image projected and the reality concealed underneath the imagery. Abortion actually functioned as a weapon to eradicate those defined as inferior, unwanted, and therefore expendable.

A document submitted at the RuSHA (Race and Settlement Main Office) Trial held in Nuremberg stripped away the facade of voluntarism surrounding the true nature of abortion:

> It is known that racially inferior offspring of Eastern workers and Poles is to be avoided if at all possible. Although pregnancy interruptions ought to be carried out on a voluntary basis only, pressure is to be applied in each of these cases.[42]

Are there any cases of forced abortions in contemporary American society?

The ideological commitment to a pro-abortion mentality is so deeply embedded that some abortionists have dropped the mask of so-called free choice and have actually recommended mandatory abortions, especially for the mentally retarded and young teenage mothers. At the National Abortion Federation Convention held in May 1980, abortion pioneer Dr. Jane Hodgson suggested the establishment of abortion as an obligatory form of immunization against teenage pregnancy viewed as a disease of epidemic proportions. "We have laws regarding other epidemics," she reasoned. "We have mandatory immunizations, but we have no law prohibiting motherhood before the age of 14." Her version of compulsory abortion consisted of "a mandate against continuing pregnancy in the very young—say, those less than 14 years."[43]

American Pro-Abortionists and The Nazi Abortion Experience

In light of the preceding facts, why do some prominent people still continue to maintain that abortions were severely limited by the Nazis?

Most of those who deny the actual extensiveness of abortion during the Nazi era are fervent proponents of abortion bent on distorting history for political purposes. Today's pro-abortion leaders have expended considerable effort promoting abortion as an indispensable civil right founded on such high-sounding values as liberty, happiness, and freedom. Any connection even implied between contemporary abortion and abortion in Germany of the past might possibly tarnish the purity of the highly positive image projected of abortion. Anti-life advocates are acutely aware that as long as massive killing of the unborn can be kept at the emotionally-remote level of minor surgical procedures and covered up with pleasant sounding abstractions, very few people are going to get upset.

The Nazi experience, probably more than any other event in history, reveals a sharply contrasting reality: the concrete, emotionally-charged and repugnant level of sheer barbarism directed against the unwanted both before and after birth. A non-biased knowledge of past horrors is likely to present a serious challenge to the euphemistic versions of the present. Only then are people apt to rise up out of their apathy, see killing for what it is in whatever historical period manifested, and become outraged enough to demand an end to the destruction. This is what today's abortion merchants fear most.

Those who dare draw any parallels between killing in Nazi Germany and destruction in contemporary American society are bound to be subjected to linguistic abuse bordering on sheer hysteria and characterized by an appalling shrillness and ferocity. An all too typical example of the unrestrained orgy of name calling aimed at individuals in the prolife movement for drawing attention to the holocaust-abortion connection is evident in the vocabulary of *Village Voice* staff writer Ellen Willis who scores the right-to-life movement as

> the most dangerous political force in the country . . . the cutting edge of neo-fascism . . . Christianity at its most authoritarian, parochial, and bigoted . . . anti-Semitic . . . apostles of brutality and repression.[44]

This particular tirade constitutes nothing more than gross rhetorical overkill designed to detract from the actual overkill of millions before birth. It is intended to intimidate and therefore discourage anyone from exploring, let alone probing in depth, the striking resemblances between past and current atrocities.

Dr. Frederick J. Taussig on Abortion

Have any American pro-abortionists ever acknowledged how widespread abortions were during the time of the Third Reich?

It would be very difficult to find an abortion advocate willing to confront such an embarrassing fact. However, there was one major figure in the U.S. abortion movement who not only told the truth about the expansion of legalized abortion in the Nazi regime, but even presented the Nazi abortion experience as a model for changing the American abortion laws!

Who are you referring to?

The late Dr. Frederick J. Taussig, an obstetrics professor at the Washington University School of Medicine in St. Louis, Missouri. Dr. Taussig stood in the very forefront of the persistent campaign waged by American physicians to strike down laws protective of human life in the womb long before the Supreme Court got into the act of legalizing mass extermination. His book, *Abortion Spontaneous and Induced: Medical and Social Aspects* (1936), served as a veritable bible for the pro-abortion forces in their efforts to obtain legal recognition of unlawful assaults on the unborn.

Just what did Dr. Taussig say about abortion in Nazi Germany?

A study of the abortion law in Germany before and during the Nazi regime led him to conclude:

> The struggle to have therapeutic indications for abortion (done by a physician) legally recognized did not meet with success until 1933, when the new enactments passed by the Hilter government established that abortion under genuine medical indications is not subject to punishment when demanded and performed by legally qualified physicians.[45]

As previously demonstrated, "genuine medical indications" were commonly interpreted to justify abortion for a wide range of factors, including social, economic, and eugenic considerations. In Nazi Germany as long as the abortion was performed by a doctor it was considered "therapeutic." The exact same situation exists currently in American society.

Provide a synopsis of legalized abortion in the Third Reich and Roe v. Wade America.

Chart 2 on page 32 includes some of the main justifications and operational facets of lawful destruction perpetrated against the unwanted unborn in Germany of the past and present-day America.

Chart 2
Abortion as the Law of the Land

The Third Reich	Roe v. Wade America
Abortion Legalization	
In 1933 the Nazi government legalized abortion for greatly expanded indications according to guidelines formulated by pro-abortion associations.	In 1973 the U.S. Supreme Court legalized abortion on demand, a position in line with resolutions enacted by pro-abortion medical associations.
Abortion and Maternal Health	
"The health of the woman—considered from all angles—is the decisive factor." (Federal Health Services Director Dr. Hamel)	"All these factors may relate to health. . . physical, emotional, psychological, familial." (U.S. Supreme Court Justice Harry Blackmun)
The Eugenic Imperative	
Unborn children suspected of being defective on the basis of information collected from their parents were destroyed in hospitals and the sick bays of concentration camps.	Unborn children identified as defective through the application of such techniques as amniocentesis and ultrasound are destroyed in hospitals and eugenics centers.
Abortion Implementation	
One-half million legal abortions were performed annually. (*Deutsches Aerzeblatt,* July 1935)	One and one-half million legal abortions are performed annually. (Alan Guttmacher Institute, 1981)
Population Control	
An "undesirable population increase." (Justification employed for aborting female Eastern workers at Auschwitz, 1944)	A defense "against an increasing population." (Justification for abortion employed by a group of high school students, 1973)
Enforced Abortions	
Mandatory abortions for the defective offspring of Eastern workers and Poles. (Document, Abortions on Eastern Workers, 1943)	Abortion as an obligatory immunization against teenage pregnancy as an epidemic disease. (Dr. Jane Hodgson, 1980)

Chapter 4

Hitler on Abortion

I have heard some people say that Hitler was strongly opposed to abortion.

Hitler is reputed to have said many things, some of which are totally false or half true at best. Keep in mind that Hitler did not invent mass killing of the born or unborn. The seeds of extermination had been planted long before he came to power.

Was he or was he not against abortion?

Hitler, obviously, did not favor abortion for Aryan women.

Individuals such as Gloria Steinem, who have characterized Hitler as unequivocably opposed to abortion, are right then?

Not at all. This is only part of the picture, and a minor one at that. Hitler's opposition to abortion possessed a definite ideological flavor: the building of a master race of Aryans. The converse of this, the tearing down of non-Aryans, necessitated a strong pro-abortion mindset. In the view of Hitler and other racists of that time, non-Aryans constituted a huge conglomeration of inferior people who threatened the survival of the superior Aryans.

Hitler dreaded, in particular, the high birth rates among the so-called surplus populations of the East. On balance, he was far more intent on promoting abortions among women in the Eastern territories than in preventing abortions among Aryan women. The reduction of the surplus populations comprised an especially urgent problem to be resolved with the utmost dispatch.

If Hitler was against abortion, as the pro-abortionists contend, how does one account for the expansion of legalized abortion in Germany during his regime?

Perhaps he was not actually that strongly anti-abortion, even for Aryan women. When the Führer came to power he did nothing to reverse the well-entrenched medical movement to broaden the range of indications for legal abortion. What he did was aid its facilitation by establishing guidelines and procedures for implementing legalized abortion in the Third Reich in accord with those supported by the Berlin Chamber of Physicians.[1] And this particular medical association was a foremost booster of abortion according to a very loose definition of health.

Although Hitler and his government encouraged Aryan women to produce alot of children, he left the matter of abortion and all its facets in the hands of a decidedly pro-abortion medical establishment. Even in the midst of Nazi propaganda aimed at increasing the Aryan population, scores of Aryan women still chose to abort their unborn children. By 1935 the medical federations publication *Deutsches Aerzleblatt* reported that the number of abortions performed in Germany each year reached half a million.[2] For the most part, such abortions were perfectly legal since they were performed by licensed physicians in approved settings according to a global definition of health.

Whatever Hitler's personal attitude toward abortion, the medical profession and not the Führer, determined the criteria for legal abortion. And they were wide open!

Was the U.S Supreme Court's reaction to American medical involvement in abortion similar to Hitler's reaction to German medical involvement in abortion?

The Supreme Court, in a manner strikingly reminiscent of Hitler, left the matter of abortion in the hands of a strongly pro-abortion medical establishment. The Court, deplorably, capitulated to the anti-life forces in the medical profession and granted legal sanction to what many doctors desired or had already done in violation of the law.[3]

What evidence is there to indicate the extent of Hitler's pro-abortion plans for people residing in the Eastern territories?

A Nazi decree of October 19, 1941 established abortion on demand as the offical policy for Poland.[4]

Hitler, however, expressed dissatisfaction with this policy. Abortion, he believed, should not be limited to Poland. He therefore ordered that abortion be extended to all populations under the control of the "Ministry of the Occupied Territories of the East."[5]

On July 22, 1942, the Führer exhibited a highly positive attitude toward abortion as an indispensable method of dealing with the non-German populations in countries under Nazi rule. "In view of the large families of the native population," he asserted, "it could only suit us if girls and women there had as many abortions as possible." Hitler also announced that he "would personally shoot" any "such idiot" who "tried to put into practice such an order [forbidding abortions] in the occupied Eastern territories."[6]

The next day Martin Bormann, acting directly under orders from Hitler, sent instructions to Alfred Rosenberg for implementing the abortion expansion policy.[7]

What are some of the major questions which should be addressed to those who still maintain that Hitler and his government were anti-abortion?

Chart 3

Questions for a Personally Opposed Politician, Adolf Hitler

1. If Hitler was opposed to abortion, why didn't he demand that Germany's strong law protective of human life before birth (enacted in 1871) be retained?

2. If Hitler was opposed to abortion, why did he leave the matter of abortion in the hands of the most vociferous pro-abortion physicians and medical organizations in Germany?

3. If Hitler was opposed to abortion, why did he permit the establishment of guidelines and procedures for legal abortion in close conformity to those developed by the Berlin Chamber of Physicians, a prominent advocate of permissive abortion under the guise of health?

4. If the Nazi government had such restrictive laws on abortion, why were there at least half-a-million abortions performed annually in Germany?

5. If Hitler was opposed to abortion, why did he say that "in view of the large families of the native population it could only suit us if girls and women there had as many abortions as possible"?

6. If Hitler was opposed to abortion, why did he order that abortion on demand be instituted as the prevailing policy for all countries under Nazi domination?

7. If Hitler was opposed to abortion, why did he threaten to shoot anyone who attempted to forbid abortions in Nazi occupied areas?

8. If the Nazi government was opposed to abortion, why did it issue an endless series of decrees legalizing the destruction of the unborn throughout the Eastern territories?

How would you summarize the position of Hitler and the Nazi government toward abortion?

Despite contemporary attempts to characterize Hitler as opposed to abortion, the historical evidence clearly and overwhelmingly supports only one possible conclusion: Hitler and his regime were adamantly pro-abortion. To depict Hitler as anti-abortion is as ludicrous as calling him anti-genocide or pro-Jewish. Both Hitler and his government had little regard for human life perceived as subpar, whether born or unborn. Even if Hitler had been personally opposed to abortion, like so many of today's "personally opposed to abortion" politicians, such personal convictions never became a significant part of either laws or policies.

Chapter 5

Bureaucratic Extermination

The killing of millions is not the product of psychopaths giving vent to uncontrolled impulses, but skilled technicians who carry out their destructive tasks in a highly rational, business-like manner. Extermination under bureaucratic auspices is characterized by such dimensions as *speed, efficiency, decor, technicism, legality, remote victims,* and *psychic numbing.*

How well do these dimensions apply to destruction in the Third Reich?

Extremely well. What made the Nazi holocaust absolutely unique, according to holocaust scholar Professor Henry Friedlander, is not the fact that millions of people were put to death. "The impulse to exterminate is old and pervasive," he concluded. "Mass murder is nothing new." It is the technological, bureaucratic components which distinguish the Nazi holocaust from all other forms of mass killing. The Nazis rationalized the killings and built factories for genocide in which human beings were processed on an assembly line that operated on the basis of productivity, profit, cost accounting, and space utilization.[1]

What about the application of these elements to contemporary American society?

Tragically, the bureaucratic aspects of mass destruction pioneered during the Nazi era are no longer unique. The technological proficiency with which today's unwanted unborn are dispatched to oblivion at least matches, and even surpasses, the proficiency with which the Nazi victims were processed out of existence.

Discuss more fully the dimensions of bureaucratic destruction and their implementation in Nazi Germany and contemporary America.

A comparative analysis of concentration camps and abortion clinics on these dimensions provides eye-opening insights into the process of bureaucratic annihilation, both past and present.

Goals

The goals of both concentration camps and abortion clinics are identical: the destruction of unwanted human lives.

Concentration camps specialized in exterminating Jews, Gypsies, Poles, asocials, and the unborn children of female slave laborers.

Abortion clinics are devoted to the task of destroying unborn children in the first trimester of pregnancy. Many abortoriums have even expanded their destructive operations to consume victims in the later stages of pregnancy.

Speed

Rudolf Höss, commandant of Auschwitz, estimated that it took from three to fifteen minutes to kill the gas chamber victims.[2] According to Auschwitz survivor Dr. Miklos Nyiszli, everybody inside the chambers died "within five minutes."[3]

At the Eastern Women's Center abortion chamber in New York City, it takes "only two to three minutes" to do an abortion.[4] Some doctors have reported that "aspiration" of the "fetal parts" can be accomplished in even less than two minutes.[5]

Auschwitz inmates injected with lethal doses of phenol died quickly: "two or three prisoners in one minute." The speediest of the phenol technicians was Josef Klehr who "injected two prisoners at a time."[6]

Dr. Ming K. Hah, reputed to be the fastest abortionist in Chicago, vacuums the unborn to smithereens at a breakneck pace: eight abortions per hour, forty per day. His productivity rate is so impressive that he sometimes performs two abortions simultaneously.[7]

Efficiency

In the Nazi death camps annihilation as an assembly-line enterprise came of age. According to holocaust scholar Raul Hilberg: "A man would step off a train in the morning, and in the evening his corpse was burned and his clothes packed away for shipment to Germany."[8]

Today, a woman can enter an abortion clinic on her lunch hour and, by the time she is due to return to work, all the remnants of her unborn baby's body and intrauterine life support membranes are obliterated by an assembly-line process which would make even the most avid Nazi technician gasp in awe!

At the Auschwitz crematorium, 17,280 corpses were disposed of "per twenty-four hour shift. And the ovens, with murderous efficiency, functioned day and night."[9]

Dr. Bernard N. Nathanson, former director of a large abortion clinic in New York City, described how proficiently his mill operated: "From eight in the morning until midnight, seven days a week, doctors working in ten operating rooms performed vacuum aspirations on an endless parade of pregnant wombs. In the peak months more than 3,000 . . . Doctors regularly worked 12-hour shifts."[10]

Decor

Neither concentration camps nor abortion clinics give the impression of being settings for mass extermination. Both have gone to considerable lengths to conceal the true nature of their activities. Both have employed decor extensively to cosmetize destruction.

Survivor Jean-Francois Steiner revealed that the flower beds surrounding the railroad station at Treblinka where the victims were selected for death gave the whole area "a neat and cheery look."[11]

An architect's report on a modern abortion clinic interior emphasizes the significance of using plants and bright colors for creating a "cheerful and anxiety-free environment."[12]

Franz Stangl, former commandant of Treblinka, disclosed how he attempted to minimize the horrors of destruction by focusing on the establishment of a pleasant atmosphere: "gardens, new barracks, new kitchens, new everything. . . There were hundreds of ways to take one's mind off it; I used them all."[13]

Most abortion clinics resemble, as one close observer so aptly pointed out, professionally decorated beauty salons.[14] Their plush interiors and furnishings are not unlike those funeral establishments, brilliantly satirized in Evelyn Waugh's *The Loved One,* so completely dedicated to the art of denying and cosmetizing death.[15]

Cleanliness

An aspect of decor highlighted in both concentration camps and abortion clinics is the existence of clean settings.

The medical front at Dachau, the locale for the horrendous freezing and high altitude experiments, was characterized as follows:

> At first glance Dachau would appear to be a model camp . . . fine showerbaths . . . spotless kitchens . . . The *Revier* (sickbay) would seem amazingly clean and tidy. It included . . . two magnificent operating theatres with a sterilization room . . . beautiful parquet floors to the wards.[16]

This, according to holocaust survivor Elie Cohen, simply served as a facade: "The Nazis—including the Nazi physicians—pursued but one aim: *extermination.* The whole medical apparatus was nothing but a *decor*, nothing but a lie intended to disguise the massacre."[17]

The same principle of cosmetizing destruction lurks beneath the slick, antiseptic veneer of today's abortion clinics. It has had a profound impact. A number of abortion clinic clients have expressed appreciation for having the opportunity of being aborted "in a sanitary hospital environment."[18]

Inside the gas chambers of Auschwitz great care was taken to ensure that "everything was spotlessly clean."[19]

The procedure room of the modern abortion clinic is commonly referred to as "a medical environment of manifest cleanliness and surgical correctness."[20]

The Nazis expressed strong opposition to pogroms (killing of Jews by street mobs) not because of an antipathy to killing per se. Pogroms were considered too messy, dirty, and capable of being exposed for what they were. The systematic destruction of millions required a setting where killing could proceed swiftly, efficiently, unobtrusively, and cleanly.[21] The camouflaging of gas chambers as bath houses epitomized the Nazi preoccupation with purging their destructive activities with the help of an antiseptic front.

By the same token, contemporary abortionists are against back-street abortions not because they abhor killing as such. Backalley butchery is deemed too unsavory an approach toward destruction, and capable of being seen for what it really is. The modern massacre of millions before birth demands an antiseptic locale where killing can be carried out quickly, proficiently, and inconspicuously. The disguising of killing centers as clinics illustrates the medical obsession with cleansing their destructive tasks of any impurities.

Music

Another element related to decor found in past and present killing centers is the presence of music.

An inmate orchestra played a medly of tangos, jazz numbers, and popular ballads during the process of selecting victims for extermination at Auschwitz. Reassuring strains of music also could be heard as they marched to the gas chambers."[22]

Today's unborn victims do not have the benefit of an orchestra to accompany them on their journey to extinction. Many clinics, however, do provide the world's most soothing music, piped in through a stereophonic system. At an abortion clinic in New York City the Beatles' *Lucy in the Sky with Diamonds* could be heard coming from a loudspeaker.[23] A woman who had her unborn child destroyed at another abortion facility recalled how the "music provided a soothing touch."[24]

Technicism

Destruction under bureaucratic auspices requires, above all, proficient technicians who carry out destructive activities in the exact same manner as any other technical procedure. Maintaining and operating the machinery of destruction become ends in themselves and override all other considerations. The implementers and operators distance themselves from the emotionally-repulsive facets of their destructive tasks by concentrating exclusively on the procedural aspects.

The individual in Nazi Germany who probably best epitomized an extreme form of technicism was Adolf Eichmann, the Nazi official responsible for planning and coordinating the final solution to the Jewish question. At his trial in Israel in 1963, Eichmann presented himself as a dispassionate civil servant who performed his duties in a meticulous, rational, and efficient manner. He emphasized harboring no personal antipathy toward Jews. In fact, he mentioned that some of his best friends were Jews. The task of dispatching millions of Jews to their deaths was portrayed as a strictly technical matter unrelated to Eichmann's or any other Nazi bureaucrat's personal disposition.[25]

Contemporary medical abortionists occupy a role similar to that of Adolf Eichmann. They utilize the most sophisticated methods to destroy millions of human lives before birth in a highly proficient manner. A strict focus on the technological dimensions of their destructive procedures helps doctors carry out some of the most barbaric acts ever devised without being bothered. Like Eichmann's attitude toward the Jews, modern physician abortionists claim they have nothing personal against the unborn. This contention is reinforced by the fact that many killers of the unborn are obstetricians who apply their technical expertise to the task of delivering as well as aborting babies.

It is this same obsessive preoccupation with technology which prompted world famous psychologist Bruno Bettelheim to provide insight into how the death camp doctor was able to pervert medical skills for destructive ends: "By taking pride in his professional skills, irrespective of what purpose they were used for."[26]

During the Auschwitz trial held in Frankfurt in 1964, details were furnished on the killing of children with injections of phenol administered directly into their hearts in the "treatment room" of Block 20 at Auschwitz. "The children," according to survivor Czeslaw Glowacki, "put their thin arms across their mouths, the poison needle jabbed between their skinny ribs, and they fell down like blades of grass and were dragged out to the other victims, to make room for those who were still playing outside."[27]

Additional testimony presented by another survivor, Polish physician Dr. Fejkiel, brought out the extreme technical orientation of those who stabbed their victims in the heart: "They all bragged of having acquired a certain degree of skill in injecting the phenol."[28]

Pride in technological destruction through injections did not end with the fall of the Third Reich. Although today's medical abortionists do not administer phenol directly into the hearts of their victims, they have come up with a technique which bears a disquieting resemblance. In June 1981 it was disclosed that doctors at Mount Sinai School of Medicine in New York City destroyed an unwanted unborn twin afflicted with Down's Syndrome by piercing his heart and draining out almost half his blood. The successful implementation of this destructive procedure required the application of ultrasound "to hit a moving target [the baby's heart] less than an inch across" with a needle.[29] The physicians who participated in this act of exterminative medicine described it as "a very gratifying experience."[30] What has been hailed as a revolutionary scientific breakthrough is much closer to a precision-type military operation conducted against an enemy!

Doctors at the Medical College of Virginia found that extracting 50 percent of fetal blood volume from an unwanted unborn twin afflicted with Tay-Sachs disease did not result in the desired outcome: death. Their final and successful resolution consisted of "embolization with a bolus of air" (death by injection of an air mass, causing blockage of the baby's circulation), after deciding against an injection of potassium because it was considered "potentially dangerous to the normal fetus."[31]

Interviews conducted by Yale psychiatrist Robert Jay Lifton of former concentration camp doctors revealed that they avoided confronting the realities of mass destruction by talking compulsively about technical matters.[32]

Equally obsessive technical accounts of abortion have the effect of camouflaging another horrendous reality: today's medical war on the unborn. As Columbia University obstetrics professor Dr. Robert E. Hall so candidly put it: "I would place the doctor in the role of a technician, simply wielding the curette."[33]

Legality

Many years ago prominent German sociologist Max Weber wrote a classic article on the nature of bureaucracy in which he set down its main characteristics, including some of those discussed here so far, such as goals, efficiency, and technicism. According to Weber, however, the most fundamental factor which distinguishes a bureaucracy from all other types of social structure is its solid grounding in legal authority. A bureaucracy owes its legitimacy to the existence of legally constituted rules and orders.[34]

Little wonder, then, that the bureaucrat is forever quoting rules and regulations to guide the performance of his tasks. His work-a-day world is dominated, not by autonomy in behavior and decision making, but by almost blind obedience to preconceived regulations buttressed by that infallible creature known as the law. In the mind-set of the bureaucrat, the laws and procedures which govern his activities must not be questioned, but simply obeyed to the letter.

All the more so when the task at hand consists of killing human beings. Then the law serves as a convenient crutch for denying personal responsibility for destruction. "What is legal is moral" is a frightening slogan invoked to justify all manner of atrocities down through history. It stands at the very core of bureaucratic extermination: the systematic, rational, assembly-line killing of millions.

At the Nuremberg Doctors' Trial in 1947, witness Walter E. Schmidt supplied the predominant rationalization for the Nazi program of extermination. "The jurists in Berlin," he testified, "told us that this was a legal matter . . . quite legal."[35]

In 1980, Dr. Michael Jackson furnished a similar justification for owning and operating six abortion clinics. "I just go by what the courts say," he explained. "I only do what's legal."[36]

Such statements as "these people were carrying out the laws of the land" and "the accused did not act wrongly because they were covered by law" formed the backbone of the argumentation employed at the Hadamar Euthanasia Trial to defend nurses who injected inmates with lethal substances.[37]

In 1975, just after being convicted of manslaughter for asphyxiating a living aborted baby, Dr. Kenneth C. Edelin declared: "I did nothing which was illegal, immoral or bad medical practice. Everything I did was in accordance with law."[38]

The jurists at Nuremberg and other war crimes trials listened with incredulity as defendant after defendant invoked the law to disavow responsibility for the atrocities. In his reflections on Auschwitz, Professor Richard L. Rubenstein states: "One of the most difficult conclusions to which we have come is that the Nazis committed no crime at Aushwitz since no law or political order protected those who were first condemned to statelessness and then to the camps."[39]

The killing of the unborn today, like the killing of the Jews during the Nazi era, is also perfectly legal since they have been defined out of the human race, rendered devoid of legal protection, relegated to statelessness, and then dispatched to the abortion chambers.

Distorted legality thus serves as the foundation of authority upon which the bureaucratic executioners of the past and those of the present have flourished in carrying out their destructive procedures.

Non-Visibility of the Victims

Bureaucratic destruction works best when the technology employed keeps the victims out of sight. If they can be rendered non-visible, a claim can be made that they do not exist. This in turn eliminates the emotionally-repulsive elements associated with killing visible victims and helps reduce destruction to the trivial level of a technical procedure.

Most Nazi victims were first removed from public view and then killed in concentration camps located in remote sections of Poland.

Although most unborn children are destroyed in large metropolitan areas, their massacre is hidden inside special facilities camouflaged as clinics.

Several years ago psychoanalyst Erich Fromm highlighted a striking similarity between the killing caused by bomber crews in World War II and the annihilation brought about by Nazi-built gas chambers. Both methods, he explained, did an excellent job of hiding victims and their fates from the eyes of the perpetrators.

Geographic distance prevented the bomber crew members from viewing the impact of their technical ministrations. Since they did not actually see people being burned, maimed, or killed, they remained emotionally-detached operators carrying out emotionally-neutral tasks.

So too for those who manned the gas chambers. Although closer geographically to their victims than the bomber crew personnel, the chamber experts remained psychologically-distant technicians because the agonies of men, women, and children being asphyxiated or trampled to death were concealed from view behind the chamber walls.[40]

The same principle holds for the application of abortion technology. In the majority of abortions perpetrated, especially those during the first 12 weeks of gestation, the uterine walls, like the gas chamber walls, prevent the doctor and his assistants from having to see the horrendous consequences of their scientific handiwork: human bodies being torn apart or sucked to oblivion. As acknowledged by Dr. Ernest Frederick on a St. Louis television program: "If you look carefully you don't see a human being in there, and that makes it much easier for the people who do abortions."[41]

Therefore, as long as the perpetrators neither touch nor see their victims, they can sustain themselves in the role of a dispassionate bureaucrat merely doing his duty. This kind of killing is limitless because nobody kills; nobody kills because there is no perceptible victim. The intervention of machinery between perpetrator and victim provides the proper amount of geographical and psychological distance to make killing at the level of a holocaust a reality. The gas chambers of the past and the vacuum aspirators of the present represent the type of destructive machinery capable of transforming incomprehensible horrors into routine banalities.

Psychic Numbing

An excessive focus on the technical, professional components of destruction leads to a particularly deplorable mentality best characterized as a state of psychic numbing. This involves a loss of capacity to feel on the part of the perpetrator and a pervasive brutalization. "What happens is that the aggressor cuts the other person off emotionally, and 'freezes' him," concluded Erich Fromm. "The other person ceases to be experienced as human, and becomes a 'thing—over there.'"[42]

The process of destroying the victim therefore is perceived as nothing more significant than operating a mechanical device which results in discarding an object or thing. The tunnel vision of the technician coupled with an abysmal lack of empathy—an inability or unwillingness to identify the victim as a human being—create the conditions necessary for the release of inhibitions against the most massive forms of destruction. "Psychic numbing," states Robert Jay Lifton, "is one of the great problems of our age.[43]

The following testimony presented at Nuremberg provides a stark glimpse into the emotionally-detached mindset of the gassing technician:

> Q. In case the inmates would not have been killed following the introduction of the gas done by you, would you have killed them with a bullet?
>
> A. I would have tried once again to suffocate them with gas, by throwing another dose of gas into the chamber. I had no feelings in carrying out these things. That, by the way, was the way I was trained.[44]

A strikingly similar mentality is evident in the comments of a medical abortionist who admitted having "harpooned the fetus" like a "fish hooked on a line" on a number of occasions in the process of injecting lethal doses of poisonous salt solution into the victim's amniotic sac. "I never had any psychological adverse reaction," he declared. "Except an occasional feeling that one was destroying life."[45]

A common method of killing individuals in the Eastern territories under Nazi occupation consisted of mass shootings in front of huge ditches. Those who pulled the trigger at point blank range did not have the luxury of avoiding the direct consequences of their actions. Although some perpetrators were bothered at first, quite a few came to see themselves as strictly professionals performing an unpleasant but necessary task.

Commenting on face-to-face killing without the psychological protection of distance available to bomber crews, psychohistorian Lifton concluded:

> While there is little ethical difference between killing someone far away whom one cannot see, and looking directly into the victim's eyes from five or ten feet away while pulling the trigger, there is a considerable psychological difference between the two acts.[46]

It is the implementation of this type of method which requires what Lifton calls an advanced state of psychic numbing.

A comparable blunting of emotionality is also an indispensable prerequisite for physicians involved in D & E (Dilatation and Extraction) abortions. This kind of destructive procedure, performed beyond the twelfth week of pregnancy, involves literally slicing apart and extracting the bodies of human beings in advanced stages of pregnancy. According to University of California (San Francisco) gynecologist Dr. Sadja Goldsmith, "wielding forceps with no-slip transverse edges, a doctor extracts the fetus piece by piece."[47]

The D & E abortionist, like the shooting squad member, does not have the benefit of operating in an atmosphere devoid of visible victims. Again, according to Dr. Goldsmith, "The gynecologist is aware of being the active agent in the D & E procedure" because he "is the one who is crushing and dismembering the fetus."[48] Experienced D & E abortionist Dr. Warren Hern agrees. "There is no possibility of denial of an act of destruction by the operator," he adds. "The sensations of dismemberment flow through the forceps like an electric current."[49]

Although there is little ethical difference between manning a vacuum machine which tears apart the tiny bodies of victims one cannot touch or see, and directly viewing the dismembered remains of much larger victims which one has just yanked out with forceps, there is a considerable psychological difference between these two acts.

While some physicians have expressed misgivings about the D & E approach toward destruction, many doctors "get used to the procedure."[50] Apparently, given time and practice, even this most blatant method of scientific butchery becomes routine and bereft of emotional revulsion. The extent of psychic numbing manifested in the utilization of D & E methodology is comparable to the most extreme forms of desensitization prevalent during the darkest days of the Third Reich.

Chart 4

The Killing Centers: The Art of Bureaucratizing and Cosmetizing Destruction

Concentration Camps	Abortion Clinics
GOALS	
The destruction of unwanted human beings before and after birth.	The destruction of unwanted human beings before birth.
METHODS	
Asphyxiation of unseen victims inside chamber walls.	Dismemberment of unseen victims inside uterine walls.
SPEED	
"Within five minutes everybody was dead" inside the chamber. (Auschwitz survivor Dr. Miklos Nyiszli, 1960)	"The abortion itself [takes] only two to three minutes." (Eastern Women's Center, 1978)
EFFICIENCY	
17,280 corpses were disposed of "per twenty-four hour shift. And the ovens, with murderous efficiency, functioned day and night." (Auschwitz survivor Dr. Olga Lengyel, 1947)	"From eight in the morning until midnight, seven days a week, doctors working in ten operating rooms performed vacuum aspirations on an endless parade of pregnant wombs." (Former abortion clinic director Dr. Bernard N. Nathanson, 1976)
DECOR	
The presence of flower beds gave the area "a neat and cheery look." (Description of railroad station at Treblinka where victims were selected for death)	Plants and bold colors create a "cheerful and anxiety-free environment." (Architect's report on the interior of a modern abortion clinic)

Chart 4 (Continued)

The Killing Centers: The Art of Bureaucratizing and Cosmetizing Destruction

Concentration Camps	Abortion Clinics
CLEANLINESS	
"Everything was spotlessly clean." (Description of gas chamber at Auschwitz)	"A medical environment of manifest cleanliness." (Description of an abortion procedure room in New York)
MUSIC	
An inmate orchestra played a medley of tangos, jazz numbers and popular ballads as the victims were dispatched to the "shower rooms."	Soothing music, piped in through a stereophonic system, can be heard as the victims are being disposed of in the "procedure rooms."
TECHNICISM	
They avoided the realities of mass destruction by talking compulsively about technical matters. (Former death camp doctors, 1980)	"I would place the doctor in the role of a technician, simply wielding the curette." (Dr. Robert E. Hall, 1970)
LEGALITY	
"The jurists in Berlin told us that this was a legal matter. . . quite legal." (Witness Walter E. Schmidt on the predominant justification for extermination, Nuremburg Doctors' Trial, 1947)	"I just go by what the courts say . . . I only do what's legal." (Abortion clinic chain owner and operator Dr. Michael Jackson, 1980)
PSYCHIC NUMBING	
"I had no feelings in carrying out these things." (Testimony of gassing technician at Nuremberg)	"I never had any psychological adverse reaction." (Abortion doctor's response to performing abortions)

Chapter 6

Experimental Barbarities

Widespread experimental exploitation of human beings does not develop out of a void. It depends on a steady supply of research expendables upon whom every conceivable procedure and indignity can be perpetrated. Only a massive program of killing is up to furnishing the prescribed types of subjects in large enough quantities.

In societies where destruction exists on a pervasive scale, it is inevitable that extensive medical manipulation and mutilation of the products of destruction will follow. Physicians are not content with simply killing human beings or pioneering some of the world's most technically advanced methods of killing. They are also intent on draining every possible ounce of scientific data out of their subjects before, during, and after expiration.

Mass experimentation, then, is essentially a by-product of mass destruction; it does not begin to prevail until widespread killing becomes a firmly established practice. Then an incomparable pool of research subjects is made available to satisfy the appetites of even the most rabidly curious scientists. In Nazi Germany the experimental population consisted primarily of concentration camp inmates destined for annihilation in the gas chambers. Today, an ever-escalating number of experimental subjects are being supplied from the ranks of unborn children slated for extermination in hospitals and abortion chambers.

"The war in the East," declared Nazi medical researcher Dr. August Hirt, "now presents us with the opportunity to remedy this shortage."[1] The shortage of which he spoke was the availability of Jewish skulls for anthropological research. "The war in the East" permitted Dr. Hirt to remedy the scarcity by severing the heads of gas chamber victims.

Today's medical war on the unborn likewise provides fetal researchers with virtually limitless opportunities to exploit to the hilt individuals and information previously unavailable for scientific scrutiny and action.

The Scope of Research

How extensive were the medical experiments carried out in the concentration camps?

The legalized extermination of Jews and others ushered in an unprecedented scientific orgy of experiments on helpless human guinea pigs. Although only twenty medical doctors were actually brought to trial at Nuremberg for crimes against humanity in conjunction with the horrendous death camp experiments, hundreds of physicians actively implicated never had to face their victims in a court of law. The Nuremberg Doctors' Trial not only furnished extensive documentation on the large number and broad range of experiments perpetrated, but also provided a showcase for the well entrenched philosophical, legal, linguistic, and medical rationalizations developed by the defendants to justify their involvement.

Most people do not realize the extent to which the concentration camp experiments had become embedded in the fabric of German medicine. Details of some of the most notorious experiments were even presented at medical conventions and published in medical journals.[2]

How extensive is fetal research in the United States?

Ever since the 1973 U.S. Supreme Court decision on legalizing the destruction of unborn children, medical scientists have waged a relentless campaign to expand the frontiers of research on human fetuses scheduled for abortion destruction. Biomedical researcher Dr. John A. Morris predicted "a whole new spectrum of research" in "the normal (and abnormal) human fetus" with the advent of "progressive liberalization of the abortion laws."[3] In the fall of 1980, researchers and philosophers gathered together at a symposium, "The Concept of Person and its Implications for the Use of the Fetus in Biomedicine," to develop additional philosophical, legal, linguistic, and medical justifications for increasing the amount of research performed on the unwanted unborn.[4]

The number of articles published in medical journals pertaining to the use of aborted babies for experimental purposes, a key indicator of research activity, has increased sharply since the early 1970s. The most recent volumes of *Cumulated Index Medicus,* an index of medical journal articles published, provide a barometer of what is happening throughout the world.[5] These listings do not cover the many experiments performed which do not get published.

In 1978, the last year for which complete statistics are available, 70,670 abortions were performed in the U.S. during the second trimester of pregnancy and later with methods (saline poisoning, prostaglandin, or hysterectomy/hysterotomy)[6] most likely to yield subjects suitable for experimentation. This represents a vast annual pool of potential research material. Little wonder, then, that the number of experiments imposed on aborted babies has risen so dramatically!

I thought that the National Commission for the Protection of Human Subjects of Biomedical and Behavioral Research enacted regulations to curtail fetal research.

At first glance this may seem to be the case, but a closer examination of the actual recommendations passed reveals an exceedingly permissive attitude regarding experimentation on unborn children before, during, and after abortion. Some of the major provisions recommended by the Commission for permitting nontherapeutic research ("research not designed to improve the health of the research subject") directed toward the fetus in anticipation of, during, or after abortion are that: "the purpose of such research is the development of important biomedical knowledge that cannot be obtained by alternative means," "investigations on pertinent animal models and nonpregnant humans (when appropriate) has preceded such research," and "the informed consent of the mother has been obtained."[7]

In actuality, these provisions allow almost any type of experimental procedure to be conducted on the unborn before, during, and after the period they are destroyed.

Ironically, no experiments can be conducted on convicted murderers in contemporary America, whether before, during, or after they are executed. Thus, prisoners scheduled for state execution enjoy greater protection against the probing intrusions of researchers than unborn children destined for medical execution!

In what respects are the principles which guided the concentration camp experiments similar to those enacted by the National Commission for fetal research?

1. The concentration camp experiments were performed before, during, and after the victims were killed.

2. The concentration camp experiments were nontherapeutic in nature: the benefits which accrued were not intended for unwanted subjects, but for wanted Aryans.

3. The purpose of the concentration camp experiments, according to the Nazi researchers, was the development of knowledge not attainable by alternative means. With regard to the death-inducing high altitude experiments conducted at Dachau, "entirely new data will be secured for science," explained Dr. Sigmund Rascher. "The problem in question," he added, "can only be solved by experiments on human beings."[8]

4. The death camp doctors claimed they performed research on animal models before using human subjects. In the sea water experiments carried out at Dachau in which "the deaths of the experimental subjects have to be expected," it was decided that "after numerous

experiments on animals," humans were to be used "because the distribution of water in the body of animals differs from that in a human being."[9]

5. Consent for concentration camp experiments was obtained from individuals other than the subjects experimented upon. Dr. Karl Gebhardt admitted that permission for the utilization of Polish women for the sulfanilamide experiments, in which many died or were made seriously ill, was not voluntary but came from the "legal authorities."[10]

Chart 5

Research on Human Expendables

CONCENTRATION CAMP EXPERIMENTS (Testimony presented at the Nuremburg Doctors' Trial, October 1946—November 1947)	GUIDELINES FOR FETAL RESEARCH (National Commission for the Protection of Human Subjects of Biomedical and Behavioral Research, 1975)
Type of Research	
Experiments performed in concentration camps were not intended to benefit the inmate subjects experimented upon (unwanted non-Aryans).	Nontherapeutic research ("research not designed to improve the health condition of the research subject") on the fetus may be conducted or supported.
Time of Performance	
Nontherapeutic experiments were conducted on camp inmates before, during, and after extermination.	Nontherapeutic research directed toward the fetus in anticipation of, during, or after abortion may be conducted or supported.
Purpose of Research	
"Entirely new data will be secured for science. The problems in question can only be solved by experiments on human beings." (Justification for the high altitude experiments performed at Dachau, Dr. Sigmund Rascher, 1942)	The development of important biomedical knowledge that cannot be obtained by alternative means is an appropriate justification for nontherapeutic research directed toward the fetus.
Previous Animal Studies	
"After numerous experiments on animals" the sea water experiments were performed on Dachau inmates.	Investigations on pertinent animal models should precede fetal research.
Consent for Experiments	
Consent for the sulfanilamide experiments came from the "legal authorities."	Consent for fetal research must be obtained from the mother.

Survival Technology for the Wanted

How were the high altitude and freezing experiments related to the development of rescue techniques?

Nazi medical scientists devoted considerable effort to developing a device for aiding German pilots forced to bail out of their planes. Before the practical application of this technology, it was considered necessary to establish the norms of human endurance at various altitudes and air pressures. In what became known as "high altitude research," the inmates of Dachau were locked inside airtight pressure chambers and exposed to atmospheric conditions simulating those encountered by German aviators in falling great distances without a parachute and without oxygen. Many subjects expired during the course of the experiments. Their deaths played an important role in furthering the development of a parachute with a barometrically controlled opening and a portable oxygen tank.[11] Such scientific advances, according to the Nazi research mentality, were not intended for unwanted inmates, but wanted German flyers.

Another matter high on the priority list of German scientific inquiry was the search for a rewarming technique capable of saving air force and naval personnel forced to abandon their crafts at sea. The determination of the best rewarming approach had to be tested before utilization in actual rescue operations. The expendables of Dachau also functioned as research subjects for this series of scientific monstrosities referred to as "cooling" or "freezing experiments." The procedure consisted of immersing inmates in enormous basins of ice cold water almost to the point of death. After removal from the water, they were subjected to various methods of rewarming. Many did not survive; they had been either chilled beyond revival or the rewarming method applied did not work. Rapid rewarming in hot baths proved to be the only reasonably effective technique tested.[12] Again, it was designed to benefit wanted Germans instead of unwanted non-Aryans.

How are the high altitude and freezing experiments related to fetal research conducted in contemporary society?

During the past several decades medical scientists have been trying to develop equipment designed to help prematurely born infants survive a host of afflictions, especially respiratory distress syndrome, a malady characterized by breathing difficulty due to lack of lung expansion. Babies aborted by hysterotomy, like the concentration camp discards, have been employed as guinea pigs for testing the operational efficacy of various extrauterine life support technologies. Hysterotomy victims are considered ideal research subjects because their conditions so closely duplicate those of their premature counterparts. The bodies of the still-living expendables are cut out of the uterus intact, and connected to some type of life-enhancing unit. Their responses are then carefully observed and recorded until death.

Swedish researchers have been able to keep aborted human subjects alive for several hours by perfusing them in a glass chamber.[13] A 980-gram human subject aborted at George Washington University Hospital was hooked up to an artificial placenta and was sustained for 5 hours and 8 minutes.[14]

Even if the equipment had the capability of preserving the subjects on an other-than-temporary basis, none of them would have survived. They are perceived as strictly the means to the end of a more effective technology. The technology is not for the benefit of unwanted intentionally-aborted castoffs, but wanted unintentionally-born premature infants.

Testing Drugs

Is it true that many drugs were tried out on concentration camp subjects just as they are being tested on contemporary fetal subjects?

A large assortment of drugs, vaccines, and pharmaceutical preparations were administered to camp inmates to assess their effectiveness in treating malaria, typhus, epidemic jaundice, cholera, gunshot wounds, and phosphorous burns. Because the drugs were new and their effects unknown, they were tested on unwanted inmates selected for gassing. Wanted German citizens were not considered appropriate material for these experiments. In order to duplicate the proper experimental conditions, the subjects were first deliberately infected with diseases or deliberately wounded.

A wide variety of current drug-related experiments have been carried out for the sole purpose of determining their effects on unborn children. Such drugs are only imposed on unwanted unborn children selected for abortion. Fetal researchers would never dream of using them on wanted babies slated for term birth because of the risks involved in applying new and untested drugs.

Give some examples of drug experiments conducted on Nazi and contemporary victims.

Dachau inmates intentionally infected with malaria were given varying doses of quinine, neosalvarsan, pyramidon, antipyrin, and combinations of these. For many, the drugs had no appreciable impact, and the subjects died from malaria. For others, overdoses of neosalvarsan and pyramidon produced fatal consequences. According to the Nazi research ethic, such experiments successfully demonstrated the limitations of certain substances in the treatment of malaria, and even identified the lethal dosage levels for different types of inmates.[15]

Fourteen women in advanced stages of pregnancy were given a high blood pressure drug, nadolol, four days before being aborted at a Phoenix, Arizona abortion clinic in 1981. The purpose of the experiment was to assess the effect of this drug on the unborn victims, to determine if it had an impact similar to that of other hypertension medications which lower fetal blood pressure and lead to possible genetic afflictions. According to Yale University researcher Dr. Maurice Mahoney, this type of research is needed "to develop a base of information on what are dangerous drug levels at different periods during pregnancy."[16]

Surely, reputable pharmaceutical firms have not been involved in exploiting mass destruction as an occasion for testing their products?

The I.G. Farben Corporation of Germany, once known as the "largest chemical corporation in the world—participating directly or indirectly in about four hundred German companies and five hundred business enterprises abroad—with the largest and most modern staff of scientists and technicians," manufactured and supplied many of the drugs and pharmaceutical products used in the concentration camp experiments. This was one of the crimes against humanity for which twenty-four top Farben executives were indicted at Nuremberg in 1947.[17]

E.R. Squibb & Sons, a leading pharmaceutical corporation with worldwide headquarters in Princeton, New Jersey, was the firm which furnished the drug nadolol for testing on unborn babies selected for abortion destruction in Arizona. According to a company representative, Squibb finances fetal research projects in other states as well.[18]

Have drug companies also been implicated in experiments solely intended to measure the destructive impact of lethal chemicals on human expendables?

Farben pioneered experiments designed to assess the destructive capacity of various substances. "Experiments on human beings (including concentration camp inmates), without their consent," according to documentation submitted to the Nuremberg tribunal, "were conducted by Farben to determine the effects of deadly gases, vaccines, and related products."[19]

The Upjohn Pharmaceutical Corporation of Kalamazoo, Michigan, manufacturers and suppliers of prostaglandin, have supported an extensive program of research into testing how effectively this drug kills and ejects from the womb unborn humans during the middle stage of pregnancy. In one of many such experiments, it was found that a single intra-amniotic instillation of 40 mg. of prostaglandin F2a successfully induced midtrimester abortion with minimal side effects for the mothers and maximally-fatal consequences for their children: "there were no live births in this series."[20]

Research Perspectives on Death and Dying

Describe some of the Nazi and contemporary experiments perpetrated against human discards.

The following excerpts furnish a scientific view of the fatalities resulting from the freezing experiments performed at Dachau:

> Upon entry into the water a severe cold shuddering appeared . . . There followed a progressive rigor . . . the rigor increased with the continuation of cooling, now and then interrupted by tonic-clonic twitchings . . . *expiration was prolonged and visibly difficult* . . . In part this was "normal, much decelerated breathing," in part an agonal form of gasping . . . Death occurred with a drop in temperature to values between 24.2° and 25.7° C.[21]

The final responses of aborted babies to the perfusion experiments conducted by Swedish physicians have been recorded in a comparably conscientious manner:

> A few minutes after the perfusions were commenced the fetuses produced a few gasps . . . they were extremely excitable to touch which incited vigorous limb movements . . . The respiratory movements came in series of 2-3 gasps at intervals of a few minutes . . . The ECG and blood pressure were recorded continuously and not terminated until signs of heart activity on the ECG ceased. This occurred in the majority of cases between the third and fourth hour after delivery. Recordings were made at a temperature of 25° C.[22]

The death of one of the victims subjected to the high altitude experiments carried out at Dachau was recorded as follows:

> After 4 minutes the VP [experimental subject] began to perspire and to wiggle his head, after 5 minutes cramps occurred, between 6 and 10 minutes breathing increased in speed and the VP became unconscious; from 11 to 30 minutes breathing slowed down to three breaths per minute, finally stopping al-

> together. . . Severest cyanosis developed in between and foam appeared at the mouth.[23]

Another carefully recorded report covers the last five hours of an aborted baby's life connected to an artificial placenta at George Washington University Hospital:

> Irregular gasping movements, twice a minute, occurred in the middle of the experiment but there was no proper respiration. Once the perfusion was stopped, however, the gasping respiratory efforts increased to 8 to 10 per minute. The fetus died 21 minutes after leaving the circuit.[24]

What conclusions can be drawn about the researchers' attitudes toward their subjects after reading the preceding accounts?

One gets the impression that what has been observed and recorded is simply the operation and demise of reflexes and physiological processes. The phraseology employed ("progressive rigor," "agonal form of gasping," "irregular gasping movements," "decelerated breathing," "severest cyanosis," and "foam appeared at the mouth") could well be interpreted to convey the agonizing, impending deaths of human beings.

When incorporated within the framework of scientific reports, such words and phrases lose their power to generate horror and revulsion at what has actually taken place. It must be kept uppermost in mind that they are not meant to project images of suffering humanity, but to embellish clinical observations with data. The mentality of science—esoteric, technical, and dispassionate—helps mask the horrendous realities of massive, systematic extermination imposed on nonconsenting subjects.

A great tragedy associated with these experiments is the researchers' perspectives. They have busily and methodically produced a variety of scientific recordings while watching their dying charges literally gasp for breath and life and then collapse into oblivion. What they have done is lost the big picture: the human being as an irreducible entity whose dignity requires the utmost respect and loving care. Instead, humanity is shorn away and relegated to the level of sheer anatomy. The subjects are perceived as simply experimental material, as disparate groups of tissues, organs, and biochemical elements.

The tyranny of experimental exploitation of destructive technology run amuck is as prevalent today as it was during the darkest days of the Third Reich! Its inexorable movement is steamrolling to oblivion many of the values which once differentiated human beings from beasts!

Scientific Butchery

To what extent have researchers exploited the remains of mass extermination?

The insatiable curiosity of medical science is not satisfied with simply observing and recording the final gasps and movements elicited from the subjects. Many past and current medical researchers have also been intent on manipulating, weighing, analyzing, and mutilating tissues, organs, and body parts in the relentless process of squeezing every possible ounce of information out of the subjects.

Under the direction of Dr. Joseph Mengele, the pathology laboratory at Auschwitz served as a center for the study of abnormalities. The hearts, brains, and other organs of inmates with defects killed in the gas chambers were dissected, preserved in alcohol, specially packed, and shipped to the Institute of Biological, Racial, and Evolutionary Research at Berlin-Dahlem. Some of the specimens were also sent to the Anthropological Museum in Berlin for the purpose of demonstrating the inferiority of the Jewish race.[25]

Physicians affiliated with the Columbia University College of Physicians and Surgeons cut out and preserved for microscopic analysis sections of the hearts, lungs, livers, kidneys, and spleens of 143 children aborted by saline poisoning. One of the major purposes of this scientific butchery was to assess the effects of saline on the fetal organs.[26]

Beating Hearts

Have past and current researchers been involved in studying the hearts of the newly destroyed?

Dr. Sigmund Rascher was preoccupied with the question of how the organs of Dachau inmates were affected by exposure to simulated altitudes without oxygen. A series of dissections performed on a subject who failed to survive the high altitude experiments revealed the following information regarding the action of the heart:

> When the cavity of the chest was opened the pericardium was filled tightly . . . The right auricle began to beat heavily, at first at the rate of 60 actions per minute, then progressively slower . . . The above described heart actions will gain particular scientific interest, since they were written down with an electrocardiogram to the very end.[27]

In a series of experiments conducted at Stanford University, Dr. Robert C. Goodlin cut open the chests and checked the heart actions of living aborted babies placed in fetal incubators. "The thorax [chest] was opened and the heart was observed directly," he explained. "When the heart was beating, the fetus was returned to the chamber and the experiment was resumed." All of the subjects expired within 11 hours.[28]

The heart actions of inmates killed in the freezing experiments carried out at Dachau were also carefully recorded. Upon immersion in the water the subject's

> heart rate went suddenly to about 120 per minute . . . it then began to become increasingly slower and to sink continuously . . . The stopping of the heart occurred either in the water or after an interval of not more than 14 minutes after removal from the water.[29]

In 1974 an American medical journal published the details of an experiment involving cutting the beating hearts out of aborted babies and placing them in a nutrient solution where their contraction rates could be examined:

> The hearts were dissected from the fetuses and were mounted in a thermostatically controlled bath . . . the hearts survived for many hours without any significant change in their spontaneous contraction rate . . . Electrograms were displayed on a polygraph and served as a basis for determination of the spontaneous heart rate.[30]

Skull Research

Have the heads of the victims been used for experimental purposes too?

Dr. August Hirt, professor of anatomy at the University of Strasbourg, displayed a painstaking commitment to proving the inferiority of the Jewish race through skull measurements. The data for this project were collected from the heads of inmates exterminated in the gas chambers. Hirt sent precise instructions to a special deputy commissioned to procure the specimens: "Following the subsequent induced death of the Jew, whose head must not be damaged, he will separate the head from the torso and will forward it to its point of destination in a preserving fluid in a well-sealed tin container."[31]

Dr. Peter A.J. Adam, professor of pediatrics at Case Western Reserve Medical School in Cleveland, Ohio, has manifested a comparably persevering dedication to the study of fetal brain metabolism. The information for his research was obtained from the heads of

12 unborn children from 12 to 21 weeks gestation killed by hysterotomy abortion. According to Adam and a team of colleagues from the Children's Hospital in Helsinki, Finland, "the head was then isolated surgically from the other organs" and perfused through the internal carotid arteries.[32] In other words, the heads of living babies were cut off and attached to a machine that pumped chemicals through the severed brains.

Prominent neuropathologist Dr. Julius Hallervorden expressed unbounded enthusiasm for pursuing research on mental and physical abnormalities. Over 500 heads severed from "unfit" Germans destroyed in the Nazi euthanasia massacre provided an ample supply of material. The containers and directions furnished by Dr. Hallervorden helped facilitate a fruitful experimental harvest: "I gave them the fixatives, jars and boxes, and instructions for removing and fixing the brains, and then they came bringing them in like the delivery van from the furniture store."[33]

Fetal researcher Dr. Martti Kekomaki of Finland possesses a passionate devotion to experiments designed to enhance the survival of premature infants. He claims to have saved many preemies by feeding them nutrients from the decapitated brains of 52 children aborted by hysterotomy. Dr. Kekomaki has elaborated upon how the procedure works: "The fetuses are fully alive when we cut their heads off . . . And then we put those organs through a rinsing machine to examine them for their nutritious substances."[34]

The brains of concentration camp subjects who died in the high altitude experiments performed by Dr. Sigmund Rascher at Dachau were cut open underwater. "An enormous amount of air embolism was found in the vessels of the brain."[35]

Various portions of the brains of babies destroyed by hysterotomy abortion were cut out and homogenized in glass tubes and compared with the hypothalami dissected from the brains of rats "killed by neck fracture." This experiment was conducted by doctors affiliated with Montefiore Hospital and Medical Center in New York City and the Harvard Medical School in Boston.[36]

Experimental Castration

Have the sexual organs of the victims been utilized for research?

An essential part of the sterilization experiments performed at Auschwitz involved exterminating at least 100 inmates exposed to high doses of X-ray in the genital area, and then cutting out their sex organs. An examination of the excised organs revealed that "high X-ray dosages destroy the internal secretion of the ovary, or of the testicles, respectively." The purpose of this research was to determine the effectiveness of X-rays for mass sterilization of Jews and others.[37]

One segment of experiments on human sexual development carried out in Canadian hospitals during the 1970s consisted of dissecting the testes, ovaries, and adrenals from 54 intentionally-aborted humans (33 males and 21 females with an age range of 10 to 25 weeks gestation). These organs were then minced, homogenized, and subjected to histochemical analysis. The purpose of the study was to provide knowledge about the onset of sexual differentiation by comparing concentrations of sex steroids in fetal testes with those in the ovaries and adrenals.[38]

Spare Parts

Is it true that the dissection of human victims has another purpose besides furnishing scientific information: the provision of organs and body parts for the wanted members of society?

In the bone, muscle, and nerve regeneration and bone transplantation experiments conducted at the Ravensbrueck concentration camp, the arms, shoulder blades, or legs of Polish female inmates were amputated "and immediately transported to the SS Hospital nearby (Hohenlychen presumably), where they were used in the attempt to heal the injured limbs of wounded German soldiers." Those subjected to these experimental atrocities were characterized as experimental "rabbits."[39]

Although the organs and body remnants of aborted babies have not been harvested on a widespread basis, this may well be in the offing. In 1972 University of California researcher Dr. Arthur Ammann transplanted human fetal thymus glands from aborted babies into older children.[40] More recently, American philosopher Mary Anne Warren expressed approval of aborting babies after 5 or 6 months of pregnancy in order to utilize their kidneys for transplantation. The morality of developing an organ farm for fetal parts rests on Warren's perception of fetuses as equivalent to "nonhuman animals."[41]

Benevolent Research

Isn't it true that the concentration camp experiments were carried out for purely sadistic reasons while the purpose of today's fetal research is to benefit science and humanity?

The benefits-to-science-and-humanity argument comprises a major justification for experimental atrocities, whether past or present. Nazi doctors became quite adept at citing a long list of benefits which accrued from their research endeavors conducted against inmates slated for destruction. American doctors invoke an endless parade of positive advances attributed to extending the boundaries of research on unborn children destined for extinction through abortion. The so-called benefits, however, are not meant for those experimented upon. In Nazi Germany the beneficiaries of research were the wanted Aryans. In contemporary America the recipients are wanted infants.

Dr. Julius Hallervorden believed that his collection of human skulls removed from the gas chamber victims of euthanasia institutions made important contributions to scientific knowledge and humanity. When he first heard about the euthanasia program he suggested to those responsible for its implementation: "If you are going to kill all these people, at least take the brains out so that the material could be utilized."[42]

An almost identical motivation prompted Dr. Martti Kekomaki to justify conducting experiments involving slicing open the stomachs and cutting off the heads of babies aborted by hysterotomy. "An aborted baby is just garbage and that's where it ends up," he declared. "Why not make use of it for society?"[43]

Dr. August Hirt supplied another equally benevolent rationale for concentration camp experiments. "These condemned men will at least make themselves useful," he said. "Wouldn't it be ridiculous to execute them and send their bodies to the crematory oven without giving them an opportunity to contribute to the progress of the society?"[44]

In 1970 the *Cambridge Evening News* attributed a similar justification for fetal research to Dr. Lawrence Lawn of Cambridge University's department of experimental medicine: "We are simply using something which is destined for the incinerator to benefit mankind."[45]

At the Nuremberg Doctors' Trial Dr. Gerhard Rose stressed the enormous life-saving legacy left by the typhus experiments. "The victims of this Buchenwald typhus test did not suffer in vain and did not die in vain," he assured the court. Countless numbers of people, he stated, "were saved by these experiments."[46]

According to the life-saving potential attributed to fetal research by Drs. Willard Gaylin and Marc Lappe, the death of the "doomed fetus" chosen for abortion "can be ennobled" through experimentation because the information obtained can be utilized for "the saving of the lives (or the reduction of defects) of other, wanted fetuses."[47]

Thus, both past and current victims of widespread legalized

killing become integral, though involuntary, partners in medical science's continuing battle against the ravages of illness and disease. One could hardly conceive of a more noble martyrdom than this! Destruction is therefore elevated to a matchless level of indispensable benevolence.

It seems extremely ironic that the expendables of Nazi Germany and contemporary society have not been considered valuable enough to deserve the right to live, but of great value as subjects to be exploited for the benefit of science and humanity.

Auschwitz survivor Dr. Gisella Pearl told how the fear of contamination with "inferior Jewish blood" was forgotten in the process of extracting blood from Jewish inmates to aid German soldiers: "We were too 'inferior' to live, but not too inferior to keep the German army alive with our blood."[48]

Unborn children in today's society, likewise, are deemed "too inferior" to merit the right to life, but their importance jumps dramatically when it comes to draining out of them every possible ounce of information, blood, and tissue on behalf of the wanted born and unborn.

The Effectiveness of Destructive Technology

An alarming number of concentration camp experiments were carried out for the sole purpose of improving the technical capacity to kill. Is this true of fetal research also?

A predominant reason for many experiments performed on both born and unborn expendables is an unrelenting search for solutions to such basics as which method of killing does the best job against which types of victims under what set of circumstances. The ultimate aim is to perfect technologies capable of annihilating an ever-increasing number and range of victims.

Long before gas chambers were installed in the death camps, numerous gassing experiments were conducted on the residents of psychiatric hospitals and euthanasia institutions. At the Hartheim euthanasia center, for example, "various mixtures of gasses were tried out to find the most effective one."[49]

Based on an impressive experimental data base of 9,000 saline abortions carried out at Mount Sinai Hospital in New York City, the volume of saline solution necessary to induce destruction and expulsion from the womb varied from 175-200 ml below 21 weeks gestation and up to 250 ml for gestations of 21 to 24 weeks.[50]

At Hartheim, "doctors with stopwatches would observe the dying patients through the peepholes in the cellar door."[51]

In American hospitals, the time of fetal death from saline or prostaglandin abortions is measured by such sophisticated devices as ultrasonic detectors or radiological techniques.[52]

At Hartheim, "the length of the death struggle was clocked down to one tenth of a second."[53] The same type of precision characterized death by phenol at the Buchenwald concentration camp: "The time between the beginning of the injection and death I estimate at about one-half second," disclosed Dr. Erwin Schuler-Ding.[54]

Experiments performed at the Columbia University College of Physicians and Surgeons on the victims of salt-poisoning abortion revealed the following information on the duration of fetal death: "The time interval between saline instillation and fetal death has varied from as early as 1 hour to as late as 7 hours, with a mean of 4 hours."[55]

A series of experiments carried out at Buchenwald produced a landmark finding in the development of destructive technology: although only 5 cc's of phenol were sufficient to do away with aged inmates, 20 cc's were usually injected to ensure a fatal outcome. "Part of the injection would have been enough for the fatal result (I estimate 5 cc.)," explained Dr. Erwin Schuler-Ding. "The rest of the dose was injected as a precautionary measure."[56]

After a careful study of 143 unborn babies killed by saline injections and an extensive review of the experimental literature on salt-poisoning abortion, physicians at Columbia University disclosed that more than enough hypertonic saline is commonly injected to induce death. "The fatal dose of sodium chloride in human subjects has been calculated at about 0.8 Gm. per kilogram," they concluded. "The amounts of sodium chloride administered during most saline abortions far exceed the lethal dosage as far as the fetus is concerned."[57]

Carbon monoxide gas, a substance first tested out on inmates in psychiatric institutions, consumed a huge number of lives in the chambers of Treblinka and Belzec. Once in a while, however, some victims temporarily survived the assaults of carbon monoxide poisoning. After being subjected to carbon monoxide gassing at Belzec for almost half an hour, a few individuals were still alive.[58] The more powerful and quicker-acting hydrogen cyanide gas, also known as Zyklon B, likewise went through numerous experimental tests before being employed on a massive basis at Auschwitz. Auschwitz commandant Rudolf Hoess paid the ultimate tribute to the destructive capacity of Zyklon B: "In all the years I knew of not a single case where anyone came out of the chambers alive."[59]

A study comparing 700 prostaglandin and 170 saline abortions revealed that "the number of live births dropped from seven with prostaglandin to none with saline."[60] Periodically, however, some individuals even survive the onslaughts of saline poisoning, although usually only temporarily. A report released by the New York State Department of Health, for example, disclosed that 26 live births followed saline-induced abortions in Upstate New York between July, 1970, and December, 1972.[61] A considerable amount of research supports D & E's unique claim to fame as the most conclusive method of destruction used during the mid stages of pregnancy, one which "never ever results in live births."[62] According to a medical abortionist with experience in employing the D & E method on victims as old as 26 weeks beyond conception, taking one's time and exercising care ensure that "you're not going to end up with a live birth."[63]

The Matter of Pain

Were pain killing drugs given to the subjects of past death-dealing experiments? Are they given to contemporary human fetal guinea pigs?

In the course of carrying out research on the doomed camp inhabitants, little or no attention was paid to alleviating the often excruciating pain associated with the death-inducing experimental procedures imposed. The administration of pain-relieving substances is entirely absent from today's terminal experiments conducted on aborted babies.

Subjects were forced to undergo the death agonies of the freezing experiments "without receiving anesthetics, which would have alleviated their pain considerably."[64]

Pain-reducing medication was not considered an appropriate component of the experiment in which the heads of aborted babies from 12 to 21 weeks gestation were severed for the purpose of studying fetal brain metabolism. "People need to understand that the fetus doesn't have the neurological development for consciousness or pain," stated Dr. Peter Adam, the leader of this project.[65]

In the bone, muscle, and nerve regeneration, and bone transplantation experiments performed at Ravensbrueck, where the arms or legs of female inmates were amputated, "it was not permitted to administer sedatives even against the most intensive post-operational pains."[66]

After viewing an aborted baby being sliced open at Dr. Martti Kekomaki's laboratory in Turku, Finland, a nurse remarked: "I didn't see any anesthetic being used for that operation." Dr.

Kekomaki acknowledged that "the fetuses are fully alive when we cut their heads off, but anesthetics are definitely unnecessary."[67]

Are aborted babies exploited for research purposes capable of experiencing pain?

Dr. Adam's comments notwithstanding, renowned pediatrician Dr. H.M.I. Liley indicated that "when doctors first began invading the sanctuary of the womb, they did not know that the unborn baby would react to pain" just as "violently as would a baby lying in a crib" by "flaying out his tiny arms, wriggling his entire body, and crying." [68]

A growing body of research conducted by fetologists indicates that unborn children may be capable of experiencing pain early in pregnancy. Beginning with the presence of sense receptors and spinal responses as early as 56 days after conception (by the end of the second month of pregnancy), "there is as much reason to believe that the unborn are capable of pain as that they are capable of sensation."[69] This capability becomes even more pronounced as the child advances through each subsequent phase of gestation. A considerable amount of fetal research is carried out when the capacity of the aborted subjects for perceiving and expressing pain is well developed.

Why don't fetal researchers at least employ pain-reducing drugs when they experiment on aborted babies?

This deplorable state of affairs is due to a glaring failure of empathy: an inability or unwillingness on the part of medical scientists to recognize their subjects as legitimate members of the human race and a subsequent refusal to treat them accordingly. Dr. Kekomaki thus justified his exercises in scientific mutilation on a perception of aborted expendables not "as babies, or even as human."[70]

Such a mentality is closely reminiscent of how the medical researchers of the Ravensbrueck camp viewed their subjects. According to the testimony of survivor Jadwiga Dzido: "We were told every day that we were nothing but numbers, that we had to forget that we were human beings."[71]

Animal Research

Were the Nazi government's regulations pertaining to animal research more stringent than those related to research on human beings?

Paradoxically, a heightened concern about the humane treatment of animals, especially when utilized in research, had developed throughout the Third Reich preceding the deplorable lack of concern toward human subjects in the concentration camp experiments. A federal law pertaining to the Protection of Animals (effective February 1, 1934) included some basic provisions on animal research:

> Persons are prohibited from performing interventions on living animals or applying treatments to them, if such interventions are associated with noteworthy pain or damage . . . Experiments may be performed only under anesthesia . . . . Reports should be made of animal experiments—we should include a clear statement of their purpose.[72]

If only the above standards for humane treatment of animals had been applied to experiments involving human subjects! Nazi doctors never used anesthetics or any other kind of pain killer when conducting experimental procedures on their captive victims. The prosecution at the Nuremberg Doctors' Trial cited the Law for the Protection of Animals as a basis for highlighting the gross incongruities between the treatment of animals and humans in experimental procedures:

> If the principles announced in this law had been followed for human beings as well, this indictment would never have been filed. It is perhaps the deepest shame of the defendants that it probably never even occurred to them that human beings should be treated with at least equal humanity.[73]

Are today's regulations governing animal research more stringent than those governing fetal research?

Ironically, the great contemporary increase in empathy toward members of the animal kingdom, including the subjects of animal research, has been accompanied by an almost total lack of empathy for the human subjects of fetal experimentation. Section 2143 (Humane standards for animals transported in commerce) of the Animal Welfare Act, enacted by the U.S. Congress in 1970, and amended in 1976, incorporated, among other things, some fundamental principles for the humane treatment of animals used in experiments:

> The Secretary of Agriculture requires, at least annually, every research facility to show that professionally acceptable standards governing the care, treatment, and use of animals, including the appropriate use of anesthetic, analgesic, and tranquilizing drugs, during experiments are being followed by the research facility during actual research or experimentation.[74]

While anesthetics are always extended to the woman having the abortion, fetal researchers never administer, let alone contemplate the administration of, anesthetic, analgesic, and tranquilizing drugs on behalf of their doomed subjects. If only the standards of humane treatment embodied in the Animal Welfare Act also applied to experiments involving human fetal subjects, many research atrocities conducted on aborted babies would never have taken place. Sad to say, the lack of empathy toward the unborn is so pronounced among contemporary fetal researchers that they probably never even consider treating their dying subjects with the same dignity commonly accorded to animals! Animal liberationist Dr. Peter Singer finds it hard to understand how "greater dignity or integrity" can be attributed "to the dying fetus than to the dying dog." According to his scale of values, "it is the dog that is the more intelligent, sensitive and autonomous being."[75]

Medical Bystanders

Surely, not many physicians in the Third Reich or in contemporary American society have actually participated in experiments on the human products of mass destruction.

While this may be true, experimental atrocities have taken place and even flourished in situations where only a minority of doctors have been directly involved. It is the silence, apathy, tolerance, or acceptance by too many members of organized medicine which has played such a crucial role in the implementation and expansion of research on human expendables.

Isn't it true that most past and present physicians have had little awareness of experimental barbarities because of their highly secret nature? Isn't this the main reason for their failure to speak out?

To the contrary, many members of the German medical profession were fully aware of the nature of the experiments performed at Auschwitz, Dachau, Ravensbrueck, and other death camps. Many members of the American medical community are also fully apprised of the horrendous research procedures imposed on unborn discards in hospitals and medical centers. In fact, unadorned accounts of even the most reprehensible experiments have been disseminated at medical conventions and published in medical journals.

At the Fourth Conference of Consulting Physicians held in Berlin, Germany (May 1943), Drs. Karl Gebhardt and Fritz Fischer gave a frank and detailed exposition of the sulfanilamide experiments in which serious wounds were intentionally inflicted on female inmates of the Ravensbrueck concentration camp for the purpose of testing the effects of sulfanilamide preparations. Some of the leading physicians in Germany heard this report. "No criticism was raised" by any of the conference attendees.[76]

At a combined meeting of the American Pediatric Society and the Society for Pediatric Research held in San Francisco, California (May 1973), Dr. Peter Adam and colleagues presented a paper containing details about the procedure used to cut off the heads of aborted babies for the purpose of studying fetal brain metabolism. Some of the leading pediatricians and pediatric surgeons in America heard Dr. Adam's disclosures. "No one even raised an eyebrow" among those in attendance.[77]

In his masterful history of Nazi Germany, *The Rise and Fall of the Third Reich,* William L. Shirer revealed that although the death camp experiments were known to "thousands of leading physicians of the Reich, not a single one of whom, so far as the record shows, ever uttered the slightest public protest." Germany's most famous surgeon, Dr. Ferdinand Sauerbruch, who eventually became an active anti-Nazi, was present at the conference in May 1943 when Drs. Gebhardt and Fischer gave their lecture on the notorious Ravensbrueck sulfanilamide experiments. Even Dr. Sauerbruch did not express any opposition to what he heard. "Sauerbruch's only argument on this occasion was that surgery was better than sulfanilamide!'"[78]

Thousands of leading physicians in contemporary America are likewise aware of equally barbaric experiments performed on unborn human guinea pigs. Very few of them exert any effort to speak out against the extensive experimental exploitation of human beings before and after they are aborted. Far too many members of the American medical community actually support the increased opportunities for research afforded by the enormous supply of human expendables slated for annihilation through abortion.

For a comprehensive summary of the major similarities between the experimental atrocities perpetrated in Nazi Germany and in contemporary society, see Chart 6 on pages 70 and 71.

Chart 6
Experimental Exploitation of Destruction

The Third Reich	Contemporary Society
Survival Technology for the Wanted	
Concentration camp inmates destined for the gas chambers were used in the freezing experiments to develop rewarming techniques for the benefit of German military personnel rescued at sea.	Unborn children slated for abortion destruction have been used in experiments designed to develop artificial placentas for the benefit of prematurely born infants with respiratory difficulties.
Testing Drugs	
The I.G. Farben Chemical Corporation supplied drugs for concentration camp experiments.	The pharmaceutical firm of E.R. Squibb & Sons furnishes the drug nadolol for fetal research.
Research Perspectives on Death and Dying	
"Progressive rigor . . . decelerated breathing . . . an agonal form of gasping . . . death occurred." (Reaction of an inmate subject to a freezing experiment in 1942)	"Irregular gasping movements . . . no proper respiration . . . the fetus died." (Reaction of an aborted human subject to an artificial placenta experiment in 1968)
Scientific Butchery	
The hearts, brains, and organs of inmates with defects killed in gas chambers were dissected, preserved in alcohol and shipped to the Institute of Biological, Racial and Evolutionary Research.	Sections of the hearts, lungs, livers, kidneys, and spleens of 143 unborn children destroyed by saline poisoning abortion were dissected and preserved for analysis at Columbia University.
Beating Hearts	
"The right auricle began to beat heavily, at first at the rate of 60 actions per minute, then progressively slower. . . The above described heart actions will gain particular scientific interest, since they were written down with an electrocardiogram to the very end." (The heart of a Dachau inmate killed in the high altitude experiments, 1942)	"The hearts survived for many hours without any significant change in their spontaneous contraction rates . . . Electrograms were displayed on a polygraph and served as a basis for determination of the spontaneous heart rates." (Hearts dissected from aborted babies, *American Journal of Obstetrics and Gynecology,* January 1, 1974)
Skull Research	
Anatomy professor Dr. August Hirt conducted research aimed at proving the inferiority of the Jewish race through skull measurements by cutting off the heads of inmates exterminated in the gas chambers.	Pediatrics professor Dr. Peter Adam conducted research on fetal brain metabolism by severing the heads of unborn babies destroyed by hysterotomy abortion and hooking them up to a machine.

Chart 6 (Cont.)

The Third Reich	Contemporary Society
Experimental Castration	
The sex organs of Auschwitz inmates exposed to high doses of X-ray were cut out and examined for the purpose of determining the effectiveness of X-rays as a method of mass sterilization.	The sex organs of unborn children aborted in Canadian hospitals were dissected and subjected to histochemical analysis for the purpose of providing knowledge about sex differentiation.
Spare Parts	
The limbs of inmates at the Ravensbrueck concentration camp were amputated for the purpose of replacing the missing limbs of wounded German soldiers.	An American philosopher has expressed approval of abortions performed after 5 or 6 months of pregnancy for the purpose of kidney transplantations.
Societal Benevolence	
"Wouldn't it be ridiculous to execute them and send their bodies to the crematory oven without giving them an opportunity to contribute to the progress of the society?" (Dr. August Hirt, 1942)	"We are simply using something which is destined for the incinerator to benefit mankind." (Fetal researcher Dr. Lawrence Lawn, 1970)
The Effectiveness of Destructive Technology	
"I know of not a single case where anyone came out of the chambers alive." (Auschwitz commandant Rudolf Hoess on the destructive capacity of Zyklon B gas, 1947)	It "never ever results in live births." (An experienced abortionist on the merits of D & E as a method of destroying unborn children, 1981)
The Matter of Pain	
The subjects were forced to undergo death-dealing experiments "without receiving anesthetics." (The Dachau freezing experiments, 1942)	"The fetuses are fully alive when we cut their heads off, but anesthetics are definitely unnecessary." (Fetal researcher Dr. Martti Kekomaki, 1980)
Animal Research	
"Experiments may be performed only under anesthesia." (Law for the Protection of Animals, February 1, 1934)	"The appropriate use of anesthetics, analgesic, and tranquilizing drugs, during experiments." (U.S. Animal Welfare Act, 1970)
Medical Bystanders	
"No criticism was raised." (Response of participants at a conference of German physicians to the Ravensbrueck death camp sulfanilamide experiments, Berlin, Germany, May 1943)	"No one even raised an eyebrow." (Response of participants at a meeting of American pediatricians to an experiment involving beheading aborted babies, San Francisco, California, May 1973)

Current Status of Fetal Research

Didn't the U.S. Congress outlaw fetal research?

On September 30, 1982 the House of Representatives voted 260-140 to prevent the National Institutes of Health from conducting or supporting "research or experimentation in the United States or abroad on a living human fetus or infant, whether before or after induced abortion, unless such research or experimentation is done for the purpose of insuring the survival of that fetus or infant."[79]

This vote demonstrates that many congressmen have taken an important step toward halting the unrestrained experimental atrocities conducted on the victims of mass abortion.

On the other hand, a substantial number of congressmen are so fully wedded to the pro-abortion mentality that they refuse to support a ban against federal funding of research imposed on living aborted babies! Furthermore, the prohibition still requires approval of the Senate. Whether the Senate will follow the lead of the House on this matter is uncertain.

Don't the existing regulations pertaining to fetal research provide sufficient protection against Nazi-style experimentation on unborn children?

The regulations currently in effect—the handiwork of several presidential commissions on biomedical ethics stacked with pro-abortion appointees—contain some highly objectionable loopholes. One of the major provisions permits the funding of almost any type of fetal research as long as "the purpose of the activity is the development of important biomedical knowledge which cannot be obtained by other means."

The development of important scientific knowledge, it should be recalled, was also a rationalization commonly invoked by the Nazi physicians to justify the experiments performed on death camp inmates.

Chapter 7

The Commercialization Of Killing

An integral aspect of mass killing, in addition to the development of sophisticated technology and the experimental exploitation of victims, is the monetary imperative. Situations in which millions are slaughtered on an assembly-line basis are closely associated with massive financial corruption.

What have been the most prominent manifestations of commercialized killing in the Nazi regime and contemporary society?

The essence of commercial extermination can be conveyed by such phrases as *useless eaters, medical mercenaries, corporate profits,* and *monetary exploitation of human body parts.*

Useless Eaters

The term "useless eaters" captures the very essence of a stark cost-callous approach toward the value of human life. The emphasis is on the saving of money by eliminating those considered not up to par.

In 1920 Dr. Alfred Hoche, a leading forerunner of the Nazi euthanasia program, stressed the heavy cost involved in operating institutions for the mentally handicapped:

> The average expenditure per idiot person is 1,300 marks. If we add up all of the idiots, they number 20,000 to 30,000. If we take an average span of 60 years, we can calculate how much capital in the form of food, clothing, energy and national resources is deducted for an unproductive purpose.[1]

Dr. Hoche's answer to reducing the above costs: euthanasia for "lives devoid of value."[2]

In 1970 the National Academy of Sciences' Institute of Medicine issued a report on the high cost of maintaining "retarded" individuals in institutions:

> It takes about $5,000–$6,000 per year to pay the costs of institutionalized care for retarded individuals. The 50,000 persons now receiving institutional care for Down's syndrome alone represent an expense of some $250–$300 million per year.[3]

The Institute of Medicine's response to decreasing this financial burden: "prenatal diagnosis in combination with selective abortion."[4]

Statistics compiled by the German Department of Health in 1941 furnished a numerical perspective on the monetary savings resulting from the euthanasia program: "The extermination has made it possible to save 88,543,980 RM per year. If we consider that a patient stays in an institution about ten years, this sum should be increased by ten . . . The quantity of foodstuffs saved represents 33,731,000 eggs and 177,088,080 pounds of vegetables."[5]

Citing figures put out by the federal government's General Accounting Office, pediatrics professor Dr. Robert Guthrie projected that the expansion of amniocentesis for the detection of genetic defects before birth followed by abortion could well yield an annual savings of $437,186,000, the amount ordinarily spent on disabilities due to genetic disorders.[6]

In 1935 Reich physician Dr. Gerhard Wagner estimated that the enormous costs imposed on German society by "congenital defectives" to be 1.2 million marks yearly.[7]

In 1981 Dr. George Ryan, president of the American College of Obstetricians and Gynecologists, calculated that passage of a human life bill intended to protect the unborn would add 400,000 babies a year to the welfare roll, "a commitment of about 40 billion dollars every year."[8]

The attitude toward the children of the poor is surely the most distressing feature of this entire cost-reduction thrust. When the outer layer of equal rights for poor women is peeled away, what remains is a cost-callous resolution to the war on poverty: a war against the poor by killing off the children of the poor!

There is nothing new here. It has always been more costly and time consuming to love and care for human beings than to destroy them. What needs to be realized is that such a morally bankrupt philosophy has its origins in Nazi ideology and practice; it bears a chilling resemblance to the war against the useless eaters of Germany and the Eastern territories under Nazi occupation.

Medical Mercenaries

Whatever the task performed in the Nazi holocaust—whether it involved selecting victims, developing destructive techniques, supervising the killing, carrying out destructive operations, or exploiting victims for experimental purposes—doctors were paid a physician's salary for their participation. Furthermore, some German doctors even viewed the horrendous concentration camp experiments as a vehicle for forging new scientific discoveries with the intention of enhancing their prestige and financial standing. The main reason Dr. Sigmund Rascher conducted the death-inducing high altitude and freezing experiments was to establish his reputation as a pioneering research scientist with the ultimate purpose of securing a prestigious appointment as a university professor.[9]

American doctors, even more so than their Nazi counterparts, are engaged in a deadly game of scientific one-upmanship to see who can come up with the latest research findings obtained from the enormous pool of human expendables slated for abortion extirpation. The increased status and financial rewards associated with high professorial rank in academic medicine is coming to depend on how many unborn victims can be salvaged for research and scholarly output before, during, or after destruction.

Experimental exploitation of the unborn is not the only area where American doctors are making a financial killing. The huge sums of money accumulated from the massive slaughter of human lives in the womb make the medical killers of the Third Reich look like paupers!

In 1970 abortionist Dr. Mark Julienne (pseudonym) told about the financial rewards attendant upon shifting from the task of healing to that of killing. "Financially, after years of struggle," he admitted, "I can't help feeling a little like the Texan who drilled for water and struck oil."[10]

Chicago legal abortionists discovered a gold mine in the prodigious supply of tax money pumped into the mushrooming specialty of exterminative medicine. In 1974 alone, Dr. Arnold Bickham derived $792,266 in Medicaid funds for performing abortions at the Friendship Medical Center.[11] During the period 1976 to 1978, three doctors were awarded Medicaid funds ranging from $465,175 to $776,636[12] for their deadly assaults against human lives before birth.

The wealthiest abortion profiteer of them all may well be a California physician, Dr. Edward Allred, who from 1970 through most of 1977 performed in the vicinity of 35,000 abortions. He owns and operates a string of abortion clinics up and down the California coast. This has made him a millionaire many times over. According to a feature article on Allred in the *Los Angeles Times*, abortions within his financial empire are carried out "on a scale so large and so efficient that they turn a profit one can only guess at. It is enough to support a staff at each clinic and maintain fulltime lawyers and accountants."[13]

Corporate Profits

The gigantic financial bonanza reaped from past and current

assembly-line killing has been facilitated further by extensive collaboration between medical mercenaries and their industrial partners.

The destruction of millions during the Nazi era was a mammoth endeavor that depended upon cooperation from government, industry, the economy, and other societal institutions.

Degesch, also known as the German Vermin-Combating Corporation, developed the Zyklon gas used to exterminate concentration camp inmates. In 1942 Degesch earned a profit of $760,368 reichsmark.[14]

In contemporary American society abortion has become big business, an industry of destruction involving a vast network of hospitals, clinics, foundations, governmental agencies, drug companies, and industrial corporations.

Just a week after the U.S. Supreme Court legalized abortion on demand as the law of the land, *Business Week* reported that the stock shares of Berkeley Bio-Engineering, manufacturer of the vacuum machine responsible for destroying unborn children during the first trimester of pregnancy, leaped from 8-1/2 to 15-3/8 in one week. The Chairman of the Board predicted that Berkeley's 1973 profits would "more than double," and expressed a hope that its 1974 earnings would "double again."[15]

None of the industrial firms in Germany during the Nazi era profited more handsomely from the destruction of human lives than the giant I.G. Farben Chemical Corporation. Farben not only exploited Auschwitz inmates for slave labor, but also produced the stabilizer for Zyklon B gas and sold drugs and poisonous chemicals to the death camps. Furthermore, Farben invested heavily in and dominated the supervisory board and policies of Degesch, manufacturer of Zyklon. "When the Final Solution added Jews to the S.S. extermination plans, Degesch profits reflected the new prosperity," concluded Joseph Borkin in his book on Farben's complicity in mass annihilation. "I.G.'s dividends on its Degesch investments for the years 1942, 1943, and 1944 were double those of 1940 and 1941."[16]

A major profiteer of the destruction against the unborn is the Upjohn Pharmaceutical Company of Kalamazoo, Michigan. Its most distinctive contribution to today's industry of eradication is the drug prostaglandin, the main purpose of which is to kill and eject from the womb victims in the middle stage of pregnancy. Upjohn not only manufactures and sells this death-inducing substance to hospitals and medical executioners, but also provides financial inducements for researchers to test and demonstrate its destructive impact on aborted discards.[17] Ever since the public announcement of Upjohn's plans for the development of another destructive product—a vaginal suppository designed to destroy the unborn in the early stages of pregnancy—its common stock has enjoyed a spectacular rise from a 12-month low of $32 a share to a high of $56. The *Detroit News* was so impressed it employed the headline: "Upjohn Stock Prices Soar with Publicity of New 'Abortion Kit.'"[18]

Upjohn's highly lucrative program of chemical warfare against unborn expendables mirrors I.G. Farben's chemical assaults on concentration camp discards. In both cases, it is the perversion of chemistry for destructive purposes fed by the insatiable passion for profit!

Monetary Exploitation of Human Body Parts

Evidence exists that the remains of those exterminated in the camps were slated for conversion into soap. Testimony presented at a session of the National Council of Danzig in Danzig, Poland on May 5, 1945, revealed the existence of a factory set up to produce soap derived from human remains at the Danzig Institute of Hygiene: "We found a cauldron with the remains of boiled human flesh, a box of prepared human bones, and baskets of hands and feet and human skin, with the fat removed."[19]

The production of soap and other ingredients from the fat of human victims did not cease with the fall of the Third Reich. Two British reporters interviewed a London gynecologist who admitted selling "foetuses to a . . . chemical factory . . . they make soap and cosmetics . . . and they . . . pay very well indeed, for babies because animal fat is very precious, gold dust in their line."[20] In April 1981 the *Gazette du Palais,* a reputable legal journal, reported that frozen human fetuses were shipped to French cosmetic laboratories for the manufacture of "beauty products used in rejuvenating the skin." These products "sold in France at high prices."[21]

A German embalmer, who assisted Dr. August Hirt in dissecting the corpses of victims exterminated in the gas chambers, testified that Hirt used human heads for something besides trying to prove the inferiority of the Jewish race through skull measurements. "One day I had prepared a head for him," the embalmer explained. "Well, do you know what the professor did with it? He gave it to the commander of the Natzweiler camp, who used it as a paperweight."[22]

In 1976 it was disclosed that a Chicago biological supply firm offered for sale the bodies and organs of aborted babies encased in a "paperweight" type of plastic block. The costs advertised in its catalogue were: $90 for a human brain, $60 for intestines, and $70 for lungs. A human foot encased in plastic was priced at $70, and "embedments of human embryos" were listed for $97.80.[23]

At Auschwitz a team of dental surgeons became quite adept at pulling gold teeth from victims exterminated in the gas chambers.

> The dead lay on their backs; the kommando pried open the contracted jaw with his lever: then, with his pliers, he extracted, or broke off, all gold teeth, as well as any gold bridgework and fillings . . . 18 to 20 pounds of it were collected daily in each crematorium.[24]

Although today's victims do not have any gold teeth to extract, other parts of their bodies possess considerable potential for yielding profits. Dr. Willard Cates, a medical bureaucrat at the Center for Disease Control in Atlanta, Georgia, has come up with a proposal for ensuring that the proper amount of money is charged for abortions: "postoperative measurements of fetal foot size." In other words, after the baby is destroyed and extracted from the womb, the medical executioner or his accomplices would examine the remains, measure the victim's foot, and assess the fee. The longer the foot, the higher the fee. Cates has even prepared a table for determining abortion charges according to estimated weeks of gestation based on fetal foot size. For example, if the aborted baby's foot measures 4.6–7.0 mm (9–10 weeks gestation), the cost of the abortion would be $175. If the abortion is performed when the fetal foot ranges in size from 11.6–17.0 mm (13-14 weeks gestation), the charge would be $225. If the aborted victim's foot measures 30.1 mm or more (19 weeks gestation or older), the fee would increase to $300.[25]

Testimony presented at Nuremberg by Czech physician Dr. Franz Blaha recounted the wide variety of commercial products obtained from the skin of victims at Dachau: "saddles, riding breeches, gloves, house slippers and ladies' handbags."[26] At Buchenwald, tatooed skin, especially "the best and most artistic specimens," was in special demand for the manufacture of lampshades.[27]

In 1976 the *Washington Post* revealed that the pathology department of D.C. General Hospital received $68,000 over a ten-year period for the sale of aborted human bodies and organs to commercial firms. The hospital's obstetrics and gynecology department was also engaged in the trafficking of aborted bodies for $75 a piece, and earned $3,535 over a 2-1/2 year period. The money was used for departmental equipment, a television set, attendance at educational meetings, and cokes and cookies for visiting professors.[28]

Chart 7

Economic Perspectives on Eradication

The Third Reich	Contemporary Society
Useless Eaters	
The enormous costs imposed on German society by "congenital defectives" is estimated at 1.2 million marks each year. (Nazi Party Health Chief Dr. Gerhard Wagner, 1935)	The passage of a human life bill would add 400,000 babies a year to the welfare roll, "a commitment of 40 billion dollars every year." (American obstetrics leader Dr. George Ryan, 1981)
Cost-Callous Savings	
"The extermination has made it possible to save 88,543,980 RM per year . . . a patient stays in an institution about ten years, this sum should be increased by ten . . . The quantity of foodstuffs saved represents 33,731,000 eggs and 177,088,080 pounds of vegetables." (Department of Health statistics, 1942)	The expansion of amniocentesis for the detection of genetic defects before birth followed by abortion could well yield an annual savings of $437,186,000, the amount ordinarily spent on disabilities due to genetic disorders. (Analysis of General Accounting Office statistics by Dr. Robert Guthrie, 1978)
Medical Mercenaries	
Doctors were paid a physician's salary for carrying out destructive tasks in euthanasia hospitals and concentration camps.	"I can't help feeling a little like the Texan who drilled for water and struck oil." (Medical abortionist Dr. Mark Julienne, 1970)
Corporate Profits	
The I.G. Farben Chemical Corporation's dividends on its investment in Degesch, manufacturer of Zyklon B gas, doubled from 1942-1944, a period when millions were being gassed to death in concentration camps. (Degesch business reports for 1942 and 1944)	The announcement by the Upjohn Pharmaceutical Company of plans for the development of a vaginal suppository for abortions was accompanied by a spectacular rise in its common stock from a low of $32 a share to a high of $56. (*Detroit News,* 1978)
Human Soap	
A factory was established in Danzig, Poland for the purpose of manufacturing soap from the remains of death camp victims. (Testimony presented to the National Council of Danzig, May 1945)	A London gynecologist admitted selling aborted babies to a chemical factory where "they make soap and cosmetics." (Reporters Michael Litchfield and Susan Kentish, 1974)
Profiteering in Body Parts	
The assembly-line extraction of gold teeth from the mouths of victims exterminated in the gas chambers. (Eyewitness account of Dr. Miklos Nyiszli, 1946)	The setting of abortion fees according to "post-operative measurements of fetal foot size"—the longer the foot the higher the fee. (Dr. Willard Cates, 1980)

Cost Benefit Analysis After Birth

Do economic factors also play an important role in determining which individuals outside the womb will be declared expendable?

An obsessive cost-accounting attitude toward the value of human life has also spilled over to the postnatal stages.

In 1971 Dr. Walter C. Alvarez expressed hope that "some day a law will have to be passed saying that the question of when to pull out the tubes must be left in the hands of the patient's physician or physicians. Such a law might save the country a few billion dollars a year."[29]

According to *The Sun* of January 11, 1973, Dr. Walter W. Sackett estimated that "$5 billion could be saved in the next half century if the state of Florida's mongoloids were permitted merely to succumb to pneumonia."[30]

A memorandum of June 4, 1977 prepared by an American bureaucrat, Robert A. Derzon, contained proposals for reducing health care costs through governmental financing of abortions and withholding of federal funds from states which fail to enact "living will" legislation. The enforced passage of "living will" laws, he reasoned, would make it easier to legally pull out the plugs on a greater number of people dependent upon respirators for survival. The savings resulting from such a plan under Medicare alone, estimated Derzon, would amount to $1.2 billion annually.[31]

The cost controllers threaten to dominate ever increasing aspects of life and death matters just as they did during the twelve-year period of the Third Reich. Today's outcome is similar to what happened in Nazi Germany: large numbers of human lives extinguished in the vicious cycle of an emotionally-detached, cutting-of-costs ideology.

Chapter 8

From Abortion To Infanticide

Once the principle is established that it is all right to do away with one category of victims, the precedent is set for doing away with other categories of victims. Dr. Leo Alexander, American medical science consultant to the Nuremberg War Crimes Trials, traced the steps of the Nazi destruction process in which euthanasia served as the forerunner to genocide:

> Whatever proportions these crimes finally assumed, it became evident to all who investigated them that they had started from small beginnings. The beginnings at first were merely a shift in emphasis in the basic attitude of the physicians. It started with the acceptance of the attitude, basic in the euthanasia movement, that there is such a thing as life not worthy to be lived. This attitude in its early stages concerned itself merely with the severely and chronically sick. Gradually the sphere of those to be included in this category was enlarged to encompass the socially unproductive, the ideologically unwanted, the racially unwanted and finally all non-Germans.[1]

What relevance does Alexander's analysis have for abortion and infanticide?

Abortion is the intentional destruction of unborn children. Infanticide is the purposeful killing of young children after birth. Acceptance of unborn baby killing has helped pave the way for approval of newborn baby killing.

How does the eugenic factor enter into this relationship?

As previously indicated, one of the leading reasons put forth to justify the medical extermination of children in the womb is the probability or proof that they are afflicted with some type of defect. Most physician-induced acts of infanticide, similarly, are directed against children born with handicaps. The logic is highly disturbing but impeccably consistent and altogether inescapable: if abortion is permitted to destroy a defective child inside the womb, why not infanticide for those children whose defects do not become evident until after birth?

Some Theoretical and Philosophical Insights

Has anyone actually employed the acceptance of exterminating unwanted afflicted children before birth as a rationale for advocating the elimination of unwanted subpar children after birth?

Many individuals, including eminent physicians, scientists, and philosophers, grasp the inexorable logic linking abortion with infanticide. These theoreticians of the slide from abortion to infant euthanasia and even beyond acknowledge that killing or withholding treatment from severely ill infants represents an ironclad and inevitable extension of destruction from inside to outside the womb. They have in essence supplied the logical and philosophical groundwork underpinning abortion as a wedge for infanticide.

Few people have exhibited more persistence than prominent situation ethicist Dr. Joseph Fletcher in pointing out the inseparable bond between abortion and infanticide. Fletcher often refers to abortion as "fetal euthanasia." He also has indicated that "it is reasonable, indeed, to describe infanticide as postnatal abortion."[2]

Fletcher has displayed a particularly intense preoccupation with using the prenatal destruction of Down's Syndrome children as a justification for their postnatal extermination. "Now, then," he reasons, "if through ignorance or neglect or sheer chance (like the forty-seventh chromosome) the damage has not been ended prenatally, why should it not be ended neonatally?"[3]

Stanford University philosophy professor Dr. Michael Tooley has likewise worked hard at building a rationale to justify abortion and infanticide. His key argument is based on the self-consciousness requirement: "An organism possesses a serious right to life only if it possesses the concept of a self as a continuing subject of experience and other mental states, and believes that it is itself such a continuing entity." Since neither the unborn nor the newborn has attained the level of self consciousness, Tooley concludes, neither possesses a serious right to live. Tooley expresses uncertainty about how long after birth it will take the child to actually reach the stage of self awareness. He considers this question of minor significance, however, because "in the vast majority of cases in which infanticide is desirable, its desirability will be apparent within a short time after birth."[4]

Among the most distinguished proponents of abortion as a wedge for infanticide are Nobel Prize winners Drs. James D. Watson and Francis H. Crick, co-discoverers in 1962 of the double helix of DNA.

In May 1973 Dr. Watson emphasized the importance of abortion of the afflicted unborn as a foundation for approval of infanticide of the afflicted newborn:

> Fortunately, now through such techniques as amniocentesis, parents can often learn in advance whether their child will be normal and healthy or hopelessly deformed. They then can choose either to have the child or opt for a therapeutic abortion. But the cruel fact remains that because of the present limits of such detection methods, most birth defects are not discovered until birth.[5]

The technical deficiencies of eugenic abortion as a method for identifying and eliminating sufficient numbers of the unwanted unfit before birth prompted Watson to offer a complementary but more conclusive solution for continuing the task of eradication begun in the womb: "If a child were not declared alive until three days after birth, then all parents could be allowed the choice that only a few are given under the present system. The doctor could allow the child to die if the parents so chose and save a lot of misery and suffering."[6]

Again, this is simply another instance of extending the option to destroy from the prenatal to the postnatal period.

Nobel laureate Crick appears to hold an attitude toward infanticide very similar to that of his illustrious colleague. In January 1978, according to the *Pacific News Service,* he indicated that "no newborn infant should be declared human until it has passed certain tests regarding its genetic endowment and that if it fails these tests it forfeits the right to live."[7]

Medical ethics professor Kenneth Vaux cited the acceptance of eugenic abortion as a precedent for defending an attempt to starve to death Siamese twins born on May 5, 1981 in Danville, Illinois. "Selective abortion for fetal disease," he stated, "is an analogy that supports a 'let die' posture in this case."[8]

Do men like Fletcher, Tooley, Watson, Crick, and Vaux reflect the mentality prevailing in the scientific and intellectual community on the significance of the link between abortion and infanticide, or are they only a small minority of individuals who speak for themselves and nobody else?

Unfortunately, they are not just isolated crackpots on the fringes of mainstream philosophy, medicine, and science, but highly influential individuals whose ideas have had a profound impact on people inside and outside the community of scholars, intellectuals, and scientists.

The extent to which the abortion-infanticide association is recognized and accepted was revealed to *Commentary* editor Norman

Podhoretz at a conference of leading scientists held in Washington D.C. Podhoretz learned that a substantial proportion of those in attendance "was by no means willing to grant mongoloids an undisputed right to live" before or after birth. One very eminent participant disclosed that "he saw no reason why anyone who accepted abortion should balk at infanticide, particularly when the infant in question was known to be defective whereas the fetus to be aborted might be normal and sound."[9]

Did anyone in Germany before or during the Third Reich acknowledge the close connection between abortion and infanticide?

As early as 1920 Drs. Karl Binding and Alfred Hoche, in their highly influential book, *The Release of the Destruction of Life Devoid of Value,* advocated legalizing doing away with incurable and deformed children and other "useless human lives." In the same year a bill was introduced in the German legislature to legalize abortion. A Berlin correspondent recognized the inextricable logic underlying both proposals. "A certain inward relation exists," he emphasized, "between the demands of Binding and Hoché, on the one hand, and the bill proposed in the reichstag by the independent social democrats that the paragraphs of the Penal Code be annulled which impose penalties on any one who brings about the death of a living embryo or fetus."[10]

Theory Into Practice

Aren't the above American and German statements merely the opinions of theorists with little basis in the real world? To what extent do they reflect the actual incidence of abortion and infanticide in Nazi Germany and contemporary America?

The quality-of-life philosophy underlying the abortion-infanticide connection has long since left the realm of theory to engulf a huge number and variety of victims in its wake. It was put into practice with a vengeance under the yoke of Nazi oppression. It is being applied with comparable intransigence in today's society where unmitigated tyranny parades under a banner of liberation.

The sequence of malevolence in both countries is important to keep in mind: legalized abortion preceded infanticide.

Medical-induced annihilation of children in the euthanasia hospitals and institutions of the Third Reich did not get off the ground until the legalized killing of unborn children had become firmly established. In 1933 the Nazi government greatly expanded the legal indications for abortion to include eugenics and a global definition of health.[11] By 1939, the basic lesson taught by permissive abortion—the right to kill unwanted and probably-defective children in the womb—had sunk in so deeply that Hitler signed a euthanasia order which had the effect of extending the massacre to unfit newborns and others considered not up to par with the Nazi quality-of-life mentality.[12]

Today's rapidly escalating medical assaults on defective or seriously afflicted newborns in the hospitals and medical centers of America did not develop out of a vacuum either. They comprise an intrinsic component of an elitist quality-of-life ethic granted legal sanctification by the U.S. Supreme Court in its abortion-on-demand decision of 1973.[13] The Court's horrendous message—the right to destroy human beings at all stages of pregnancy—unleashed a legacy of destructive energy which has spilled over to consume an increasing number of postnatal expendables, especially handicapped newborn children.

Several years after the Supreme Court's abortion decision, pediatrics professor Dr. Eugene F. Diamond etched an alarmingly incisive portrayal of the American medical profession's inexorable movement from abortion to infanticide:

> We in the medical profession now stand awash in the blood of millions of aborted unborn children. We put aside our curettes and our salt syringes and, consigning the damp pulp of the most-recently slaughtered fetus to the ovens, we lift our eyes above the windows of the abortorium and gaze into the nursery.[14]

Dr. Diamond's comments are even more valid today than when they were first expressed. They also capture equally well the most virulent period of the Third Reich when members of the medical profession embarked on a slippery slope which led relentlessly from abortion to infanticide and beyond.

Wasn't medical infanticide of the unfit more prevalent during the Nazi era than it is today?

This is true right now, but the acceptance as well as the practice of physician-inflicted infanticide has grown enormously since the Supreme Court decision supportive of massive abortion, and it shows ominous signs of moving ever more swiftly and implacably in the direction of Nazi medicine.

What have been the main methods used to exterminate unwanted children born with defects in Nazi Germany and today's America?

Imposed starvation and the administration of lethal substances.

Enforced Starvation

Give some examples of how handicapped children were starved to death in Germany of the past and America of the present.

The children of foreign workers in countries under Nazi rule were given "racial examinations" to measure their degree of fitness. Those who passed were sent to homes under the auspices of the Lebensborn (fountain of life) to be Germanized. Those who failed were dispatched to special homes where they eventually expired, many due to a policy of imposed starvation. An inspector's report on one such institution revealed that "the home receives only a pint of milk and a piece and a half of sugar per day per baby. With these rations the babies are sure to die of malnutrition in a few months."[15]

In 1971 it was brought to public attention that a child born with Down's Syndrome plus duodenal artresia (an intestinal blockage) at the Johns Hopkins University Hospital in Baltimore was allowed to die because his parents would not grant permission for the performance of the necessary corrective surgery. The child was placed in a remote part of the hospital with a foreboding sign, "Nothing By Mouth," placed on his bassinet. It took him 15 days to die of starvation and dehydration! At Johns Hopkins this form of infanticide, referred to euphemistically as allowing "nature to take its course," was deemed a legally appropriate mode of action.[16]

Non-voluntary starvation was a prime weapon used against defective and disturbed children languishing in the "children's divisions" of psychiatric and euthanasia hospitals throughout Nazi Germany. Dr. Pfannmüller, head of the Eglfing-Haar mental hospital, gave a stark demonstration in 1939 of how the "natural and simple" method of death by starvation worked at his institution. "Food was not withdrawn from the children all at once," he explained, "but by gradual reduction of the rations." Dr. Pfannmüller picked up one of the children, "a whimpering bundle of skin and bones," and "showed around the child like a dead rabbit." He then said, "This one, for example, may take another two or three days."[17]

On April 9, 1982, a baby boy, known only as Infant Doe, was born with Down's Syndrome and a deformed esophagus in a Bloomington, Indiana hospital. His parents—backed up by the hospital, the doctors, and the judicial system of Indiana—not only refused permission for the needed surgery, but also refused permission for him to be fed intravenously. Under what was defined as one of two "medical options" chosen (denial of treatment, food, fluids or any kind of nourishment), this handicapped infant died painfully of starvation and dehydration within six days. An attorney directly involved in trying to save the child's life disclosed that Infant Doe cried for four of these days.[18]

Aren't the Johns Hopkins and Bloomington cases very rare compared to the number of babies starved to death in the euthanasia hospitals and children's homes of the Third Reich?

What was done to the handicapped newborn children in these two cases, tragically, represents only the tip of the entire reprehensible iceberg of infanticide perpetrated under the guise of benign treatment in many American hospitals and prestigious medical centers. Dr. Bob Hall, chief neonatologist at Children's Mercy Hospital in Kansas City, characterized the practice of permitting deformed or defective newborns to die by withholding treatment and nourishment as a "commonplace" phenomenon. He estimated that it accounts for around 14 percent of all deaths occurring in special care nurseries throughout the United States.[19]

Eugenic Infanticide

Wouldn't it be more humane to spare unwanted defective newborn babies the prolonged agony of imposed starvation death by ending their misery quickly and painlessly with a terminal injection?

A growing number of contemporary physicians and other elitists exploit the horrors of starvation destruction as a strategy designed to obtain public and legal support for the administration of "mercy" shots to terminate the lives of infants considered not worth living.

Today's proponents of "merciful" infanticide should be reminded that their approach is not new. Its roots are securely embedded in one of history's darkest chapters. It was the Nazi medics and their assistants who developed the practice of eugenic infanticide to the state of a fine art.

Provide some examples of beneficient infanticide as advocated and practiced in Nazi Germany and contemporary America.

During the Nazi era the theory of benevolent infanticide was applied extensively. The method of putting to death physically handicapped and mentally deficient children and others was commonly referred to as "an injection of mercy to relieve them of their incurable and painful suffering."[20] Defense attorneys at the Nuremberg Doctors' Trial in 1947 invoked the concept of "humaneness" to justify the killing of children in euthanasia hospitals. "From a medical standpoint," they asserted, "it is a humane motive to shorten the lives of children not fit to live."[21]

Writing in the *New England Journal of Medicine* in 1976, Dr.

James Lachs indicated that "the only way to treat" hydrocephalic children "humanely" is to "mercifully" put them "to death."[22] On the Donahue television talk show of March 10, 1982, American philosophy professor Mary Anne Warren decried the cruelty associated with the growing practice of starving handicapped newborns to death. She advocated, instead, the kind, quick, painless, and direct method of lethal injection. Hardly anyone in the audience bothered to challenge such a noxious Nazi-style medical ethic. In fact, several women jumped on the quality-of-life bandwagon and chimed in with stories which reinforced Warren's prescription for the problem of the unwanted handicapped newborn child.[23]

The Killing-of-Horses Analogy

Why have handicapped children in Germany of the past and America of the present been compared to horses?

When horses are crippled they are put out of their misery by the quick and humane method of shooting. When this approach is applied analogously to defective newborn children, it is meant to justify the humaneness of quick-acting solutions for doing away with unwanted subpar children.

As far back as 1904, Dr. Ernst Haeckel, physician, biologist, and Nazism's most vociferous philosopher, likened those "who are born every year with an hereditary burden of incurable disease" to horses which "are rightfully put to death and relieved from pain when they fall hopelessly ill."[24]

In 1982, before a presidential commission appointed to study biomedical and behavioral ethics, that ever ubiquitous philosopher Mary Anne Warren compared the severely disabled newborn child to a horse with a broken leg which should be killed to spare it from the agony of a slow painful death.[25]

Administration of Lethal Substances

Have death-inducing substances actually been used against disabled children in Nazi Germany and contemporary America?

At the Hadamar Euthanasia Hospital Trial in 1947, Nurse Heinrich Ruoff revealed that a dosage of 2-1/2 to 3 cc. of morphine or scopolamine was sufficient to do away with the afflicted children of Hadamar.[26]

Two doctors affiliated with Yale University told a reporter in 1981 that physicians on the staff of the intensive care nursery at Yale-New Haven Hospital in Connecticut "have helped parents give their defective infants lethal drug overdoses."[27]

Chart 8
The Abortion-Infanticide Slope

The Logic of an Irrevocable Bond

"If through ignorance or neglect or sheer chance (like the forty-seventh chromosome) the damage has not been ended prenatally, why should it not be ended neonatally?" (Dr. Joseph Fletcher, April 1968)

"Because of the present limits of such detection methods [the use of amniocentesis to identify candidates for abortion], most birth defects are not discovered until birth. If a child were not declared alive until three days after birth, than all parents could be allowed the choice that only a few are given under the present system. The doctor could allow the child to die if the parents so chose and save a lot of misery and suffering." (Dr. James D. Watson, May 1973)

"Selective abortion for fetal disease is an analogy that supports a 'let die' posture [the attempted starvation death of Siamese twins born in Danville, Illinois on May 5, 1981] in this case." (Medical ethics professor Kenneth Vaux, June 1981)

Infanticide as a Method of Treatment

Nazi Germany	Contemporary America
Enforced Starvation	
"Food was not withdrawn from the children all at once but by gradual reduction of the rations . . . This one, for example, may take another two or three days." (Eglfing-Haar Hospital, 1939)	A newborn child with Down's Syndrome, Infant Doe, was denied treatment, food, and fluids. It took him six days to die of starvation and dehydration. (Bloomington Hospital, 1982)
Nature's Way	
A "natural and simple" method. (Imposed starvation of children at Eglfing-Haar Hospital, 1939)	Allowing "nature to take its course." (Imposed starvation of infant at Johns Hopkins Hospital, 1973)
Eugenic Infanticide	
"From a medical standpoint, it is a humane motive to shorten the lives of children not fit to live." (Nuremberg Defense, 1947)	"The only way to treat" hydrocephalic children "humanely" is to "mercifully" put them "to death." (Dr. James Lachs, 1976)
The Killing-of-Horses Analogy	
Those "who are born every year with an hereditary burden of incurable disease" are like horses which "are rightfully put to death and relieved from pain when they fall hopelessly ill." (Nazi philosopher Ernst Haeckel, 1904)	The severely disabled newborn child is similar to a horse with a broken leg which should be destroyed to spare it from the agony of a slow painful death. (American philosopher Mary Anne Warren, 1982)
Administration of Lethal Substances	
Nurses gave deadly doses of morphine and scopolamine to handicapped children. (Hadamar Euthanasia Hospital, 1942-1945)	Physicians aided parents in giving "lethal drug overdoses." to "their defective infants." (Yale-New Haven Hospital, 1981)

It is not surprising to learn that an obstetrician who performs abortions played an instrumental role in the starvation death of a Down's Syndrome infant at a Bloomington, Indiana hospital in 1982.[28] Pediatrician Anne Bannon's disturbing description of the Bloomington baby's condition on his last day of life "in a modern hospital in the richest country in the world" lays bare the stark brutality intrinsic to one end of the irrepressible abortion-infanticide spectrum:

> Baby Doe's shrunken, thin little body, with dry cyanotic skin, extremely dehydrated, breathing shallowly and irregularly, lay passively on fresh hospital linens. Blood was running from a mouth too dry to close. Death by starvation was near. Too late for fluids. Too late for surgery. Too late for justice.[29]

This portrait is a chilling duplicate of how the unwanted subpar children of Nazi Germany were disposed of in euthanasia hospitals. Sheer barbarism, deplorably, is not a quality confined to the Nazi medical community.

Chapter 9

Racist Foundations of Violence Against Jews and the Unborn

Those bent on genocide have commonly subjected their victims to an orgy of name calling as a preparatory step to their extermination. The war of words directed against the victims usually precedes the actual war by at least decades. The killing phase represents the translation of noxious attitudes into practice.

Many of the derogatory labels concocted are saturated with racist-type terminology.

The Concept of Race

Could you define racism? I thought it meant discrimination on the basis of skin color or membership in a particular type of racial or ethnic group.

Before defining racism it is necessary to understand the meaning of the word race. At the most general level, all of us are members of the same human race, whether we be black or white, Jew or Gentile, born or unborn, young or old, sick or healthy, imperfect or perfect, male or female.

In addition to our common membership in the human species, the concept of race covers many distinctions made among human beings. It has been used to include the following: 1) Any group of individuals united or classified together on the basis of common history, nationality, or geographical distribution; 2) A group of individuals related by common descent, blood, or heredity; 3) A class or kind of people unified by a community of interests, habits, or characteristics; 4) A group of tribes or people forming an ethnic stock; 5) A group of people more or less distinct from all others; 6) Any group, class, or kind, especially of persons; 7) A local geographical or global human population distinguished as a more or less distinct group by genetically transmitted physical characteristics.

There is nothing inherently invidious about making distinctions between various groups of human beings whether the differences are related to skin color, cultural traditions, place of residence, size, physical appearance, age, or a host of other characteristics.

In fact, the field of anthropology began in the eighteenth century as the result of scholars attempting to account for both similarities and diversities manifested by individuals and groups in various cultures throughout history.[1]

Racism and Its Characteristics

How, then, does the concept of racism differ from that of race?

Racism enters the picture when a hierarchy of worth is imposed on the classifications used to distinguish groups of human beings from one another. A hierarchical principle of perceiving others dominates the mindset of the racist. The diverse segments of individuals within the human race are thus assessed according to a scale of value; those considered superior at the top, and those rated as inferior at the bottom. This may even degenerate into a master-slave race mentality.

Frequently the racist considers some individuals or groups so inferior that they no longer even merit the designation human. They are relegated to such subhuman or nonhuman levels as animals, beasts, insects, indiscriminate masses, or even trash. Although black people and Jews have commonly occupied the lowest rungs on the superiority-inferiority continuum, almost every group at one time or another has suffered the dire consequences of being placed in such positions.

Anything which minimizes or detracts from the humanity of individuals or groups is a form of racism.

The racist resorts to an almost endless variety of criteria for defining fellow human beings out of the human race. Some of the most typical ones invoked include skin color, ethnic status, place of residence, physical appearance, traditions, language, age, and many others. Racists also invariably perceive themselves as members of the most favored groups. Derogating others serves to bolster their feeling of superiority.

How long has racism existed?

Racism has had a longstanding history, dating back many centuries before the birth of Christ. The practice of relegating individuals to the level of superior and inferior races was endowed with scientific respectability in the writings of eighteenth century European naturalists and anthropologists. By the mid 1800s, much of the racist thought was synthesized by Comte Arthur de Gobineau in his highly influential *The Inequality of Human Races* (1853–55).[2] The white race was portrayed as containing the highest quality of human development while the black and yellow races were categorized as possessing various deficiencies and negative qualities. Although Gobineau classified Jews as valid members of the superior white race, his racist-oriented notions provided the foundation for the anti-Semitism which began to flourish toward the close of the nineteenth century. It was but a short step from the presumption of the inherent inequality of the races to the complete dehumanization of those placed on the lowest ends of the hierarchy-of-importance gradations.

How did racism operate against Jews before and during the Third Reich?

The German racial theorists concentrated on two basic races: a master race of Aryans consisting of good Germans, and an inferior race of non-Aryans populated primarily by Jews. Jews were reduced to such a low level of inferiority that they were no longer considered legitimate members of the human race, but merely some sort of subspecies. Much of the propaganda disseminated depicted Jews as repulsive forms of subhumanity, much closer to the animal than the human kingdom.

How can racism be applied to abortion in contemporary society? I have never heard pro-abortionists support the idea of a master race of Aryans.

Today's abortion proponents are much too calculating in their manipulation of language to acknowledge such a fact. Rather than overtly subscribe to a master race ideology, they have exploited a far more subtle but equally malignant distinction: the born-unborn dichotomy. According to this principle of differentation, the born, especially adults in good health, are analogous to a master race, while the unborn, especially the unwanted variety, occupy the lowest position as did the Jew in Germany. The unborn are cut off from the rest of humanity by the imposition of derogatory linguistics strikingly similar to the terminology used to depersonalize the Nazi victims.

The Language of Racism

What have been some of the most common words employed to dehumanize the European Jews of the past and the unborn of contemporary America?

The orgy of name calling includes such terms as *question, nonperson, subhuman, nonhuman, animal, parasite, mass, trash,* and *garbage.*

The Jewish Question

What was the Jewish Question and how did it relate to racism?

The Jewish question functioned as a convenient slogan for raising doubts about the nature of the Jews, their racial origins, and their position in the hierachy of racial supremacy. From the nineteenth century on, an almost ceaseless controversy raged as to whether Jews were human, subhuman, or not human at all. To the anti-Semites, the humanity of the Jews was not an indisputable fact, but a question to be resolved by debate and argumentation. The predominant answer to the Jewish question was expressed by Foreign Office Minister Paul Karl Schmidt in 1943: "The Jewish question is no question of humanity."[3]

The Jewish question provided a crucial forum for the degradation of the Jews through the imposition of racist-infested stereotypes. German historian Joachim Fest referred to the notions about Jews of the time as "insane ideas."[4]

Surely, those who questioned the humanity of the Jews must have been crackpots.

Some were, most were not. The relegation of Jews to a level far below the threshold of humanity was the handiwork not of madmen or mobs, but leading intellectuals, including scientists and doctors. It was the intellectual community which gave these absurd ideas credibility and helped make them fashionable. This is all fully documented in many books, including *Jews in the Eyes of the Germans,* by Professor Alfred D. Low, and *From Prejudice to Destruction,* by Professor Jacob Katz.[5]

The Question of the Unborn

What is the relationship between the Jewish question and abortion in contemporary society?

The modern-day counterpart to the Jewish question is the question of the humanity of the unborn. As in Germany of the past, an intense debate is raging, this time it is the status of the unborn as a human, subhuman, or nonhuman at issue.

Today's anti-prenatal forces dispute the humanity of the unborn just as blatantly and vociferously as the anti-Semites disputed the humanity of the Jew. They often portray the beginning of human life in the womb, and therefore the humanity of the unborn, as an irresolvable question instead of an established scientific fact. "The question is unresolvable," according to Dr. Norman Fost of the University of Wisconsin–Madison Medical School.[6] Dr. Leon Rosenberg, a Yale University geneticist, reduces the onset and humanness of life before birth to the level of a "question" and not a "scientific matter."[7]

Nonperson

In what sense is the word "nonperson" a racist term?

The word "nonperson" and such closely associated concepts as "nonpeople" and lack of "legal personality" are racist in both a rhetorical and legal sense.

Semantically, the term "nonperson" implies that the individual so labeled is inferior and lacks those fundamental qualitites which bona fide members of the human race possess. Basically, it is a designation of contempt intended to detract from one's humanity.

The assumption underlying "legal nonpersonhood" is that some individuals and groups are considered so far below the level of humanity they do not even deserve the rights which any ordinary citizen enjoys. In essence, the "legal nonperson" designation serves as a device for defining the victims out of the human race and beyond the protection of the law where they can be manipulated, exploited, and annihilated with impunity.

How has the "nonperson" concept been employed against Jews during the Third Reich and unborn children in contemporary American society?

Hannah Arendt, in her monumental study *The Origins of Totalitarianism* (1951), indicated that throughout history the hallmark of totalitarian governments, whether fascist or communist, has been to treat those deemed stateless and expendable as "legal nonpersons"[8]

According to the above criterion, today's America qualifies as a totalitarian state. The American government considers unwanted unborn children expendable and, as a consequence, treats them as "legal nonpersons."

German legal scholar Ernst Fraenkel came across a 1936 decision of the highest court of Germany, the *Reichsgericht*, which helped facilitate removing Jews from the law's protection. According to Fraenkel's analysis of this particular German Supreme Court decision, "The Reichsgericht itself refused to recognize Jews living in Germany as 'persons' in the legal sense."[9]

When the U.S. Supreme Court in 1973 ruled that unborn children could not be legal persons, this constituted a veritable death sentence for millions! In a manner strikingly similar to the 1936 German high court decision which stripped away legal personhood from Jews, Associate Justice Harry Blackmun, author of the American pro-abortion Supreme Court decision (Roe v. Wade), concluded: "The word 'person,' as used in the Fourteenth Amendment, does not include the unborn."[10]

A further step in the direction of denying legal personhood to

Jews occurred on March 28, 1938, when a law was passed depriving the Jewish religious congregrations of legal protection. Historian George L. Mosse, in *Toward the Final Solution: A History of European Racism* (1978), reveals that from this point on Jews were no longer considered "legal personalities."[11]

Ironically, although the late Supreme Court Justice William O. Douglas experienced little difficulty in reducing the human being before birth to the status of a "legal nonperson," he was not willing to do the same thing to the wilderness, ships, and corporations. In Roe v. Wade (1973), Douglas joined the majority in denying legal personhood to the unborn child. In Sierra Club v. Morton (1971), however, he proposed that legal personhood be conferred on a "valley, an alpine meadow, a river or a lake" just as it has been bestowed on ships and corporations.[12]

The phrase "non-people," a variation of nonperson, occupied a prominent spot in the anti-Semitic literature of Germany. Among the dehumanized stereotypes inflicted on Jews by Otto Weininger in his book *Sex and Character* (1903) was the expression "non-people."[13]

In contemporary America the "nonperson" epithet comprises one of the dominant terms invoked to keep the public from perceiving the unwanted unborn as a legitimate member of the human race. San Francisco State University philosopher Mary Anne Warren, like many others in the upper rungs of academia, refers to the "fetus" as "an entity far below the threshold of personhood."[14]

Subhuman and Nonhuman

Give more examples to show how closely the pro-abortionist attitude toward the unborn resembles the Nazi racist attitude toward the Jews.

The basic posture has been to characterize both Jews and the unborn as subhuman or nonhuman.

The term "Jewish," according to the German racists, "designated the physical traits of a human subspecies—ugly mollusclike, sensuous."[15] In a speech in May 1923, Adolf Hitler asserted: "The Jews are undoubtedly a race, but not human."[16] University of Strasbourg anatomy professor Dr. August Hirt, committed to proving the inferiority of the Jewish race through measurements on skulls severed from gas chamber victims, viewed Jews as "a repulsive yet characteristic subhumanity."[17]

What about contemporary abortionists' portrayals of the unborn?

In the journal *Society* (March/April 1976), Columbia University sociologist Dr. Amitai Etzioni called for the development of "procedures and criteria for determining who and what shall live or die and which fetuses are tissue and which are human." He contended that most scientists and much of the public view the "previable" fetus as "not alive, not human, and basically a piece of tissue." Etzioni's version of subhuman semantics consisted of portraying the first four and one-half months of fetal development as "the subhuman stage" and the unborn during this period, "subhuman and relatively close to a piece of tissue."[18] This preoccupation with creating derogatory categories is alarmingly close to the Nazi approach toward deciding which individuals or groups were expendable. Incredibly, Etzioni, a Jew, resorts to the very same demeaning terminology against the unborn as the Nazis used against his ancestors!

Situation ethics professor Dr. Joseph Fletcher does not confine his subhuman semantics to the so-called previable stage of pregnancy, but has frequently referred to the unwanted unborn, whatever his or her stage of development, as merely "subhuman life in utero."[19] Equally pervasive is the fabrication spread by many medical abortionists and abortion chamber counselors that the fetus is "not a live human being" or "not a human being" at all.[20]

What was the publication *The Subhuman*?

This was a pamphlet published by the RuSHA (Race and Settlement Main Office) in 1942. It contained many stereotypes of Jews in both printed and pictorial forms. This piece of propaganda enjoyed wide circulation: it was translated into fourteen languages; almost four million copies were printed in German alone. The following excerpts reveal its main thrust:

> The sub-human, that biologically seemingly complete creation of nature with hands, feet and a kind of brain, with eyes and mouth, is nevertheless a completely different, dreadful creature. He is only a rough copy of a human being, with human-like facial traits but nonetheless morally and mentally lower than any animal . . . Sub-human, otherwise nothing. For all that bear a human face are not equal.[21]

Have similar characterizations been employed to dehumanize unborn children?

For Dr. Howard I. Diamond of New York and many like him, "the fetus is nothing."[22]

Another portrayal of the unborn, comparable in style of expression to that etched of Jews by the Nazis, was furnished in 1978:

> Fetuses, especially those as old as five or six months, elicit our sympathy . . . because they look disconcertingly like people; their physical features are recognizably human. But this sympathy is misplaced . . . While a fetus of five or six months may, perhaps, possess some flickering of sensation, or some capacity to feel pain, this is equally true and probably even more true of creatures like fish or insects . . . a proper respect for the right to life requires that it not be respected where it does not exist.[23]

Animal

How were animal analogies used to dehumanize the victims of the past?

The black people of Africa were one of the first groups reduced to the level of beasts. Anthropologist Peter Camper, in 1792, declared that Negroes were closer to apes and dogs than to men.[24] In 1850, Scotch anatomist Robert Knox described the black African inhabitants as resembling the "inchoate nature of animals."[25] The Boers' exploitation of Black Africa was based on a view of the natives as "just another form of animal life."[26]

It was during the mid to late nineteenth century that Jews began to be subjected to animalistic terminology. In 1895 Hermann Ahlwardt gave an anti-Semitic speech in the *reichstag* in which he said Jews belonged to "a different race" than Germans. More specifically, he classified them as "beasts of prey."[27] In *The Release of the Destruction of Life Devoid of Value* (1920), Drs. Karl Binding and Alfred Hoche equated worthless individuals to "very low animal life."[28] This book played a significant role in generating the type of demeaning images which helped fuel the holocaust against the Jews.

During the Nazi era the animal analogies, a foremost staple of racist thought, continued unabated. Treblinka commandant Franz Stangl characterized the situation of Jews in concentration camps as equivalent to "cattle" in their pens before being herded into the slaughterhouse.[29] The extermination of Jews and others in Kamenetz-Podolski was founded on a perception of the victims as "monkeys in human form."[30] Dr. August Hirt justified performing poisonous gas experiments on human subjects at the Natzweiler-Struthof concentration camp because "the prisoners here are animals before all else."[31]

Are animal analogies employed to denigrate life in the womb?

Abortionists have frequently depicted life before birth as constituting nothing more than an animal stage of development on the evolutionary scale. Such a contention is a remnant of the long-discarded theory of ancestral recapitulation in which fetal development is perceived as going through vegetative and animal phases before reaching the human stage. Human life is thus hypothesized as beginning either late in pregnancy or not until birth.[32]

When nurses in a New York hospital became distraught at the sight of an aborted baby who moved, the attending physician remarked that this was nothing more than "a reflexive response of a spinal animal."[33] In the mindset of Dr. Howard I. Diamond the unwanted unborn child exists at a level lower than even that of animals. "I feel sorry for a starving cat," he stated. "A fetus that nobody wants—that's not sad."[34] Philosopher Mary Anne Warren places the unborn on a par with such "problematic entities" as "nonhuman animals."[35]

Explain again how these animal associations are related to racism.

Racism involves reducing segments of the human race to inferior statuses. The imposition of animal imagery onto blacks, Jews, the unborn, and others has the effect of relegating them to one of the lowest levels of inferiority possible. "Likening the so-called inferior races to animals," concluded historian George L. Mosse, "put them low on the chain of being and, by analogy, robbed them of their humanity."[36]

Parasite

To what extent has the word "parasite" been used to disparage Jews and unborn children?

Jews were persistently portrayed as grasping, unscrupulous, foreign, and dangerous "parasites" intent on exploiting and destroying the institutions and people of Germany. Some of the propaganda depicting Jews as parasites took on a Darwinian twist: "an arrested development in evolution, a fossil that lacked the strength or roots to nourish itself."[37]

As long ago as 1910, sexologist Havelock Ellis called the fetus a "parasite performing no function whatsoever."[38] Today, one of the overriding images projected of unborn children is that of a dangerous, ravenous, festering "parasite" determined to ravage the woman's body by insidiously sapping her health and life.

As far back as 1802, leading German intellectual Johann Gottlieb von Herder characterized the Jewish people as "a parasitic growth on the trunk of other peoples."[39]

Leading feminist editor Gloria Steinem asserted on cable television in 1981 that a woman should have a right to abortion just as she has a right to remove "any parasitic growth" from her body.[40]

In 1818 Christoph Heinrich Pfaff, a German scientist "of high intellectual standards and genuine liberal convictions," conjured up a commonly-held image of the Jew as "a rapidly growing parasitic plant that winds round the still healthy tree to suck up the life juice until the trunk, emaciated and eaten up from within, falls moldering into decay."[41]

American physicians with impeccable liberal sentiments such as psychiatrist Natalie Shainess have likened the fetus to "a parasite" which has the capacity "to murder its mother."[42]

In 1895 Hermann Ahlwardt delivered an anti-Semitic speech before the *reichstag* in which he denounced Jews as "exploiters, parasites." He added that "these parasites must be made harmless by a special law."[43]

Women undergoing abortions in Hawaiian hospitals during the early 1970s described their experience as getting rid of "an intestinal parasite."[44]

In *Mein Kampf*, Adolf Hitler referred to the Jew as "a *parasite* in the body of other peoples."[45]

According to an early edition of the radical feminist tract *Our Bodies, Ourselves: A Book By and For Women,* the unborn acts as "a parasite within the mother's body."[46]

Mass

Is there any evidence that the word "mass" has been used to reduce Jews and the unborn to a less-than-human status?

A plan for the subjugation of Jews and others in the Eastern territories rested upon a set of demeaning images foisted on the victims. Among the most prominent were such phrases as a "mass of primitive European types," a "dull and obtuse mass," and "this primitive mass."[47]

In 1971 an interview was conducted with former Treblinka commandant Franz Stangl in his prison cell. The reporter asked how it was possible to preside over the destruction of almost one million men, women, and children. He replied: "It had nothing to do with humanity . . . it was a mass . . . I rarely saw them as individuals. It was always a huge mass."[48]

Prominent American obstetrician-gynecologist William J. Sweeney's willingness "to abort a woman if that's what she wants" is based on a perception of the fetus before 12 weeks as "just an amorphous mass"[49]

In 1970 nurses involved in performing abortions in Hawaiian

hospitals became so upset by the sight of "fetal parts sucked or scraped out in the operating room" or "dead fetuses or pieces of limbs, fingernails and hair" that they threatened to resign. Two psychiatrists, Drs. Walter F. Char and John F. McDermott, were called in to quell the disturbance. They consoled the nurses that "what is aborted is a protoplasmic mass and not a real, live, grown-up individual."[50]

This form of racism has even infected some Roman Catholic nuns. On the Donahue show of June 16, 1982, a member of the National Coalition of American Nuns characterized the unborn child as "a mass."[51]

Trash, Garbage

The reduction of human beings, born or unborn, to the despicable level of parasites and masses must represent the most extreme forms of racism imaginable.

Even more extreme variations of racism exist. Demeaning designations of the victims as *trash, rubbish, debris, garbage,* or some kind of disposable *waste* places them at the very bottom of the sub-human scrap pile.

Can you provide specific examples of this type of terminology from Nazi Germany?

According to leading holocaust scholar Leon Poliakov, in *Harvest of Hate: The Nazi Program for the Destruction of the Jews of Europe,* "even in their subconscious mind the Germans had been trained to consider the Jews as pariahs, the refuse of humanity."[52]

In *The Rubbish Heap* (1942), Lucien Rebatet's characterization of Jews as rubbish provided the basis upon which he advocated their deportation and destruction.[53] On June 21, 1942, a police officer charged with exterminating Jews and others wrote about the targets of his destructive activities in the following manner: "There are four actions a week. Sometimes Jews, sometimes Bohemians, partisans, and all kinds of trash."[54]

Poland, the major locale for the systematic execution and disposal of millions, was dubbed the "trashcan of Europe" by Nazi semanticists.[55] When confronted with the task of body disposal at Treblinka, one of Poland's largest killing centers, Christian Wirth stood next to the enormous pits full of blue-black corpses and asked: "What should we do with this garbage?"[56]

Is the same type of language used against the unwanted unborn?

Very much so. In July 1967, *Obstetrics and Gynecology* published an article by Dr. Dorothea Kerslake and Donn Casey in which the products of suction abortion were described not as the torn-apart remains of tiny human beings, but simply as "debris from the conceptus" which "passes visibly into the glass container, either whole or piecemeal." The authors even include a chart estimating the "amount of debris withdrawn" according to when (in weeks gestation) the abortion was carried out.[57]

A year later an American biologist, Dr. Garrett Hardin, reasoned that the early fetus never has been regarded "as a human being" because it "may, with impunity, be flushed down the toilet or thrown out with the garbage."[58] In May 1970, an abortion clinic spokesman in England referred to the unborn before viability as "so much garbage."[59]

The degrading terminology has continued into the 1980s with a vengeance. During the summer of 1980, a Finnish doctor invoked the garbage analogy to justify the brutal experiments which involved cutting off the heads and slicing open the stomachs of babies aborted fully alive. "An aborted baby is just garbage and that's where it ends up," explained Dr. Martti Kekomaki. "You must see it like this: these fetuses are just refuse."[60]

On February 4, 1982, in a backyard in Woodland Hills, California, workmen found a huge storage container with the bodies of at least 1,000 aborted babies, each one suspended in formaldehyde in a plastic jar. Additional investigation revealed a grand total of over 16,000 aborted corpses! To Assistant Coroner Richard Wilson, this grisly discovery did not constitute "evidence of foul play," but merely the possibility of "health code" violations "covering the disposal of medical waste."[61]

The Power of Racist Terminology

Is language powerful enough to actually precipitate a holocaust?

One of the most compelling findings to come out of the Nazi holocaust was the indispensable role of language in fostering mass destruction. Racist-type terminology is an equally significant ingredient in the success of today's medical war on the unborn.

Show how the derogatory linguistics have furthered past and present holocausts.

SS General Erich Bach-Zelewski, the commander of a Nazi extermination squad, acknowledged the ultimate consequence of racist thinking. "It's my opinion," he asserted, "that when the doctrine that the Slavic race is inferior and the Jews not even human has been preached for years and decades, such a result [the holocaust] is inevitable."[62]

The reduction of the unborn to an inferior nonhuman level has become so well entrenched that it too has reached the level of a full-fledged doctrine. And it is this ideology which provides the fuel to power the massive killing of human beings in utero.

Holocaust scholar Raul Hilberg identified the main functions of the demeaning stereotypes heaped on the Jews: "They are used as justifications for destructive thinking; they are employed as excuses for destructive action."[63]

Today's degrading stereotypes imposed on the unborn serve identical purposes: to stimulate destructive thinking and facilitate destructive action.

Helen Fein, author of *Accounting for Genocide,* declared that annihilation could not have been chosen "had not the victims been previously defined as basically of a different species, outside of the common conscience, and beyond the universe of obligation; this was the precondition."[64]

The precondition for the contemporary medical holocaust against the unborn consists of defining the victims out of the human race by relegating them to a subhuman species and therefore unworthy of both public empathy and legal protection. The importance of definitions has been underscored by Dr. Garrett Hardin:

> Whether the fetus is or is not a human being is a matter of definition, not fact; and we can define in any way we wish . . . it would be unwise to define the fetus as human (hence tactically unwise ever to refer to the fetus as an "unborn child").[65]

Hilberg also emphasized the vital role played by definitions in the legalized extermination of European Jews. "When in the early days of 1933 the first civil servant wrote the first definition of a 'non-Aryan' into a civil service ordinance," he concluded, "the fate of European Jewry was sealed."[66]

Ever since January 22, 1973, when the U.S. Supreme Court removed unborn children from the law's protection by defining them as "nonpersons," the unwanted unborn have been doomed to undergo a carnage unprecedented in American history.

In a reference to the killings at Auschwitz, columnist Anthony Lewis stressed the enormous amount of evil done "when human beings think of another group as less than human."[67]

Pittsburgh radio talk show host Mark Schreiber linked the pro-abortion subhuman semantics to the linguistics created by the perpetrators of other barbarities: "This argument that the human unborn baby is less than human is the same type of argument that the most vicious killers the world has ever known used in justifying their atrocities."[68]

Chart 9
The Racist Scale of Inferiority

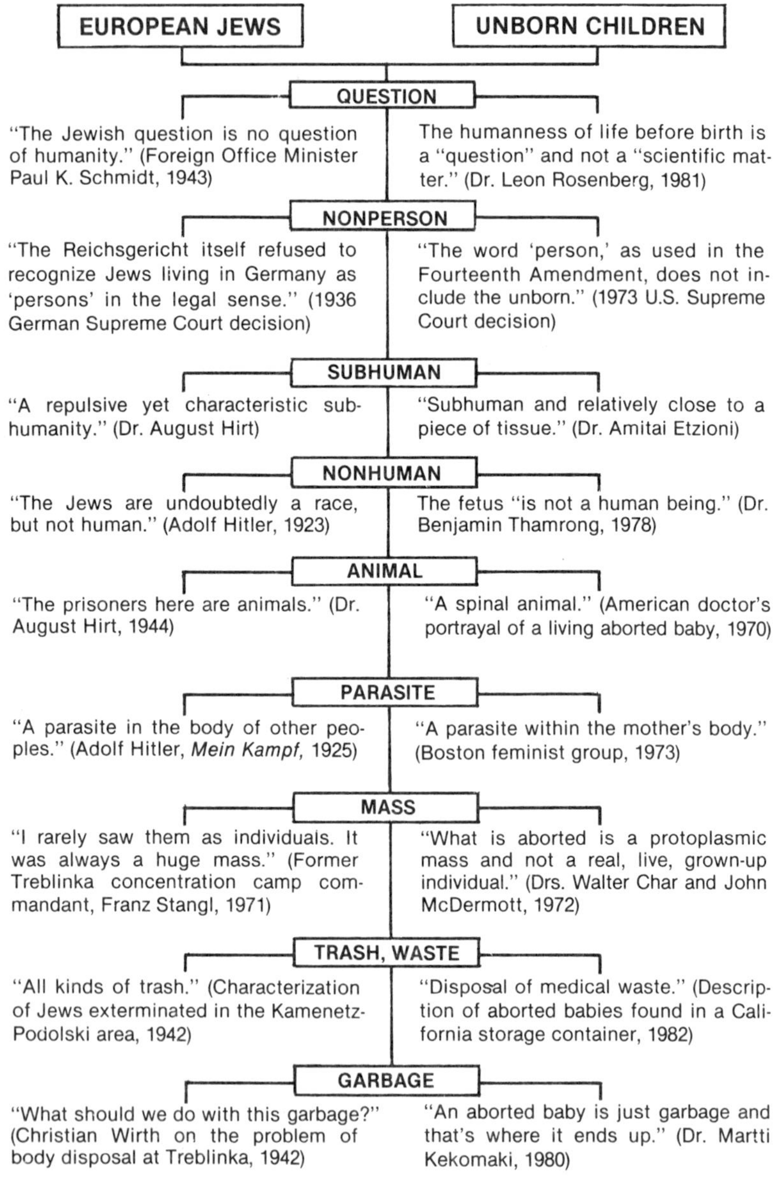

Chapter 10

The Semantics of Mass Destruction

The intentional extermination of human lives, especially when carried out on a vast scale, is an inherently distasteful endeavor which somehow must be rationalized. One way of accomplishing this is to cover up destruction with abstract, inoffensive or misleading language. That is, to call what is done to the victims something other than killing.

Can killing actually be transformed into something other than killing through the perversion of language?

Many people underestimate the power of language to transform harsh realities into pleasant or emotionally-neutral phenomena. To paraphrase a famous statement uttered many years ago by sociologist W.I. Thomas and analyzed by sociologist Robert K. Merton: if people define situations as real they are real in their consequences.[1] What is significant, according to this perspective, are not the concrete, objective facts of massive killing, but the subjective perceptions and definitions imposed on them by the perpetrators and their most ardent supporters.

How does this all relate to what is known as the self-fulfilling prophecy?

The self-fulfilling prophecy in essence is an originally false definition of the situation which becomes true if repeated often enough. When applied to large-scale destruction, the process involves the following steps:

1) The perpetrators become involved in destroying human lives.

2) They falsely define what they are doing as something other than killing.

3) In their mindsets, destruction becomes non-destruction through the power of language and definitions repeated over and over again.

4) According to this process of linguistic hocus-pocus, killing is unlimited because no one destroys, but simply carries out "technical" tasks devoid of any stigma or emotional repugnance.

Semantic Gymnastics: A Strategy for Annihilation

Do you have any documentation to show that the perpetrators of Nazi Germany and contemporary America have intentionally distorted language to conceal their destructive activities?

There is ample evidence to indicate that a major tactic employed by past and present perpetrators is the utilization of terminology as an indispensable weapon for furthering the destruction of millions. This is not an unwitting, accidental, or unconscious process, but a direct, intentional, and conscious decision to subvert words for malevolent purposes.

Beginning with the American scene, what is probably the most forthright and comprehensive strategy of linguistic perversion for destructive ends was unveiled in 1970 by the California Medical Association in an editorial written by Dr. Malcolm Watts entitled: "A New Ethic for Medicine and Society." The following excerpts provide a revealing glimpse into the ideology and semantics underlying exterminative medicine:

> The traditional Western ethic has always placed great emphasis on the intrinsic worth and equal value of every human life regardless of its stage or condition. This ethic has had the blessing of the Judeo-Christian heritage and has been the basis for most of our laws and much of our social policy. The reverence for each and every human life has also been a keystone of Western medicine and is the ethic which has caused physicians to try to preserve, protect, repair, prolong, and enhance every human live which comes under their surveillance. This traditional ethic is still clearly dominant, but there is much to suggest that it is being eroded at its core and may eventually even be abandoned . . . .
>
> What is not yet so clearly perceived is that in order to bring this about hard choices will have to be made with respect to what is to be preserved and strengthened and what is not, and that this will of necessity violate and ultimately destroy the traditional Western ethic with all that this portends. It will become necessary and acceptable to place relative rather than absolute values on such things as human lives, the use of scarce resources and the various elements which are to make up the quality of life or of living which is to be sought. This is quite distinctly at variance with the Judeo-Christian ethic . . . .
>
> The process of eroding the old ethic and substituting the new has already begun. It may be seen most clearly in chang-

> ing attitudes toward human abortion. In defiance of the long held Western ethic of intrinsic and equal value for every human life regardless of its stage, condition, or status, abortion is becoming accepted by society as moral, right and even necessary. It is worth noting that this shift in public attitude has affected the churches, the laws, and public policy rather than the reverse. Since the old ethic has not yet been fully displaced it has been necessary to separate the idea of abortion from the idea of killing, which continues to be socially abhorrent. The result has been a curious avoidance of the scientific fact, which everyone really knows, that human life begins at conception and is continuous whether intra- or extra-uterine until death. The very considerable semantic gymnastics which are required to rationalize abortion as anything but taking a human life would be ludicrous if they were not often put forth under socially impeccable auspices. It is suggested that this schizophrenic sort of subterfuge is necessary because while a new ethic is being accepted the old one has not yet been rejected.[2]

What are the most significant features of this statement?

1) It highlights the fact that abortion represents a concerted assault on the very core of the Judeo-Christian ethic and heritage. Sad to say, the leaders and followers of some religious denominations still fail to grasp the blatantly anti-Christian and anti-Jewish nature of today's pro-abortion juggernaut. It is nothing short of bizarre to behold the leaders of various Christian and Jewish groups defending a principle and a movement whose avowed purpose is to ultimately destroy the most fundamental ethic of both Christianity and Judaism: "intrinsic and equal value for every human life regardless of its stage, condition or status."

2) Clearly, the purpose of the semantics outlined by the California Medical Association editorial is to replace the Judeo-Christian sanctity-of-life ethic with an elitist quality-of-life ethic. "Semantic gymnastics" is an extremely apt phrase since it conveys the severe twisting and distorting of language necessary to deny such fundamental scientific facts as human life begins at conception and abortion kills human life in the womb. In fact, these denials are considered absurd enough to be dubbed "ludicrous" and "this schizophrenic sort of subterfuge."

Schizophrenia, by the way, is a psychotic disorder characterized by loss of contact with the environment and disintegration of the personality expressed as a disorder of feeling, thought, and conduct. The word subterfuge means deception by artifice or strategem in order to conceal, escape, or evade.

Thus, the CMA (California Medical Association) likens the contention of abortion as something other than taking a human life to a falsehood so extreme that it borders on mental illness. The incredible thing about what is admittedly a strategy of pathological lying is that it is actually endorsed as the appropriate way to promote a quality-of-life ethic: "This schizophrenic sort of subterfuge is necessary because while a new ethic is being accepted the old one has not yet been rejected."

3) The transformation of blatant lies into incontestable truths stands a much better chance of success at the hands of prestigious professionals. If, in the not too distant past, the ordinary person went around saying that human life did not begin at its true beginnings (conception), and abortion did not destroy that life, few people would have been impressed. However, when such patent nonsense is put forth under that most impeccable auspice, organized medicine, it is magically elevated from the level of fiction to that of fact.

4) Public acceptance of the two great lies propagated in the CMA editorial—human life does not begin at conception and abortion does not kill human beings—also depends on the psychology of the *big lie,* a notion so conscientiously advanced by Adolf Hitler: if the lies are repeated often enough they are eventually perceived as incontrovertible facts. In the years since announcement of the big lie as a basic strategy for gaining acceptance of abortion, the slogans designed to conceal the harsh truths of unborn baby killing have been repeated relentlessly. Never has Hitler's concept of the big lie been so completely successful in its application!

How would you summarize the goals and strategic principles of semantic gymnastics?

Chart 10
Semantic Gymnastics

Goals

1) Destruction of the Judeo-Christian ethic of intrinsic and equal value for every human life regardless of stage, condition, or status
2) Creation of an elitist quality-of-life ethic with relative values placed on human lives

Strategy for Implementation

1) Avoid the scientific fact that human life begins at conception
2) Separate the idea of abortion from the idea of killing
3) Do this under socially impeccable auspices

What additional reformulations does a closer analysis of semantic gymnastics reveal?

Avoidance of the scientific fact that human life begins at conception has readily led to a denial that human life begins at quickening, or any other point in pregnancy. This in turn has fostered a perception of the unborn throughout the entire duration of pregnancy as not human, but simply a form of subhumanity. The restatement of this principle thus reads: *subhumanity of the victims.*

Separation of the idea of abortion from the idea of killing has resulted in calling what is done to those who are aborted something other than killing. This in turn has spawned an endless list of euphemistic phrases to conceal the destruction of unborn children. Thus this principle can be restated to read: *the euphemisms of destruction.*

Did the CMA statement go beyond abortion?

The CMA did not confine its ideology and vocabulary of duplicity to abortion, but engulfed other victims as well:

> Medicine's role with respect to changing attitudes toward abortion may well be a prototype of what is to occur . . . One may anticipate further development of these roles as the problems of birth control and birth selection are extended inevitably to death selection and death control.[3]

In other words, if semantic gymnastics can be used to deny the humanity of the unborn, they can also be employed to deny the humanity of individuals after birth. If semantic gymnastics can be invoked to call abortion something other than killing, they can also be employed to call euthanasia, infanticide, and other medical atrocities something other than killing.

The Holocaust Mentality

How do semantic gymnastics pertain to the holocaust of Nazi Germany?

The goals and principles underlying semantic gymnastics are identical to those that provided the semantic and ideological foundation for the Third Reich. In Nazi Germany the Judeo-Christian sanctity-of-life ethic was replaced by an elitist quality-of-life ethic which emphasized the quality of life for Aryans at the expense of life for those who did not measure up to the Aryan criteria of worth.

The victims of the Third Reich, like contemporary victims, were viewed as subhuman creatures, and it was this type of imagery which sealed their doom. The subhumanity label encompassed a wide range of victims, including the unborn, the German handicapped, Jews, Gypsies, Poles, Russians, asocials, and others.

What was done to the Nazi victims, like what is being done to today's victims, was called something other than killing. The Nazis had a stong aversion to calling things, especially destructive activities, by their rightful names. They avoided the word kill just as persistently as do contemporary abortionists. The Nazi wordsmiths likewise generated a host of euphemistic phrases to cover up the killing of millions.

What is the relationship between semantic gymnastics and the holocaust mentality?

Semantic gymnastics represents a strategy of linguistic corruption for fostering and implementing programs of mass extermination. A holocaust mentality represents a more advanced phase of semantic gymnastics in which the distorted language becomes so well entrenched that it can be said to have reached the stage of a full-fledged mentality: a more or less fixed outlook or way of thought. It is a holocaust mentality because the nature of the semantics developed (benign or emotionally-insignificant acts performed on subhuman entities under socially impeccable auspices) possesses an unerring capacity to promote, support, and perpetuate the destruction of enormous numbers of victims.

Therefore, the terminology employed in a holocaust mentality is built on two very different but perfectly complementary principles. The first principle emphasizes highly negative, degrading images of the victims. The second principle requires a radical shift in semantic strategy: highly positive or inoffensive portrayals of what happens to the victims.

What types of words do the above principles cover?

The first principle encompasses such concepts as *question, nonperson, subhuman, nonhuman, animal, parasite, mass, trash, waste,* and *garbage.* The second principle includes such expressions as *selection, choice, evacuation, emptied, removal, cleanup, pregnancy interruption,* and *humaneness.*

Is the phrase holocaust mentality meant to refer to the killing in Nazi Germany and contemporary America?

Yes. During both periods the distorted semantics manufactured have become pronounced enough to reduce horrendous atrocities to the level of routine tasks.

How would you summarize the major elements of the holocaust mentality in the form of a chart?

Chart 11
The Holocaust Mentality of Nazi Germany and Contemporary America

Goals

1) Destruction of the Judeo-Christian ethic of intrinsic and equal value for every human life regardless of stage, condition, or status
2) Creation of an elitist quality-of-life ethic with relative values placed on human lives

Linguistic Strategy for Implementation

1) Dehumanization of the Victims
   (The victims are called something other than human)

   A. Question
   B. Nonperson
   C. Subhuman
   D. Nonhuman
   E. Animal
   F. Parasite
   G. Mass
   H. Trash, Waste
   I. Garbage

2) The Euphemisms of Destruction
   (What is done to the victims is called something other than killing)

   A. Selection, Choice
   B. Evacuation
   C. Emptied
   D. Removal
   E. Cleanup
   F. Pregnancy Interruption
   G. Humaneness

Aren't the terms listed under Dehumanization of the Victims identical to those included in a previous chapter?

Since these terms were analyzed in the chapter on "Racist Foundations of Violence Against Jews and the Unborn," this chapter will focus on an examination of the language employed to conceal the killing: the euphemisms of destruction.

Why is the word euphemism used to characterize such words as

selection, choice, evacuation, emptied, removal, cleanup, pregnancy interruption, and humaneness?

The word euphemism is from the Greek *euphemismos* (to use words of a good omen) and the French *euphanai* (to speak well). In English, euphemism refers to the use of mild, agreeable, or inoffensive expressions to describe harsh, delicate, or otherwise unpleasant things. The words *selection, choice, evacuation, emptied, removal, cleanup, pregnancy interruption,* and *humaneness* illustrate the diversity of euphemistic phrases manufactured to deny, conceal, or minimize an extremely harsh reality: the wholesale destruction of human lives.

Were those who resorted to euphemistic terminology to describe the fate of Jews and other victims aware that such terms were designed to cover up the killing?

The architects of the final solution were very cognizant of the power of language to facilitate mass annihilation. They consciously and systematically perverted semantics in pursuing their destructive tasks.

Nuremberg War Crimes consultant Dr. Leo Alexander indicated that the Nazi perpetrators "made a fetish of euphemisms" in order "to deceive outsiders" and "to rationalize their basic aims away."[4] An analysis of Nazi reports on the killing operations reveals painstaking efforts "to avoid the use of direct expressions such as 'to kill' or 'murder.'"[5] According to concentration camp survivor Germaine Tillion, official Nazi communications regarding "the most terrifying realities" were frequently "juggled and camouflaged from the very beginning" by the insertion of "bland and innocent terminology."[6] After examining tens of thousands of Nazi documents on the holocaust, historian-political scientist Raul Hilberg could not find any mention of the word kill in any of them.[7]

In addition to California Medical Association editor Dr. Malcolm Watts' advocacy of semantic gymnastics as an indispensable strategy for covering up the extermination of unborn children, have any other semantic gymnasts acknowledged the essential link between the perversion of language and the concealment of destruction in the womb?

Most American medical perpetrators are not about to admit that the procedures they are carrying out actually destroy living, growing human beings in utero. Nor are they apt to reveal that they are lying when they call what they are doing something other than killing. Both admissions would be completely contrary to the well established image of physicians as professionals unequivocally dedicated to healing and truth-in-telling.

Periodically, however, some members of the healing arts have admitted to and even proposed the use of semantics to gloss over the brutalities of unborn baby killing. In a 1971 issue of *Clinical Obstetrics and Gynecology,* a leader in the nursing profession expressed a recognition that "the basic contradiction between destruction and creation is difficult to ignore" when medical personnel become involved in performing abortions. She offered a plan for dealing with this vexing dilemma: "Through public conditioning, use of language, concepts and laws, the idea of abortion can be separated from the idea of killing."[8] How such a program was implemented on the practical level was revealed at a symposium on abortion held in 1971 in Los Angeles:

> If you say, "Suck out the baby," you may easily generate or increase trauma; say instead, "Empty the uterus," or "We will scrape the lining of the uterus," but never "We will scrape away the baby."[9]

Harsh Realities and Linguistic Distortions

Your analysis so far has emphasized the importance of language in bringing about destruction at the level of a holocaust. Can you provide some specific examples to show how what has actually been done to the victims contrasts with what the perpetrators say has been done to them?

As these contrasts are being examined, two major factors will stand out:

1) An extreme gap between the actual fate of the victims and the linguistic portrayals of their fate.

2) A striking similarity between the euphemisms manufactured to conceal the destruction of Nazi victims and those concocted to blanket the extermination of contemporary victims.

Selection, Choice

The designation "selection" was one of the major code words devised to cover up the killings in the concentration camps. According to Nazi terminology, no one was exterminated at Auschwitz, Treblinka, or Dachau, but inmates merely underwent the process of "selection." And it was doctors who made these "selections."

At the Belsen Trial held in 1945, former Auschwitz physician Dr. Fritz Klein furnished details about the extensive involvement of doctors in the death selection process:

> When the transports arrived at Auschwitz it was the doctor's job to pick out those who were unfit or unable to work. These included children, old people and the sick. I have seen the gas chambers and crematoria at Auschwitz, and I knew that those I selected were to go to the gas chamber.[10]

In the official Nazi version of what happened nothing was said about gas chambers, crematoriums, or the fate of the victims. The only phrases employed were "these selections" or "the selecting."[11]

Today, the word "choice" is one of the main designations invented to conceal the destruction of the unborn. According to contemporary abortionists no one is killed, but "choices" are simply being made.

In 1976 the number of human lives destroyed before birth annually on a worldwide basis was estimated at 40 to 55 million. Rather than being appalled at the enormity of such a global slaughter, the authors of the United Nations study announcing this estimate depicted the number of abortions as representing a positive, sweeping change in line with the "freedom of choice."[12]

Toward the latter part of July 1944, women who had contracted scarlet fever at Auschwitz were dispatched to the chambers where they were gassed to death. This destructive process was characterized as a "selection."[13]

In June 1981 it was learned that doctors at Mount Sinai Hospital in New York City had killed an unborn twin afflicted with Down's Syndrome by stabbing him in the heart with a needle, causing cardiac arrest, and then extracting half his blood. The physicians who performed this barbaric act of medical mayhem called what they did: "Selective Birth in Twin Pregnancy with Discordancy for Down's Syndrome."[14] *Newsweek* decided to place the destructive procedure under the revealing heading: "A Choice in the Womb."[15]

Death camp doctors thus had the *right to select,* just as contemporary women in consultation with physicians have the *right to choose.* In the Third Reich there were no specifics given about the selection of whom for what. In contemporary society neither are there any specifics conveyed about the choice of whom for what.

The right to select, the right to choose are deplorable slogans. Underneath these democratic-sounding phrases lurks an especially hideous form of tyranny: *the right to choose to kill.* Just as the Nazis claimed *the right to select* who would expire in gas chambers, today's perpetrators insist upon the *right to choose* who will perish in abortion chambers!

This is a perversion of the first order because it exploits the language of rights as a pretext for taking away the most fundamental right of all: the right to life. It is an arrogant, elitist assumption of the awesome power to destroy those who cannot defend themselves, an extreme manifestation of the strong victimizing the helpless. The catch words "selection" and "choice" represent a blatant sham because the individuals most drastically affected, the victims, are the very ones who are denied the right to choose. Someone else determines their fate—death by someone else's selection. This is not freedom, but the worst kind of oppression!

No one should be entrusted with the right to choose the destruction of anyone else. The major reason Nazi Germany came to be is that some individuals took it upon themselves to choose who would survive and who would not.

Evacuation

During the latter part of 1941, 15,000 Jewish women and children were killed in the area of Serbia by asphyxiation in mobile gas vans. As the gas seeped into the overcrowded cabin sections of these deathmobiles, the victims suffered agonizingly, gasping for breath in their futile attempts to escape suffocation, frequently mauling and crushing each other in the process. The official Nazi report on the fate of these victims contained no specifics. It simply stated that they had been "evacuated."[16]

In the early 1970s, 4,463 unborn children from 7 to 19 weeks gestation were killed in North Carolina hospitals. The destructive procedures involved either dismembering the small bodies by sharp-edged instruments called curettes, or tearing apart and obliterating their perviously intact bodies through the pressure exerted by vacuum machines. Such stark details are entirely absent from a medical journal article describing this massacre. The acts of medical mutilation perpetrated, instead, were completely obscured by the phrase "the uterus was evacuated."[17]

In 1942, more than 2,450 mentally ill patients were taken from two psychiatric hospitals and shot to death on the outskirts of Riga. Again, the Nazi communiques had nothing to say about what happened to the victims. A hospital doctor disclosed he was instructed to write on the sick lists simply: "evacuated by SS."[18]

From 1970 through the greater part of 1977, California millionaire-abortionist Dr. Edward Allred was personally responsible for destroying 35,000 human lives before birth, including some 7,000 mid-trimester killings by salt poisoning. When asked by a reporter what happens in an abortion, Dr. Allred made no reference to the killings, but replied: "the contents are evacuated."[19]

Emptied

The assault against Jews living in the ghettos of Europe began in

1942. Many victims were shot, starved, or worked to death. Those who survived these ordeals were sent to the gas chambers of Auschwitz, Treblinka, Sobibor, and Belzec. This mammoth destruction process was commonly placed under the euphemistic expression: the ghettoes were "emptied out."[20]

Most unborn children in contemporary America are destroyed by suction aspiration abortion. The damage is done by an electric pump which tears apart and sucks out the destroyed remains of living, growing bodies through a transparent tubing into a collecting bottle. "The uterus," according to a benevolent portrayal of this wholesale slaughter etched by the National Abortion Rights Action League, "is gently emptied."[21]

On February 13, 1943, the residents of a ghetto located in Salonika, Greece, were deported to concentration camps in death transports. The only thing known was the official authorization which stated that "the Baron de Hirsch ghetto would have to be emptied."[22]

A massive killing project involving the destruction of 5,000 unborn human beings between 14 and 24 weeks gestation with lethal doses of saline took place in a New York City hospital from February 1971 to February 1972. The phrase "empty the uterus"[23] served as a convenient semantic device for camouflaging what happened.

Removal

By August 15, 1940, thousands of Jews had been expelled from Krakow and deported to the killing centers. The term "voluntary removal" was manufactured to conceal the fate of the victims.[24]

In 1967 an American medical journal supplied details on the techniques involved in tearing apart and reducing to an indistinguisable mass the bodies of 500 unborn children by a vacuum aspirator. One of the main designations used to obscure what really happened was "remove foreign tissue from the walls of the uterus."[25]

Huge numbers of Polish Jews were exterminated in the death camps during the early 1940s. At a health conference held in the summer of 1943, the Nazi Generalgovernor of Poland, Hans Frank, characterized this as the "removal of the Jewish element" and emphasized what an important contribution this "removal" made to the health of Europe.[26]

Roosevelt Hospital in New York City was the setting for the killing of 71 unborn human lives between 13 and 20 weeks of gestation by injections of prostaglandins during the early 1970s. The harsh realities of what happened to the victims were buried under the expression "remove the products of conception."[27]

Cleanup

In 1942 Heinrich Himmler issued an order for the extermination of the entire Jewish population in the generalgovernment. The communique was entitled: "A Total Cleanup."[28]

Planned Parenthood of New York City provided a comparatively antiseptic coverup of how unborn victims are torn apart by a vacuum machine. Their version of what occurs is "a final cleanup with a small curette."[29]

During the spring of 1942, a police sergeant led a massive assault against Jews in the Kamenets-Podolski area. In a private letter sent to a police general, the sergeant described the destructive operation in the following manner: "We are cleaning up considerably."[30]

A physician abortionist interviewed by a reporter in 1973 furnished a thoroughly immaculate rendition of destruction in the womb. He referred to abortion as "cleaning out the uterus."[31]

The supply of lethal products by German industrial firms made the gassing of millions a reality. This component of the destruction process was commonly referred to as a "cleansing operation."[32]

An equally unsullied portrait of unborn baby killing can be found in a pamphlet put out by the National Abortion Rights Action League. According to this piece of propaganda, the uterus is merely "cleaned with a curette."[33]

The Nazi imagery of destruction as "cleaning up" or "cleansing" was in close harmony with the conception of Jews as unclean, sinister, inhuman, or foreign elements which threatened to pollute the purity of the Aryan race. What could be more sanitary than the "cleaning out" of elements so harmful to the public health! Such antiseptic terminology aided the killers, symbolically as well as psychologically, to whitewash their activities to themselves and to others.

Today's medical abortionist characterizations of intrauterine killing as a "cleanup" process is in perfect accord with the prevailing images of the entity in the womb as foreign tissue, a tumor, or a cell mass. Abortion is then readily transformed into a procedure involving "cleaning out" foreign elements from the womb, just as the Jews defined as impure elements had to be "cleansed out" of the ghettoes. Abortion takes on increased credibility as a "cleaning" operation because of who performs the abortion and where it is performed. What could be more hygienic than destruction at the hands of well-scrubbed medical executioners in the spotless "procedure rooms" of hospitals and abortion clinics!

Pregnancy Interruption

In the decades before the establishment of legalized abortion under the Nazi regime, physicians and medical organizations waged an intense campaign to legalize the killing of unborn children. An essential part of the propaganda disseminated was to say nothing about what abortion does to the victims.

Instead, German doctors chose to rely on the convenient abstraction "interruption of pregnancy." In 1929, for example, the Berlin Chamber of Physicians passed a resolution recommending that the law be changed to allow for "interruption of pregnancy."[34]

During the period prior to the legalization of abortion by the U.S. Supreme Court, doctors and medical associations likewise led the way in attacking laws protective of human life before birth. The portrayal of unborn baby killing as merely the "interruption of pregnancy" played an essential role in molding public opinion. In just one article, psychiatrist Dr. Harold Rosen resorted to this form of linguistic hypocrisy over 35 times! His recommendation for legalizing the destruction of the unborn featured the expression "interruption of a pre-viable pregnancy."[35]

Many unborn children of women relegated to slave labor were aborted in the sick ward of the I.G. Farben plant located at Auschwitz. This large-scale destruction of the unborn went under the designation, "Interruption of Pregnancy of Female Eastern Workers."[36]

Salt osmotic shock was the method chosen to do away with thousands of unborn children in a New York City hospital during the early 1970s. One of the phrases selected to mask the killings was "interruption of midtrimester pregnancy."[37]

Humaneness

A highly benevolent method of concealing the horrors of mass destruction has been to portray them as a type of humane service. The projection of killing as an act of charity endows it with an incredible aura of respectability.

Euthanasia administrator Viktor Brack testified at the Nuremberg Doctors' Trial that one of his main jobs was to ensure that the euthanasia program "was being carried out in a humane manner."[38]

Doctors affiliated with the University of Hawaii Medical School recommended that hospitals planning unrestricted abortions "design an abortion program that is humanized."[39]

The massive slaughter in the concentration camps was saturated with a language of benevolence. The destruction of millions by gassing evolved as a result of Heinrich Himmler's wish to develop a more "humane" method of killing than shooting.[40]

American psychiatrist Zigmond M. Lebensohn is fond of referring to abortion as "the practice of humanitarian medicine at its very best."[41]

During a banquet in honor of the Treblinka concentration camp perpetrators, public health professor Dr. Pfannenstiel remarked that the "beauty of the task" performed at Treblinka represented a "humane cause."[42]

Writing in a leading American medical journal, Dr. Michael S. Burnhill referred to abortion as "a consistently high quality, humane service."[43]

The transformation of both past and current destruction into humanitarian endeavors is intended to facilitate and sustain the involvement of the perpetrators in mass extermination while maintaining positive self-concepts. Otherwise it would not be possible either psychologically or morally to carry out destructive activities on such an extensive scale. The main recipients of the compassionate vocabulary are meant to be the perpetrators and not the victims. "The 'humaneness' of the destruction process," declared Hilberg, "was evolved not for the benefit of the victims but for the welfare of the perpetrators."[44]

Furnish an overview of the discrepancies between the actual fate of the victims and the perpetrators' euphemistic versions of their fate.

These striking contrasts are shown in Chart 12 on pages 120 and 121.

Chart 12
Semantic Camouflage in the Service of Holocausts Past and Present

Nazi Germany		Contemporary America	
HARSH REALITIES (What Actually Happened)	**LINGUISTIC DISTORTIONS** (Perpetrator's Version of What Happened)	**HARSH REALITIES** (What Actually Happened)	**LINGUISTIC DISTORTIONS** (Perpetrator's Version of What Happened)
	SELECTION, CHOICE		
The right to decide which inmates would be dispatched to the gas chamber.	"Selection"	The right to decide which unborn children will be dispatched to the abortion chamber.	"Choice"
	EVACUATION		
The suffocation of 15,000 women and children in gas vans.	They were "evacuated." (Nazi report, 1941)	The killing of 4,463 unborn children in North Carolina hospitals.	"The uterus was evacuated." (Dr. David A. Edelman 1974)
	EMPTIED		
The dispatching of Baron de Hirsch ghetto inhabitants to the gas chambers.	The "ghetto would have to be emptied." (Dr. Max Merten, 1943)	The destruction of unborn children.	"The uterus is gently emptied." (National Abortion Rights Action League)
	REMOVAL		
The annihilation of Polish Jews.	"Removal of the Jewish element." (Hans Frank, 1943)	The extermination of 71 unborn human lives by injections of prostaglandins.	"Remove the products of conception." (Dr. Thomas F. Dillion, 1974)

Chart 12 (Cont.)

Nazi Germany		Contemporary America	
HARSH REALITIES (What Actually Happened)	**LINGUISTIC DISTORTIONS** (Perpetrator's Version of What Happened)	**HARSH REALITIES** (What Actually Happened)	**LINGUISTIC DISTORTIONS** (Perpetrator's Version of What Happened)
	CLEANUP		
The destruction of the Jews in the generalgovernment.	"A total cleanup." (Order of Heinrich Himmler, 1942)	The dismemberment of unborn children with a suction machine.	"A final cleanup." (Planned Parenthood of New York City, 1973)
	PREGNANCY INTERRUPTION		
The killing of the unborn at Auschwitz.	"Interruption of pregnancy of female Eastern workers." (Labor Office memo, 1944)	The salt poisoning of 5,000 unborn children in a New York hospital.	"The interruption of midtrimester pregnancy." (Dr. Thomas D. Kerenyi, 1973)
	HUMANENESS		
The destruction of nearly one million people at the Treblinka concentration camp.	"The beauty of the task" represents a "humane cause." (Dr. Pfannenstiel, 1942)	The destruction of unborn children in the first trimester of gestation.	"A consistently high quality, humane service." (Dr. Michael S. Burnhill, 1975)

The incredible distortions of language employed by past and current perpetrators to conceal their involvement in mass destruction can be aptly summed up by a Yiddish proverb: The truth can walk around naked, only lies must be clothed in euphemism.

Chapter 11

The Medicalization of Annihilation

The perversion of medicine in the service of killing is accompanied by a redefinition of barbaric acts as valid medical procedures. An astounding bit of alchemy sets in whereby the physician healer not only becomes a killer, but in the process of this most radical of transformations, destruction loses its most repulsive features and becomes incorporated into the fabric of respectable medical practice. Doctors can then continue to view themselves as healers while perpetrating destruction on a massive scale.

The redefinition of killing as healing also leads inevitably to a redefinition of the victims as diseases. What better way for the doctor to retain his image as healer than by reconceptualizing destruction as a distinctly medical task designed to eliminate individuals who have been reduced to the level of disease entities!

Medical Linguistics and Mass Destruction

How was the medicalization of annihilation manifested in Nazi Germany?

A study conducted by psychiatrist Robert Jay Lifton of former Nazi death camp doctors underscores how readily they justified their participation in Germany's holocaust as a strictly medical matter. "Doctors," Lifton found, "were key figures in a process of murder in the name of therapy." Nazi ideology and language were replete with biological and medical references. The slogan "Nazism is applied biology" served as an inducement for physicians to join the Nazi party and view themselves as "vast revolutionary biological therapists." Medical involvement in genocide was projected not as killing but as a "medical operation" or even a "health measure" against Jews and other undesirables perceived as diseases and such disease carriers as vermin and lice.[1] Moral and psychological considerations were rendered impotent as mass extermination of the victims was elevated to the unimpeachable status of curing illnesses, combatting epidemics, and removing infected body parts.

How is medicalized killing manifested in contemporary society?

Today's medical assaults against the unwanted unborn, like the Nazi onslaughts against Jews and others, are portrayed not as the wholesale destruction of bona fide human beings, but simply as legitimate "medical procedures" conducted to counteract sickness and excise diseased tissue and body contents. American doctors are so fully implicated in destruction that the killing of the unborn is now the most frequently performed surgical operation in America, outstripping even tonsillectomy.[2] Under the guise of treatment, the destructive activities of physician abortionists are literally saturated with an antiseptic, medically-impeccable vocabulary. The medical semantics deployed by American physicians to conceal their destructive procedures are almost exact replicas of the terminology manufactured by the Nazi doctors to camouflage extermination with medical respectability.

What are some of the major linguistic expressions used to pervert medical skills for malevolent purposes in both the Nazi era and contemporary society?

Medical operations or *procedure; eradication of germs, infections, epidemics; removal of infected appendix* or *gangrenous growth; treatment for disease; charitable organizations;* and *service.*

Medical Operation or Procedure

"Operation" *(aktion)* was one of the most widely employed code words used to conceal all types of destructive actions. It frequently appeared in a variety of combinations: "cleaning operations" and "pacification operations" blanketed the killing of Jews in the Eastern territories; "Operation Reinhard" was the cover designation for the extermination of Polish Jews; "large-scale operation" was intended to obscure the destruction of the Warsaw ghetto.[3]

The word "operation" was readily adopted by Germany's doctors of infamy. When Dr. Robert Jay Lifton interviewed former death camp physicians he found that their involvement in the killing "came to be projected as a medical operation."[4]

Today, an alarming number of American physicians accept Dr. Carl O. Rice's euphemistic version of unborn baby killing as merely "a minor surgical operation."[5]

A similar concept, "procedure," has served as a favorite standby to disguise past and contemporary medical atrocities.

The gassing of lice-infested female inmates was considered an appropriate public health measure for ridding the Auschwitz women's camp of lice. This became commonly known as "this procedure."[6]

Plunging a needle directly into the heart of an unborn twin afflicted with Down's Syndrome is now deemed an acceptable medical procedure at New York's Mount Sinai School of Medicine for eradicating congenital disease. In the medical journal article describing this destructive operation the word "kill" is nowhere to be found. The phrase "the procedure" is mentioned fourteen different times![7]

Eradication of Germs, Infections, Epidemics

On October 3, 1943 in Poznan, Heinrich Himmler compared the killing of Jews to having "exterminated a germ," and warned his generals to stay away from dead Jews to avoid becoming "infected by that germ."[8]

A major foundation of psychiatrist Natalie Shainess' fervent defense of abortion on demand is a perception of unwanted pregnancy as equivalent to an "alien germ."[9]

The medical treatment of scarlet fever epidemics among women at Auschwitz resulted in reducing the victims to ashes in the crematorium. The official version of what happened was contained in a report authored by Dr. Josef Mengele: the "intensive struggle against the propagation of infection."[10]

Psychiatrist Natalie Shainess furnished another infected metaphor for justifying abortion as a valid medical procedure: unwanted pregnancy as an "unseen infection deep in the body."[11]

Typhus epidemics among Jews forced into the Warsaw ghetto provided the Nazis with additional derogatory terminology intended to equate the victims with the disease with which they were afflicted. A prime example of this was the slogan "Jews-Lice-Typhus," which was circulated extensively throughout Poland.[12] A health conference was held on July 9, 1943 to commemorate the deportation of over 400,000 Jews from the Warsaw ghetto to the death camps. The removal of the "typhus epidemic," it was announced, made a significant contribution to the health of Europe.[13]

In contemporary American society the presentation of pregnancy as an "epidemic" has become widespread. Planned Parenthood Federation of America, a foremost proponent of abortion as an indispensable medical response to pregnancy viewed as a problem of "epidemic" proportions, published a booklet in 1976 which referred to the U.S. teenage birth rate as constituting "an epidemic of adolescent pregnancies."[14] A definition of teenage pregnancy as a disease of "epidemic" dimensions prompted Dr. Jane Hodgson to promote enforced abortion as a type of "mandatory immunization" designed to prohibit "motherhood."[15]

Removal of Infected Appendix or Gangrenous Growth

Former Auschwitz physician Dr. Fritz Klein described the extermination of Jews as analogous to a "good doctor" who "takes a scalpel and removes an appendix full of pus" on the assumption that "the Jews are the pus-filled appendix in the body of Europe."[16]

In 1968 Dr. Alan F. Guttmacher likened the destruction of the unborn to "operating on an appendix or removing gangrenous bowel."[17]

Auschwitz survivor Dr. Ella Lingens-Reiner once pointed to the crematorium chimneys and asked Dr. Fritz Klein: "How can you reconcile that with your Hippocratic Oath?" Klein replied: "When you find a gangrenous appendix, you must remove it."[18]

At an abortion conference held in New York in 1955, Dr. Robert Laidlaw called for a change in the law which would allow the doctor to do abortions just as it permits him to perform other legitimate medical procedures. Laidlaw placed abortion in the same medical category as operating on "a ruptured appendix."[19]

Another former death camp doctor supplied a similar version of genocide as a form of surgery. "If you have a gangrenous growth," he explained, "you have to remove it."[20]

American psychiatrist Jerome M. Kummer has compared abortion to "an appendectomy for acute appendicitis or amputation to remove a gangrenous or cancerous limb."[21]

Treatment for Disease

A decree of April 5, 1943, signed by Reich health leader Dr. Leonardo Conti, gave the authorization to establish "sick bays" for the purpose of destroying the unborn children of female Eastern workers. What went on in these facilities was referred to as "the treatment."[22]

Before the American Anthropological Association in 1970, Dr. Warren M. Hern portrayed pregnancy as an "episodic, moderately extended chronic condition." This provided him with a foundation from which to promote abortion as "the indicated treatment."[23]

The destruction of children at the Eglfing-Haar psychiatric institution was disguised by the terms "the treatment" and "was treated."[24] The killing of Down's Syndrome children at the Eichberg euthanasia hospital went under the heading: "treatment of idiotic children."[25]

In 1973 Planned Parenthood of New York City declared that "ending" a woman's pregnancy "is no more unnatural than treating an illness that can cripple her."[26] "In a girl under 18," asserted Planned Parenthood board member Dr. James Irwin, "we consider pregnancy a disease."[27]

At the Hadamar euthanasia hospital, patients about to be killed by lethal injections were told that the substances administered were for "treatment of their lung disease."[28]

A meeting of Planned Parenthood Physicians in 1976 provided Dr. Willard Cates and colleagues with a forum for prescribing abortion as the "preferred medical treatment" for unwanted pregnancy viewed as "a sexually transmitted disease" of "epidemic proportion." Gonorrhea was identified as the "number one sexually transmitted disease," with unwanted pregnancy holding down the second slot. Cates and associates, however, rated abortion "10 times more effective for treating unwanted pregnancies than is penicillin for treating gonorrhea." The title of the paper presented by Dr. Cates at this meeting was: "Abortion as a Treatment for Unwanted Pregnancy: The Number Two Sexually Transmitted 'Disease.'"[29]

These disease-ridden metaphors created by elitist medical bureaucrats have had a profound impact on women. The prestigious textbook *Williams Obstetrics* found it noteworthy to report that "for some women pregnancy is a venereal disease."[30]

An exchange of letters between Reich Governor of Poznan Arthur Greiser and Heinrich Himmler regarding the fate of tubercular Polish nationals under Nazi occupation illustrates how the destruction-disguised-as-treatment hoax was put across linguistically. In the first letter, Greiser requested permission from Himmler to take appropriate steps against the "public plague" of 35,000 Poles infected with open tuberculosis while the "special treatment" of 100,000 Jews had been almost completed. Himmler's reply reinforced the image of a medical resolution to the problem: "I have no objection to having protectorate people and stateless persons of Polish origin, who live within the territory of the Warthegau and are infected with tuberculosis, handed over for special treatment as you suggest."[31]

The astonishing extent to which the transformation of mass killing into an acceptable treatment for disease has become enshrined as a modern dogma of organized mainstream medicine in America was revealed in a legal brief submitted to the U.S. Supreme Court on August 27, 1982 by the American College of Obstetricians and Gynecologists, the American Medical Association, the American Academy of Pediatrics, and the Nurses Association of the American College of Obstetricians and Gynecologists. The intention of this *amici curiae* (friends of the court) brief was to strike down an ordinance enacted by the City of Akron, Ohio, which contains only the most minimal regulations for performing abortions. The physician's responsibility "to provide care and treatment," according to the rhetoric fashioned by these groups of medical elites, includes abortion defined as a legitimate component of "medical care or treatment."[32] Echoing the type of semantic hocus-pocus pioneered by the Nazi doctors and such American physicians as Dr. Willard

Cates and others, the brief emphasizes the impressive safety record of abortion compared to other medical procedures:

> A patient undergoing an abortion faces about the same risk of death as does a patient receiving an intra-muscular injection of penicillin for gonorrhea. A tonsillectomy is twice as risky, and an appendectomy is nearly a hundred times as risky, as a legal abortion.[33]

The essential role that medical jargon has played in covering up the harsh realities of unborn baby killing is undeniable. The elevation of abortion from a destructive act to a highly respectable medical treatment, and the reduction of the unborn from a human entity to a disease entity, deserve an honored position among the most successful semantic sleight-of-hands ever pulled off!

Block 20 at Auschwitz, the place where adults and children were injected in the heart with lethal doses of phenol, was known as the "treatment room."[34]

Today a similar designation, the "procedure room,"[35] is frequently employed to indicate the locale where the bodies of unborn children are literally torn apart and reduced to indistinguishable fragments by the force of a suction machine.

Charitable Organizations

The Nazi euthanasia program was so heavily infused with altruistic imagery that the agency responsible for transporting the victims to the killing centers was called the "Charitable Transport Company for the Sick."[36] The actual killing of physically and mentally ill patients was coordinated by an organization known as the "Charitable Foundation for Institutional Care."[37]

Contemporary abortion, similarly, has gained considerable acceptance as a "charitable" enterprise. This is nowhere more perversely illustrated than in the Internal Revenue Service's practice of granting "non-profit" tax exempt status to abortion chambers under the highly benevolent classification of "charitable organizations" engaged in "promoting health."[38]

Service

Closely allied with a benevolent portrayal of destruction is the transformation of annihilation into a highly valued "service" on behalf of patients or clients. The acceptance of killing as a type of "service" illustrates the awesome power of terminology in league with technology to camouflage the perpetration of the most horrendous atrocities.

Beginning on June 22, 1941, specially trained killing units, composed of many intellectuals, followed upon the heels of the German army in a search-and-destroy mission directed against Jews, Gypsies, communists, and the insane in the Eastern territories under Nazi subjugation. Most of the victims were shot to death in front of huge ditches.[39] These extermination squads became known as "special service groups."[40]

Each year in America over 1.5 million unborn children are slaughtered in a variety of settings, including abortion chambers, hospitals, and doctors' offices. Researchers at the Alan Guttmacher Institute of the Planned Parenthood Federation of America have developed a longstanding pattern of calling the individuals, groups, and facilities responsible for this massive eradication of human lives "service providers."[41]

A comparison between the harsh realities of unborn baby killing and the semantic camouflage concocted by physicians to mask their destructive operations can be found in Chart 13 on pages 130 and 131.

Chart 13
The Language of Exterminative Medicine

Nazi Germany		Contemporary America	
HARSH REALITIES (What Actually Happened)	**LINGUISTIC DISTORTIONS** (Perpetrator's Version of What Happened)	**HARSH REALITIES** (What Actually Happened)	**LINGUISTIC DISTORTIONS** (Perpetrator's Version of What Happened)
	MEDICAL OPERATION		
The killing of human beings in concentration camps.	"A medical operation." (Former death camp doctors, 1979)	The killing of unborn children in hospitals and clinics.	"A minor surgical operation." (Dr. Carl O. Rice, 1973)
	PROCEDURE		
The gassing of lice-infested female inmates at Auschwitz.	"This procedure." (Dr. Ella Lingens, Auschwitz Trial, 1964)	Piercing the heart of an afflicted twin in utero at New York's Mount Sinai Hospital.	"The procedure." (Drs. Thomas D. Kerenyi and Usha Chitkara, 1981)
	INFECTION		
The gassing of women afflicted with scarlet fever at Auschwitz.	"The intensive struggle against the propagation of infection." (Dr. Josef Mengele, 1944)	A justification for unborn baby killing.	A perception of unwanted pregnancy as "an unseen infection." (Dr. Natalie Shainess, 1970)
	REMOVAL OF APPENDIX		
The extermination of Jews at Auschwitz.	"When you find a gangrenous appendix, you must remove it." (Dr. Fritz Klein, 1944)	The destruction of unborn children.	"Operating on an appendix or removing gangrenous bowel." (Dr. Alan F. Guttmacher, 1968)

Chart 13 (Cont.)

Nazi Germany		Contemporary America	
HARSH REALITIES (What Actually Happened)	**LINGUISTIC DISTORTIONS** (Perpetrator's Version of What Happened)	**HARSH REALITIES** (What Actually Happened)	**LINGUISTIC DISTORTIONS** (Perpetrator's Version of What Happened)
TREATMENT OF DISEASE			
Lethal injections administered to patients at the Hadamar Euthanasia Hospital.	"Treatment of their lung disease." (Nurse Heinrich Ruoff, Hadamar Trial, 1947)	The promotion of abortion for unwanted unborn children.	"Treatment for unwanted pregnancy: the number two sexually transmitted disease." (Dr. Willard Cates, 1976)
CHARITABLE ORGANIZATIONS			
Killing centers for physically and mentally ill patients.	"Charitable Foundation for Institutional Care." (Official designation of organization responsible for implementing the euthanasia program)	Killing centers for the unborn.	"Charitable organizations" engaged in "promoting health." (Official designation given to abortion chambers by Internal Revenue Service)
SERVICE			
Extermination squads responsible for shooting to death millions in the East.	"Special service groups." (Routine regimental reports, 1941)	Individuals, groups, and facilities responsible for the destruction of over 1.5 million unborn children each year.	"Service providers." (Stanley K. Henshaw, Alan Guttmacher Institute, 1982)

One of the best definitions of prejudice formulated is: *being down on something you are not up on.* The reduction of human expendables ("being down on something") to the level of diseases and cancerous growths is due largely to an incredible lack of knowledge or outright distortions ("something you are not up on") conveyed by medical executioners regarding the nature of human life, especially the unwanted variety.

The medicalized destruction of millions in the Third Reich and today's society owes its phenomenal success to a lethal combination of factors: highly negative stereotypes of the victims induced by ignorance and misinformation. The elevation of barbaric acts to the ultimate heights of respectability as benevolent medical procedures represents an awesome display of extreme prejudice backed up by semantic gymnastics and raw medical power gone awry.

Chapter 12

Subversion of Hippocrates And His Oath

The most significant authority doctors must reject in order to justify sustained participation in mass destruction is Hippocrates, the Father of Medicine. It is the Oath bequeathed to medicine by Hippocrates which not only embodies the highest ethical standards for physicians, but also condemns killing inside and outside the womb.

I thought Hippocrates was a religious fanatic who tried to impose his sectarian views on everyone in the medical profession.

To the contrary, Hippocrates was a pagan who truly believed in the sanctity of all human lives and made this the very foundation of his Oath. He presents a formidable challenge to doctors intent upon perverting medical skills for destructive purposes.

Before Hippocrates

What was the role of physicians before the time of Hippocrates?

The sorcerer, owing to a knowledge of harmful and beneficial substances derived from a study of plants and animals, performed two basic functions: he prescribed and administered drugs designed to heal some and to kill others. In a culture dominated by ignorance and superstition, the sorcerer-physician combined the dual task of curing those afflicted by supernatural forces and eliminating those defined as causing their afflictions.[1]

What did anthropologist Margaret Mead say about the doctor's role in ancient times?

"Throughout the primitive world the doctor and the sorcerer tended to be the same person," she concluded. "He with the power to kill had the power to cure, including specially the undoing of his own killing activities. He who had the power to cure would necessarily also be able to kill."[2]

When was the role of the physician as healer-killer first questioned?

When a greater understanding of the natural causes of diseases began to replace superstition. One of the most significant challenges came in the form of a treatise entitled "The Sacred Disease," authored by the Greek physician Hippocrates, which maintained that epilepsy and other illnesses were not due to such malignant forces as evil spirits, angry gods, or unscrupulous enemies, but arose from natural causes.[3]

How eminent was Hippocrates?

Hippocrates is universally recognized as the Father of Medicine, the "wisest and the greatest practitioner of his art" and the "most important and most complete medical personality of antiquity."[4]

The Hippocratic Oath

When was the Hippocratic Oath formulated and what were some of its main components?

It was formulated in the fifth century before Christ. It states in part:

> I swear by Apollo Physician, by Asclepius . . . I will use treatment to help the sick according to my ability and judgment, but never with a view to injury and wrong-doing. Neither will I administer a poison to anybody when asked to do so, nor will I suggest such a course. Similarly, I will not give to a woman a pessary to cause abortion . . . Into whatsoever houses I enter, I will enter to help the sick, and I will abstain from all intentional wrong-doing and harm, especially from abusing the bodies of man or woman, bond or free.[5]

Why is the Hippocratic Oath considered so important?

According to anthropologist Mead, the Oath marked a turning point in the history of civilized society because "for the first time in our tradition" it effectuated "a complete separation between curing and killing."[6] This meant that never again would physicians be expected or allowed to kill anyone in any manner as part of their range of professional tasks. From this point on, doctors were to be entirely and preeminently healers of the sick.

The Oath's main principle, *primum non nocere,* first do no harm, is the very cornerstone of humane medical practice, an unwavering beacon which has guided doctors for centuries. Since physicians had been so heavily invested in destruction as well as curing before the time of Hippocrates, it is not surprising that the Oath contains explicit condemnations of both abortion and mercy killing. Hippocrates was insistent on removing physician from association with all forms of destruction, whether they involved killing the child before birth or the adult during the last stages of life.

Are there any exceptions or qualifications to the sanctity of life ethic so deeply etched in the Oath?

None whatsoever. It represents an ethic completely dedicated to healing, protecting, and caring for individuals at all phases of the human life cycle. This point is underscored by Mead:

> With the Greeks the distinction was made clear. One profession, the followers of Asclepius, were to be dedicated completely to life under all circumstances, regardless of rank, age, or intellect—the life of a slave, the life of the Emperor, the life of a foreign man, the life of a defective child.[7]

What are the implications of the Hippocratic Oath for the role of the physician and for the profession of medicine?

The Oath provided the doctor with a code for professional conduct of the highest ethical standards. It was meant to confer on the physician the kind of professional autonomy needed to withstand attempts by others to reinstate the dark age of exterminative medicine. With Hippocrates and his Oath the course of humane medicine was set with conspicuous clarity: the doctor as a servant, protector, and healer of the sick, and never again as an instrument to be exploited by the state or any other pressure group bent on distorting medical skills for destructive purposes.

This, in Mead's assessment, is "a priceless possession which we cannot afford to tarnish," especially in light of the fact that "society is attempting to make the physician into a killer—to kill the defective child at birth, to leave sleeping pills beside the bed of a cancer patient."[8]

American medical science consultant Dr. Andrew C. Ivy testified to the indispensability of the Hippocratic Oath for the profession of medicine at the Nuremberg Doctors' Trial where twenty physicians were charged with crimes against humanity committed in the euthanasia hospitals and concentration camps of the Third Reich: "The moral imperative of the oath of Hippocrates I believe is necessary for the survival of the scientific and technical philosophy of medicine."[9]

A penetrating analysis by Dr. Herbert Ratner highlights the great importance of Hippocrates and his Oath for the establishment of medicine as a learned profession dedicated to the service of humanity:

> In the golden age of ancient Greece, medicine emerged as the prototype of the learned professions. The contribution of Hippocrates, the father of medicine, was to incorporate the rights of the patient, as well as the obligations of the physician, into the Oath.

> Hippocrates' profound grasp of the nature of a learned profession serving one of man's basic needs makes the Hippocratic Oath one of the great documents and classics of man, a fact not only signified by its universal inclusion in collections of the great books of western civilization, but by the universal veneration accorded it by physicians, singly and collectively, through the ages.[10]

Ratner also focuses on the significance of the Oath for keeping medicine true to its healing tradition:

> It is the Oath—a code of ethics which holds steadfast to a moral obligation in conformity with the definitive nature of a learned profession (here medicine)—which is the prime protector of the purity of the medical art. By imposing on its members an obligation to remain resolute against the assault of a sick society, the Oath, properly constituted, becomes the one hope of preserving the unconfused role of the physician as healer.[11]

It should be noted once more that Hippocrates was a pagan whose antipathy toward killing did not arise out of a religious foundation, but came from a medical orientation. He perceived any kind of killing as completely foreign to the role of the physician. With Hippocrates the commandment "Thou Shalt Not Kill," an injunction which transcends all races, religions, and creeds, was finally extended to the highly appropriate sphere of medical practice.

German Assaults

To what extent did attacks on the Hippocratic Oath serve as a pretext for Germany's medical holocaust?

Unrelenting assaults on the core of the Hippocratic Oath comprised an integral part of the insidious erosion of respect for human life which culminated in the heavy involvement of doctors in the destruction and experimental exploitation of human lives during the Nazi era.

When did the process of discrediting the Oath begin?

As early as 1920 Drs. Karl Binding and Alfred Hoche, forerunners of the Nazi euthanasia program, characterized the Hippocratic Oath as outdated. This portrayal provided a convenient justification for advocating the destruction of "life devoid of value." In the words of Dr. Hoche: "Not even the Hippocratic Oath is really binding anymore."[12]

Are there any statements which show how the Hippocratic Oath was denigrated by German doctors involved in the Nazi holocaust?

At a trial held in 1961, a public health physician convicted of killing mentally handicapped patients during the Nazi era admitted that he was "in favour of killing worthless life." When reminded that such an attitude was in violation of the Hippocratic Oath, "he denied ever having sworn to preserve life."[13]

The onslaught against Hippocrates was very much in evidence at the Nuremberg Doctors' Trial. All twenty of the physicians charged with crimes against humanity, declared the prosecution, "violated the Hippocratic commandments which they had solemnly sworn to uphold and abide by, including the fundamental principles never to do harm—'primum non nocere.'"[14] Some of the physician defendants even openly stated that "the oath of Hippocrates is obsolete today."[15] In his final statement before the Nuremberg tribunal, defendant Dr. Helmut Poppendick cited a prominent medical professor from Heidelberg to support his view of the Hippocratic Oath as being unrelated to the legality of euthanasia and experiments on human beings. "The oath of Hippocrates," he stated, "has nothing to do with the problem."[16]

The Declaration of Geneva

When was the Declaration of Geneva formulated and what are some of its key provisions?

The Declaration of Geneva, also known as the Geneva Code, was enacted in Geneva, Switzerland in 1948 by the World Medical Association. It states in part:

> Now being admitted to the profession of medicine, I solemnly pledge to consecrate my life to the service of humanity . . . . I will practice medicine with conscience and dignity. The health and life of my patient will be my first consideration . . . . I will maintain the utmost respect for human life from the time of its conception. Even under threat I will not use my knowledge contrary to the laws of humanity.[17]

How is the Declaration of Geneva related to the Hippocratic Oath?

The Geneva Code is a modern reaffirmation of the Hippocratic Oath adopted out of the ashes of the medical holocaust in Nazi Germany. It retains the "do no harm" principle and sanctity-of-life ethic so deeply etched in the older statement of medical conduct. The phrase "I will maintain the utmost respect for human life from the time of its conception" places the physician in the role of a healer totally and unequivocably dedicated to the service of *all* human beings, both born and unborn, from the *earliest* point of their existence.

What is the World Medical Association?

An organization which, in 1948, consisted of thirty-nine national medical societies throughout the world, including the American Medical Association.[18]

Why did the World Medical Association adopt the Declaration of Geneva?

As a reminder of the atrocities perpetrated by physicians in the Third Reich and "as a check upon any repetition, anywhere in the world, of the German doctors descent into savagery."[19]

Did the World Medical Association propose that the Geneva Code, the modern version of the Hippocratic Oath, be taken by every doctor upon graduation from medical school?

Absolutely. It recommended that this Oath "be read by every doctor on receipt of his diploma." Again, the indispensable rationale for its recitation: "May those who recite it as they enter the noble Hippocratic fellowship ever recall the deeds that necessitated its drafting—determined never to let such things happen again."[20]

American Assaults

What impact has the Hippocratic Oath had on physicians in contemporary America?

One would think that after what occurred in Nazi Germany, doctors would never again participate in any activities even remotely associated with killing. One would think that the reassertion of the do-no-harm principle of the Hippocratic Oath contained in the Geneva Code would be sufficient to deter present-day physicians from repeating the crimes against humanity perpetrated by the German doctors. One would think that the Oath and its modern version would help doctors resist any efforts to turn them into instruments of destruction.

What has happened, deplorably, is just the opposite. Instead of abandoning their destructive practices, many contemporary physicians have decided to attack the Oath, and along with it, the reputation of Hippocrates.

Why are today's doctors trying to discredit Hippocrates and his Oath?

Their efforts are motivated primarily by a need to rationalize participation in the modern slaughter of the unwanted unborn. It would be untenable as well as embarrassing to continue killing unborn human lives at the current assembly-line rate and still retain an

Oath so clearly opposed to such repulsive operations.

Can you furnish some examples of attacks directed against the Hippocratic Oath in contemporary American society?

During the course of presenting oral arguments before the U.S. Supreme Court on October 11, 1972, for the abolition of abortion laws, pro-abortion attorney Sarah R. Weddington was asked why a discussion of the Hippocratic Oath had not been included in any of the voluminous briefs submitted to the Court. "The Hippocratic Oath," she replied, "does not pertain to that." [the woman's constitutional right to an abortion][21]

According to St. Louis abortionist Dr. Bolivar M. Escobedo, "The Hippocratic Oath is nothing but a ritual or symbolic act that bears no legal force."[22]

Dr. William Petersen, chairman of the department of obstetrics and gynecology at the Washington Hospital Center and an expert in performing midtrimester abortions, defends his destructive activities by relegating the Oath of Hippocrates to a state of obsolescence. The Oath, he claims, was "carried down from olden times. Many of our old traditions had been changed by present-day demands."[23]

The U.S. Supreme Court on the Hippocratic Oath

What did the U.S. Supreme Court say about the Hippocratic Oath in its 1973 decision legalizing abortion?

First, the Oath is interpreted not as an expression of the highest ethical standards, but merely as a piece of sectarian dogma representing just a small segment of the Greek population, the Pythagoreans.[24] In a pluralistic society such as contemporary America, what better way to thoroughly malign individuals than by giving the impression that they are trying to force their particular brand of sectarian morality onto the rest of society!

Second, the universality of the Oath is weakened further by pointing toward "evidence of the violation of almost everyone of its injunctions."[25] The image the Court wishes to convey here is widespread deviations; the logical conclusion being there must be something seriously wrong with a code so frequently violated in so many different ways. The focus is therefore shifted away from the behavioral violations and toward the Oath's alleged deficiencies; it is the Oath that is in error and not the behavior that deviates from it.

Finally, the Court resorts to name calling when it refers to the "apparent rigidity" of the Oath and how it is simply a "Pythagorean manifesto" which "echos Pythagorean doctrines" proposed in a spirit of "uncompromising austerity."[26] The demise of the Oath and its veracity is thus finalized in a volley of disparaging terms.

What kind of scholarship did the Supreme Court base its interpretation of the Hippocratic Oath on?

The slandering of the Hippocratic Oath has nothing to do with either scholarship or objective historical research. The rhetoric emanating from the pen of Associate Justice Harry Blackmun represents a highly partisan attack intended to provide historical support for the legalized destruction of unborn children. Excessive reliance was placed almost exclusively on the opinion of one physician. The late Dr. Ludwig Edelstein[27] is cited as the authority for the Court's excursions in historical fantasy and distortion. Against such extremely slanted interpretations, the Oath stood little chance of survival. So have, tragically, countless human lives!

The Oath and American Medical Schools

I thought that all medical students were supposed to commit themselves to the ethical principles embodied in the Hippocratic Oath before receiving their diplomas.

No longer is the Hippocratic Oath or even its modern counterpart, the Declaration of Geneva, a required part of graduation ceremonies at American medical schools. An extensive survey conducted by Scottsdale, Arizona cardiologist and right-to-life leader Dr. Carolyn F. Gerster reveals that the Hippocratic Oath has been abandoned by almost every medical school in America. Those few which still retain it, she found, do so only in a most diluted form. For example, the sanctity-of-life ethic manifested by Hippocrates' explicit strictures against abortion and mercy killing has been expunged and replaced by such respectable-sounding phrases as "I will give no drugs and perform no operation for a criminal purpose" or "I will abstain from all that is illegal."[28]

From this, Gerster furnishes an essential parallel in urgent need of exposure: only one other time in modern history was the Oath "completely dropped from use in medical schools—during the twelve years of the Third Reich."[29]

Is recitation of the Geneva Code a required part of graduation ceremonies at Northwestern University medical school?

A censored version of the Declaration of Geneva minus two key passages (*I will maintain the utmost respect for human life from the time of its conception* and *Even under threat I will not use my knowledge contrary to the laws of humanity*) is recited by medical students at Northwestern University (Evanston, Illinois) during graduation ceremonies. On June 18, 1982, however, a small group of students in the 180-member Northwestern medical school graduating class distributed to their fellow students a circular calling for a return to the Hippocratic tradition as a means of counteracting the heavy participation of their medical professors in abortion.

One side of the circular contained an uncensored adaptation from the Geneva Code. The other side included a statement entitled "A Modest Protest" in which the dissenting students pleaded with their classmates to let them recite the oath in its entirely, including the passages omitted in the printed graduation booklet. The protesting students pointed out that the Declaration they were being instructed to take was not the true Oath of Hippocrates but was actually an incorrect version of the Geneva Code. They then provided the following historical perspectives:

> The Geneva Oath was first composed in 1948 as a response to the atrocities of the Nazi Holocaust. The doctors living in 1948 were frightened to learn that their German counterparts were actively involved in many of Hitler's mass extermination programs. In fact, many German physicians easily acquiesced to societal and institutional pressures for a "genetically pure" Aryan Race; thus paving the way for later campaigns directed against "inferior humans," such as the Jews and Poles.
>
> As medical students, we see many of these same authoritarian attitudes at work in our own society. Like the Germans, we have become preoccupied with "improving our race." [30]

"When the time came for the recitation of the oath," disclosed reporter-columnist Joseph T. Gill, "the dean of the medical school reluctantly and with evident embarrassment and distaste announced that since the full statement was in the hands of the graduates those who wished to recite it in full would be allowed to do so whereas those who did not should remain silent when that paragraph was reached."[31] Despite the fact that all the students had a copy of the uncut version of the Oath and information on the historical circumstances responsible for its enactment, 160 graduating doctors remained silent while only about twenty of their classmates made a public commitment to the most scared ethical standards underlying the practice of humane medicine!

The most basic principles embodied in the Hippocratic Oath and its modern counterpart, the Declaration of Geneva, and the medical assaults directed against them are summarized in Chart 14 on pages 142 and 143.

Chart 14
Milestones in Medical Ethics and their Violations

I. Before Hippocrates

The physician in the role of sorcerer functioned as both a killer and a healer.

II. The Oath of Hippocrates (460-377 B.C.)

"I swear by Apollo Physician, by Asclepius . . . I will use treatment to help the sick according to my ability and judgment, but never with a view to injury and wrong-doing. Neither will I administer a poison to anybody when asked to do so, nor will I suggest such a course. Similarly, I will not give a woman a pessary to cause abortion . . ."

A. Background Information

The Oath was formulated in the 5th Century B.C. by the pagan physician Hippocrates, "the wisest and the greatest practitioner of his art" and the "most important and most complete medical personality of antiquity."

B. Importance

1. A turning point in the history of medicine.

"For the first time in our tradition there was a complete separation between killing and curing . . . One profession, the followers of Asclepius, were to be dedicated completely to life under all circumstances regardless of rank, age, or intellect." (Anthropologist Margaret Mead, 1963)

2. Survival of the medical profession.

"The moral imperative of the oath of Hippocrates I believe is necessary for the survival of the scientific and technical philosophy of medicine." (Dr. Andrew C. Ivy, American medical scientific consultant to the prosecution, Nuremberg War Crimes Trials, 1947)

III. The Third Reich (1933-1945)

Doctors destroyed unborn and born expendables on a massive scale.

IV. The Declaration of Geneva—A Modern Reaffirmation of the Hippocratic Oath (1948)

"Now being admitted to the profession of medicine, I solemnly pledge to consecrate my life to the service of humanity . . . I will maintain the utmost respect for human life from the time of its conception. Even under threat, I will not use my knowledge contrary to the laws of humanity."

Chart 14 (Cont.)

A. Background Information

The Declaration was enacted by the World Medical Association, comprising thirty-nine national medical associations including the American Medical Association, in September 1948 in response to the German physicians' involvement in crimes against humanity during the Nazi era.

B. Recommendation

That this Declaration be recited by every doctor upon graduation from medical school.

C. Purpose

1. A reminder of the depths of degradation to which German doctors had sunk in the Third Reich.
2. An attempt to prevent the recurrence of medical atrocities.

V. Contemporary Society (1973 – ?)

Doctors are destroying millions of unborn human lives and growing numbers of postnatal discards.

VI. Discrediting the Hippocratic Oath

Germany	America
"Not even the Hippocratic Oath is really binding anymore." (Euthanasia proponent Dr. Alfred Hoche, 1920)	"The Hippocratic Oath is nothing but a ritual or symbolic act that bears no legal force." (Abortionist Dr. Bolivar M. Escobedo, 1979)
"The oath of Hippocrates has nothing to do with the problem." [the legality of euthanasia and experiments on human beings] (Dr. Helmut Poppendick, Nuremberg Doctors' Trial, 1947)	"The Hippocratic Oath does not pertain to that." [the legality of the woman's constitutional right to an abortion] (Sarah R. Weddington, Oral Arguments in Supreme Court Abortion Decisions, October 1972)
"The oath of Hippocrates is obsolete today." (Testimony of physician defendants at the Nuremberg Doctors' Trial, 1947)	The Oath was "carried down from olden times. Many of our old traditions had been changed by present-day demands." (Abortionist Dr. William Peterson, 1980)

A Return to Sorcery

For over 2,000 years the role of the physician as healer had remained undisputed. Only two times, both in the 20th Century, has this indispensable legacy been seriously challenged: during the Third Reich and in contemporary society!

One of the most blatant assaults on the very core of the Hippocratic Oath came in 1972 when one hundred professors of obstetrics and chairmen of the obstetrics-gynecology departments from the leading medical schools in America issued a formal pronouncement in favor of abortion on demand. "For the first time, except perhaps for cosmetic surgery," they proclaimed, "doctors will be expected to do an operation simply because the patient asks that it be done. Granted, this changes the physician's traditional role, but it will be necessary to make this change if we are to serve the new society in which we live."[32]

The doctor's traditional role as healer bequeathed to medicine by Hippocrates was indeed altered, and radically so, to include extermination of the most unwanted and vulnerable human lives! According to medical professor and Hippocratic Oath scholar Dr. Herbert Ratner, the notion of "exterminative medicine" incorporated in the above statement "in which the physician serves as killer is as monstrous as expecting the learned profession of law to serve injustice, or of the ministry to serve vice and sin, and to promote hell as well as heaven."[33]

The demise of the Hippocratic Oath has resulted in unleashing an unprecedented era of unrestrained killing by the very profession which had once been so uncompromisingly dedicated to human life at all stages of development. Abandonment of the Oath has also had the effect of recycling many of today's physicians back to the dark age of the sorcerer where killing and curing once again share a perverse state of professional compatibility.

Chapter 13

The Media as Agents of Destructive Propaganda

Destruction at the level of a holocaust cannot be perpetrated unless the derogatory names directed against the victims and respectable language created to conceal what happens to them extend beyond the private domain of the killers to penetrate and pollute the public conscience. The media thus serve as indispensable allies in the creation and maintenance of a holocaust by disseminating the dehumanizing and deceptive linguistics to a vast audience.

After Hitler came to power the German press, the world's most diverse and independent conveyor of information, was reduced to an agent of the Ministry of Propaganda. Images of Jews and other victims as insignificant or subhuman elements dominated the contents of news accounts considered appropriate for public consumption. Nowhere could be found any descriptions or pictures of those exterminated in the death camps. What the media presented to the German people, instead, were idyllic versions of Jews being "removed" from ghettos and "evacuated" to the "East" for purposes of "resettlement" in the "bath houses" of "labor," "concentration," "recreation," or "resettlement camps."

An alarming number of journalists in America's media establishment have likewise become highly effective agents for circulating the dehumanizing and euphemistic semantics blanketing the mass killing of human lives before birth. Many reporters have shown no reluctance about employing horrifying but truthful words and pictures in covering the massacre of My Lai villagers, the annual slaughter of baby seals, or even the threatened extinction of snail darters. The vast majority of the media, in contrast, *avoids like a plague* either words or pictures depicting the harsh realities of today's medical war on the unwanted unborn. These gatekeepers of public information specialize in transmitting the benevolent portrayals of abortion as merely the "evacuation" or "removal" of "contents" or "products" in the antiseptic "procedure rooms" of "reproductive health clinics" or "ladies centers."

Manipulation of the Media

What was the status of the German media when the Nazis came to power?

When the Nazis took over control of the government in 1933, Germany, a country of some 66 million people, was the world's leading producer and consumer of the printed word. The range and diversity of publications surpassed any other industrial country. This prodigious output included 7,000 periodicals in all fields of knowledge and interest, 30,000 books published annually (40,000 books are published each year in America today, a country of some 226 million people), and 4,703 daily and weekly newspapers. Germany's metropolitan areas had many dailies: Hamburg 10, Cologne 8, Stuttgart 8, Leipzig 5, Frankfurt 6, and Berlin 20 (most of the largest cities in contemporary America have no more than one or two daily newspapers). In addition, the local small-town and political party presses flourished. Eighty-one percent of the newspapers were family owned.[1]

The Nazi regime succeeded in reducing this diverse and highly autonomous system of mass communications to the level of parrots and puppets of Nazi propaganda. Nazi culture, with its emphasis on the Aryan ideal of superiority and derogation of those who failed to measure up, dominated every facet of German life, including art, literature, drama, architecture, science, family living, and the military.[2] The media served as an indispensable instrument for spreading Nazi ideology throughout Germany.

Do the media of contemporary American society also serve as mouthpieces for anti-life propaganda?

Very much so. A rare inside view of how readily the media succumbed to the lies and deceit manufactured by the pro-abortionists is provided by Dr. Bernard N. Nathanson, former director of the largest abortion clinic in the Western world and a founder of the National Abortion Rights Action League. In a major address delivered at the National Right to Life Convention in 1980, Dr. Nathanson disclosed the strategy employed in the late 1960s and early 1970s to seduce the media into acceptance of a pro-abortion mentality. "We fed a line of deceit, of dishonesty, of fabrication of statistics and figures. We coddled, and caressed, and stroked the press," he declared. "We, in one short year, succeeded in striking down the abortion laws of New York State."[3]

In another speech, presented almost a year later, Nathanson again elaborated on the process involved in exploiting the media for malevolent purposes: "We, of course, stroked the media shamelessly. We played on them. We took them out to lunch. We wined them and dined them and gave them all sorts of exclusives . . . We were embarked on what looked like a historic crusade, a sweeping social revolution, and they loved it.''[4]

Never has the media's complicity in spreading blatant falsehoods been so fully uncovered! The ease with which the mainline mass communications have been duped into incorporating and circulating prevaricated propaganda churned out by physician executioners and their most avid accomplices casts a dark cloud of disbelief over the image of independent, factual reporting so carefully nurtured by the gatekeepers of public information.

The media are hard put to discredit someone like Dr. Nathanson in the usual fashion: as a narrow-minded bigot devoid of compassion and experience in the real world. His alarming revelations are not the ravings of a disgruntled religious fanatic with a sectarian axe to grind (a persistently imposed media stereotype), but the forthright conclusions of an articulate, liberal, and professed atheist. They are not the disclosures of an outsider, but of someone who has stood at the very core of mass destruction, saw it for what it was, and has acknowledged and changed his previously distorted perceptions.

When Dr. Nathanson was a staunch abortionist, he occupied an honored position as the darling of the media. The press and other media outlets just about doted on every word and idea which he and his cohorts concocted. Now that Nathanson has decided to challenge the monstrosity he helped create and the media's role in sustaining it, those who control what the public is allowed to read or view have attempted to ignore him. The hope is that the lack of media coverage will prevent his disclosures from reaching beyond the right-to-life movement.

What percentage of the American media has been influenced along the lines indicated in Dr. Nathanson's revelations?

A recent study of 240 journalists and broadcasters working for the most influential media outlets in America (the *New York Times,* the *Washington Post,* the *Wall Street Journal, Time* magazine, *Newsweek, U.S. News and World Report,* the news departments at CBS, NBC, ABC, PBS, and major public broadcasting stations) shows a pronounced capitulation to the beneficient images of abortion constructed by the killers of the unborn and their most vociferous apologists. Ninety percent of what is so aptly characterized as ''the media elite'' has assimilated the ''right to decide'' pro-abortion rhetoric as a prominent part of their social gospel.[5]

To what extent are the pro-abortion attitudes of the media elite reflected in their coverage of abortion?

An overwhelming amount of evidence points to a heavy pro-abortion slant in the media elite's reporting of abortion. In fact, the media of contemporary America is as much a captive of the pro-abortion party line regarding the nature and fate of unborn children as the German media was a prisoner of Nazi rhetoric on the identity and destiny of European Jews!

What evidence exists to substantiate the comparability of the German and American media as agents of past and current holocausts?

Some of the major comparisons relate to such factors as *subhuman semantics,* the *cosmetics of killing, neutralized language,* the *visual evidence of destruction, media schizophrenia, atrocity propaganda,* and *acceptance of distorted linguistics at face value.*

Subhuman Semantics

Give some examples of how the German and American media have derogated the victims.

By the time of the Third Reich the practice of questioning the humanity of the Jews had become a national obsession. A major reason for the widespread acceptance of Jews as questions instead of human beings can be attributed to the persistence with which the German media, especially the press, helped spread such propaganda. Scores of books, newspapers articles, pamphlets, and speeches were intended to distort the nature and origins of the Jewish people. As early as 1880, the subhumanity of the Jew comprised a major theme of a book entitled *The Jewish Question.*[6] After the Jews had been deported from the Reich, the press was instructed to deal with "the Jewish question" relentlessly and without letup.[7] During a visit to Slovakia, German Foreign Office Press Chief Paul Karl Schmidt announced to members of the press: "The Jewish question is no question of humanity."[8]

The incessant questions raised about the human status of Jews as illustrated in the slogan "the Jewish question" were summed up by sociologist Irving Louis Horowitz: "The Jew as a 'national question,' the Jew as a 'cultural question,' the Jew as an 'economic question'—always a question, never a person."[9]

Today the humanity of the unborn is called into question as tenaciously as that of the Jew before and during the Nazi era. And the mainstream media has played a major role in bringing this about. Mass communications in American society has devoted inordinate attention to doctors and scientists who attempt to sow seeds of doubt about the unborn child's humanness by contending that they do not know when human life begins. *Time* magazine chose to characterize life before birth as "the unresolvable question."[10]

On April 24 and 25, 1981, eight medical scientists testified before a Senate subcommittee convened to examine the nature of intra-uterine existence and its beginnings. Seven of them provided compelling scientific-based evidence that the entity within the womb is an actual human being from conception onward. Only one individual, Yale University geneticist Dr. Leon E. Rosenberg, portrayed the beginning of life before birth and therefore the humanness of the unborn as simply a "question" and not a "scientific matter."

An article which appeared in the *New York Times* of April 25, 1981, included not only extensive coverage of Dr. Rosenberg's remarks, but also his picture. None of the testimony of those who presented the scientific case for the humanity of the unborn was quoted. Dr. Rosenberg was described in glowing terms: "one of the nation's leading geneticists" and "chairman of the department of human genetics at the Yale University School of Medicine and former president of the American Society of Human Genetics."[11]

In contrast, the article contains little or no information whatsoever about the outstanding credentials and achievements of the seven scientists who contradicted Dr. Rosenberg's excursions into mythology, especially Dr. Jerome Lejeune, Professor of Fundamental Genetics at the University Rene Descartes in Paris. Not only is Dr. Lejeune regarded by many as the world's leading geneticist, his achievements are considered so monumental that he had even been nominated for a Nobel Prize. Obviously, this is the kind of information a reporter finds it convenient to omit, particularly when it is so potentially disruptive to the overriding image being projected of the unborn as a question rather than a human being.

In 1942 two newspapers, *Lemberger Zeitung* and *Krakower Zeitung,* launched a rhetorical war against Gypsies, one of the prime groups targeted for annihilation. The series of anti-Gypsy articles which appeared in these publications were based on a view of the victims as "an entire race of parasites."[12]

On January 25, 1981, a medical doctor used an American television program as a forum to justify the contemporary medical war on the unborn with identical terminology. "The fetus," he declared, "isn't a human body but is more or acts more like a parasite."[13]

Cosmetizing Destruction

How, specifically, have the German and American media camouflaged the killing?

While millions of men, women, and children were being slaughtered in the death camps, German newspapers fed to the public euphemistic portrayals of what were commonly referred to as "resettlement camps." A German newspaper editor, Fritz Fiala, wrote a highly positive article on life at Auschwitz, which appeared in newspapers throughout Europe. In it, the Jews were said to have their own rabbis, doctors, and officials. There was mention made of warm water, a children's kitchen, and an abundant supply of food. Also featured were pictures showing a Jewish coffee house, a group of smiling nurses, and well-nourished young men. The overall image of loving concern intended was expressed in a quotation allegedly coming from one of the inmates interviewed: "I wish the whole world knew with how much humanity Germany has treated us here."[14]

The media of contemporary American society overwhelmingly describe today's killing centers for the unwanted unborn in the same highly positive manner that the German press characterized the killing centers for the unwanted expendables of the Third Reich! An all too typical example of the indispensable role played by the press in cosmetizing mass destruction is the coverage given to an abortion chamber by the *St. Louis Post-Dispatch.* Through the use of both words and pictures, the reader is treated to scenes of the clinic's roomy and attractive interiors. One picture shows women decorating a room, while another focuses on smiling staff members seated in a beautifully furnished reception room. Also highlighted is a picture of an immaculate procedure room equipped with a suction machine. The dominant impression projected is a wholly idyllic one of empathetic people offering tender loving care in a pleasant and benevolent environment.[15]

As the killing escalated in the Eastern territories so did the positive portrayals concocted by the German media. A host of articles published in German language periodicals "painted life on the 'Jewish reservations' to the east in the rosiest colors."[16]

Many members of the American media have constructed comparably positive versions to offset the enormity of destruction perpetrated in abortion chambers. A writer in the *Saturday Review,* exuding an air of unblemished benevolence, characterized abortion clinics as "clean, tastefully decorated, and staffed by kind people."[17]

The Neutralization of Extermination

Give some examples of how the German media employed neutral language to camouflage the holocaust.

The language manufactured to conceal the extermination of Jews and others was saturated with neutral, passionless terms. "The reporters," concluded holocaust scholar Raul Hilberg, "were trying to avoid the use of direct expressions such as 'to kill' or 'murder.'''[18] The replacement of such emotionally-charged words as "kill" and "destroy" with such emotionally-neutral concepts as "selection" and "removal" was a major step toward neutralizing the horrors of mass killing. With unpleasant words and their associated emotions out of the way, the perpetrators found it far easier to kill because what they did was linguistically and therefore psychologically defined as a strictly technical procedure devoid of any emotional significance.

The neutral semantics which dominated the Third Reich constituted a blatant sham, not only because of the horrendous atrocities they were intended to conceal, but also because they were so heavily weighted in favor of the oppressors. As Hilberg so aptly put it: "Neutrality is a zero quantity which helps the stronger party in an unequal struggle."[19]

Are there any counterparts in today's media to the neutral linguistics created by the Nazi propagandists?

Contemporary public opinion makers emphasize a language of neutrality in covering the subject of abortion. The use of the terms "anti-abortion" and "abortion-rights" is, explained *New York Times* news editor Alan M. Siegal, "as close as we've been able to come to neutral language." At the *Washington Post,* writers and editors have been instructed "to be careful and to stay as neutral as possible" in selecting terminology on abortion. NBC News' idea of neutrality is either "pro-abortion or anti-abortion." Editor Gilbert Millstein elaborated further that NBC News considers the phrase "pro-life" too "loaded" for inclusion in news stories, but added: "if someone wanted to use 'pro-choice,' I'd say that was fine."[20]

This so-called neutral language represents a mere pretense of objectivity in reporting. All along the semantics of neutrality has comprised an essential ingredient of the propaganda manufactured by those who are doing the killing and their most ardent defenders. The medical executioners of the unborn have continually stressed the importance of imparting information about the "procedure" of abortion in a "neutral way."[21] By adopting this bland, euphemistic style of reporting, the members of the media have played an immense role in obscuring the harsh realities buried underneath the deceptive linguistics, therefore making mass destruction credible to a vast audience!

Abortion and the Media

Did the German media play an important part in supporting and promoting abortion?

Yes, particularly abortions among women residing in the Eastern territories under Nazi rule. In a memorandum of April 23, 1943 entitled "Plan East," Professor Alfred Wetzel unveiled a media-based campaign stressing a highly negative view of childbearing and childrearing, and a highly positive image of abortion:

> Every propaganda means, especially the press, radio, and movies, as well as pamphlets, booklets, and lectures, must be used to instill in the Russian population the idea that it is harmful to have several children. We must emphasize the expenses that children cause, the good things people could have had with the money spent on them. We could also hint at the dangerous effect of child-bearing on a woman's health . . . . It will even be necessary to open special institutions for abortion, and to train midwives and nurses for this purpose. The population will practise abortion all the more willingly if these institutions are competently operated. The doctors must be able to help out without there being any question of this being a breach of their professional ethics.[22]

How is the "Plan East" strategy related to the American media's role in pushing for and perpetuating abortion?

Much of its contents sound exactly like today's media parroting the propaganda disseminated by Planned Parenthood, Zero Population Growth, the National Abortion Rights Action League, and numerous medical organizations. The "Plan East" campaign, with its emphasis on a cost-callous approach toward eliminating the unwanted before birth, has been fully operational in the United States for at least a decade or more.

One of the major themes of a feature article on "Those Missing Babies" in the September 16, 1974 issue of *Time* was the great expenses involved in raising children and the many recreational activities a couple can enjoy by deciding against having children. "The cost of parenthood in the U.S. today is colossal," *Time* reminded its readers. "Young working couples can now enjoy luxuries like skiing and vacation houses . . . Many are reluctant to sacrifice these for what they consider to be the dubious rewards of having children."[23] The resemblance this quotation bears to one of the major tenets of "Plan East" is striking.

Although "Plan East" recommended the subtle tactic of hinting at the dangerous effect of childbearing on a woman's health, the media of contemporary America employ direct and categorical statements blaring out a persistent message: childbirth is much more dangerous than abortion.[24] In 1975 the American Home Economics Association in conjunction with the National Foundation-March of

Dimes, the American Medical Association, and the U.S. Federal Government sponsored a week-long institute for health experts and home economists. According to a reporter from the *St. Louis Post-Dispatch,* the overriding concern of this conference was a warning to young women that "having a baby can be hazardous to your health. It can kill you."[25]

The creation of special institutions for abortion incorporated in "Plan East" has been extensively established in contemporary society. The bulk of intrauterine killing occurs not in hospitals but in today's special institutions for abortion: abortion clinics. The Planned Parenthood journal *Family Planning Perspectives* announced that "in 1978, 75 percent of abortions took place in non-hospital facilities."[26]

The slogan "safe and legal abortions" performed in antiseptic settings, the modern version of Plan East's competently-operated abortion institutions, has been incessantly highlighted by the media and has played a significant role in inducing the public to embrace a veritable abortion culture. A typical rendition of abortion clinic operations can be found in many periodicals, including the following description provided by *Nursing Outlook* of July 1973: "On a busy day, I'm always amazed at how smoothly and efficiently the service is running."[27]

The current destruction directed against the unborn, as intended in "Plan East," has gained the ultimate level of respectability as a valid component of professional medical ethics. In 1967 the House of Delegates of the American Medical Association enacted a series of resolutions in support of legalized abortion for a wide range of indications. The *Journal of the American Medical Association* reported that medical involvement in abortion is "considered consistent with the principles of ethics of the American Medical Association."[28]

It is highly likely that a vast majority of today's media establishment never heard of either Professor Wetzel or the "Plan East" media program for promoting abortions among women in countries occupied by the Nazis during the early to mid 1940s. Nevertheless, the contemporary media elite's treatment of abortion is a carbon copy of the Nazi-induced pro-abortion media propaganda tactics set forth in "Plan East" by Professor Wetzel.

These astonishing resemblances illustrate an important principle: the errors of the past will continue to be repeated in the present as long as the facts associated with historical atrocities remain unknown or are intentionally suppressed.

Chart 15 on page 154 contains a summary of the main provisions of "Plan East" and their modern applications.

Chart 15
The Media Promoters of Abortion

"Plan East," April 23, 1943 "Every propaganda means, especially the press, radio, and movies, as well as pamphlets, booklets, and lectures, must be used to instill in the Russian population" (and other countries under Nazi rule) the following ideas:	**Modern Applications of "Plan East"** The newspapers, television networks, magazines, movies, books, and journals of contemporary American society serve as tools for propagating the following ideas among the public:
"We must emphasize the expenses that children cause, the good things people could have had with the money spent on them."	"The cost of parenthood in the U.S. today is colossal . . . couples can now enjoy luxuries like skiing and vacation houses . . . Many are reluctant to sacrifice these for what they consider to be the dubious rewards of having children." (*Time,* September 16, 1974)
"We could also hint at the dangerous effect of child-bearing on a woman's health."	"Having a baby can be hazardous . . . It can kill you." (*St. Louis Post-Dispatch,* June 27, 1975)
"It will even be necessary to open special institutions for abortion."	"In 1978, 75 percent of abortions took place in nonhospital facilities." (*Family Planning Perspectives,* January/February 1981)
"The population will practise abortion all the more willingly if these institutions are competently operated."	"On a busy day, I'm always amazed at how smoothly and efficiently the service is running." (Description of the operation of an abortion clinic, *Nursing Outlook,* July 1973)
"The doctors must be able to help out without there being any question of this being a breach of their professional ethics."	Medical involvement in abortion is "considered consistent with the principles of ethics of the American Medical Association." (*Journal of the American Medical Association,* August 14, 1967)

Media Schizophrenia: A Double Standard of Reporting Morality

Give some examples of typical media coverage of the Nazi war against the Jews, capital punishment, the killing of Vietnamese villagers, the

destruction of dolphins, the slaughter of baby seals, the threatened extinction of snail darters, the extermination of birds, and the medical war on the unborn.

The Nazi War Against the Jews

On August 1, 1942 the German journal *Ostland* reported nothing about the massive killing of Polish Jews but simply referred to their "removal." In the November 15, 1942 issue of *Ostland* an announcement was made about the "conclusion of the resettlement of the Jews."[29]

Capital Punishment

A guest editorial which appeared in the *St. Louis Post-Dispatch* on May 2, 1978 provided graphic details regarding the methods involved in executing prisoners convicted of capital crimes. Some of the phrases highlighted were "incredible pain," "strangulation," "breaking of the neck," "death by asphyxiation," "barbaric," and "sordid destruction."[30]

The Killing of Vietnamese Villagers

On March 16, 1968 a company of American soldiers led by Lieutenant William L. Calley shot to death hundreds of unarmed civilians, including many women and children, in the Vietnamese hamlet of My Lai located in the village of Song My. *Newsweek* employed the following terms to describe what happened: "Broken and covered with blood," "wanton slaughter," "the massacre," "cold-blooded slaying," "acts of brutality," and "the tip of a blood-soaked iceberg."[31]

It takes little imagination to accurately predict what would happen if today's reporters exposed the atrocities concealed beneath the benign images fabricated by the medical executioners of the war on the unborn as conscientiously as they uncovered the barbarities hidden underneath the benevolent impressions devised by the military executioners of the Vietnam War.

The Slaughter of Baby Seals

A detailed account of the annual killing of baby harp seals appeared on the front page of the *Washington Post* on March 22, 1976. Reporter William Claiborne used such words as "trails of blood," "the carnage," "clubbing the pups to death," "a slaughterhouse," and "barbaric" to characterize what occurred. Also highlighted was a picture of a baby seal being struck in the head and a picture of seal pelts ready for pickup, with their skinned carcasses in the foreground.[32]

The Destruction of Dolphins

An extensive article on "the slaughter" of dolphins in the *Chicago Tribune* of March 16, 1980 furnished stark accounts of "the dolphin war" in which Japanese fishermen "stabbed and slashed the dolphins to death" and fed them into a "shredding machine" with "whirling steel teeth" which "spat out chunks of red meat." The remains were then removed from the "pools of blood" and readied for "conversion into fertilizer." Accompanying these explicit descriptions are a series of equally graphic pictures. One of them shows fishermen wielding long-bladed knives against dolphins trapped in a net. Another portrays a bunch of slain dolphins hanging from a pole, ready for reduction to fertilizer.[33]

Would the *Chicago Tribune,* or any other mainline newspaper for that matter, dare do a feature story on what medical abortionists really do to the unborn? Would the *Tribune* cover the massacre of the unborn as thoroughly and graphically as it covered the slaughter of dolphins? Would any media establishment newspaper give an honest account of how the vacuum machine tears apart living human bodies inside the womb? Would those members of the press who pride themselves on publishing "all the news that's fit to print" reveal how the sharp-edged curette slashes and slices up human beings in utero? Would the watchdogs of mass communications furnish factual accounts of the prolonged agony experienced by unborn children in their desperate struggles against the invasion of lethal instruments, poisonous solutions, or corrosive substances? Would the guardians of public information show pictures of aborted bodies crammed into trash bags?

The answers to the above questions, tragically, are all emphatic no's. The media are not about to expand their watchdog role from seals and dolphins to unborn children. They are so heavily implicated in the conspiracy of silence, denial, and distortion which shrouds today's medical war on the unborn that to probe further would be to indict themselves as well as those who are doing the killing!

The Threatened Extinction of Snail Darters

During its 1977-78 term the U.S. Supreme Court halted the completion of a multi-million dollar dam in order to grant legal protection to snail darters, tiny fish which had been officially declared an endangered species. A guest editorial published in the *St. Louis Post-Dispatch* of August 14, 1978 hailed the decision and described the plight of snail darters and other threatened species in ominous terms: "Extermination of fellow species," "a biological massacre," "species destruction," and "massive extinction."[34]

The Extermination of Birds and Unborn Children

The ironclad tenacity of the press's schizophrenic attitude toward destruction was flagrantly displayed in two editorials which appeared next to one another in the *New York Times* of February 19, 1975.

The first commentary, entitled "Abortion Error," expresses considerable dismay over the conviction of Dr. Kenneth C. Edelin for manslaughter in the case of a late-term abortion. The decision of the jury is characterized as "a blow not only to physicians who perform legal abortions but also to the women who need these operations or may need them in the future." The Times editorial cites "the historic Supreme Court verdict legalizing abortion" as a basis for predicting the reversal of Dr. Edelin's conviction, but still bemoans the fact that "the damage done to the cause of rational abortion may be much harder to undo than the conviction itself."[35]

Immediately following upon the heels of the preceding editorial is one with an entirely different slant entitled "Bird Massacre." The United States Circuit Court of Appeals for the District of Columbia is taken to task for having "upheld the legality of killing millions of starlings, grackles and redwing blackbirds that roost near military installations in Kentucky and Tennessee." Other culprits identified are the city of Paducah, Kentucky and the Army for initiating a policy of spraying the birds "with a detergent that removes protective oil from their feathers, causing them to die." The writer does not hesitate to emphasize that "the poignant spectacle of millions of dead and dying birds ought to make Army and municipal officials reconsider this hideous project, particularly as they cannot achieve their objective by this mass slaughter." Plans generated for dealing with the birds are likened to "the kind of repeated bird massacres that exterminated the once-common passenger pigeon."[36]

The uses of language in these editorials are light years apart. It takes a quantum leap backwards in logic to accomodate the sharply divergent semantic versions conveyed. The first one conceals destruction under a thick blanket of euphemistic terminology, while the second pushes destruction to the forefront with a barrage of blunt words and phrases. The U.S. Supreme Court decision upholding the legality of killing millions of human beings before birth is referred to as "the historic Supreme Court verdict." The U.S. Circuit Court of Appeals, in contrast, is severely rebuked for upholding "the legality of killing millions of starlings, grackles and redwing blackbirds." To the Times semanticists, the killing of unborn humans is simply a matter of "legal abortion," "these operations," "an action" or "rational abortion." The killing of birds, on the other hand, is saturated with such concepts as "bird massacres," "killing," "the slaughter," "dead and dying birds," "hideous project," "mass slaughter," and "exterminated."

The editorial writers of the *New York Times* are not the only ones who specialize in concealing the extermination of unborn children under a blanket of deceptive linguistics. The *Reader's Digest* of November 1973 chose the phrase "an essential and humane medical service" to introduce Dr. Alan F. Guttmacher's article in support of legalized abortion.[37] An editorial in the *Washington Post* of July 2, 1980 covered up the harsh realities of annihilation in the womb with such standard slogans as "freedom of choice," "exercising her choice" and "freedom to decide."[38] The November 1981 issue of *Life* continued the tradition of camouflaging unborn baby killing by resorting to such semantic standbys as "terminate a pregnancy," "vacuum aspiration procedure" and "right to choose."[39]

The Open Secret

Despite the fact that the Nazi media suppressed the truth about the holocaust, didn't this terrible secret soon become common knowledge?

Historian Walter Laqueur, in *The Terrible Secret: Suppression of the Truth About Hitler's 'Final Solution',* indicates that information about what really happened to the Jews in the concentration camps and territories of the East was known early.[40] From the very onset of the massacre, the underground press of Poland sent out reports, communiques, and dispatches full of details about death camp operations to neutral and allied countries. The media of the free world, it was hoped, would transmit knowledge of the horrendous atrocities being perpetrated to all corners of the globe.

Many members of the Allied press, including Britain and the United States, refused to believe the bad news. Even when media coverage was given to the extermination of Jews, it was at best disseminated with an air of skepticism or only half-heartedly.

On June 25 and June 30, 1942, for example, the London *Daily Telegraph* finally gave extensive coverage to the grim reality of "More than 1,000,000 Jews Killed in Europe." The *New York Times* of June 30, 1942 published a very brief account of this story on page 14.[41] The placement of this story indicated that the *Times* editors still possessed considerable reservations about its authenticity. "If it was true that a million people had been killed this clearly should have been front page news; it did not, after all, happen every day," concluded Laqueur. "Since they were not certain they

Chart 16
Media Schizophrenia and the Selective Reporting of Destruction

DESTRUCTIVE ACTIVITIES	TYPICAL MEDIA COVERAGE
The Nazi War Against the Jews	"Removal" of the Polish Jews. (*Ostland,* August 1, 1942) "Conclusion of the resettlement of the Jews." (*Ostland,* November 15, 1942)
Capital Punishment	"Incredible pain . . . strangulation . . . breaking of the neck . . . death by asphyxiation . . . barbaric . . . sordid destruction." (Guest editorial, *St. Louis Post-Dispatch,* May 2, 1978)
The Killing of Vietnamese Villagers	"Broken and covered with blood . . . wanton slaughter . . . the massacre . . . cold-blooded slaying . . . acts of brutality . . . the tip of a blood-soaked iceberg." (*Newsweek,* December 8, 1969)
The Destruction of Dolphins	"The dolphin war . . . stabbed and slashed the thrashing dolphins to death . . . the slaughter . . . pools of blood." (*Chicago Tribune,* March 16, 1980)
The Slaughter of Baby Seals	"Trails of blood . . . the carnage . . . clubbing the pups to death . . . a slaughterhouse . . . barbaric."(*Washington Post,* March 22, 1976)
The Extermination of Birds	"The slaughter . . . millions of dead and dying birds . . . hideous project . . . bird massacres." (*New York Times,* February 19, 1975)
The Extinction of Snail Darters	"Extermination of fellow species . . . a biological massacre . . . species destruction . . . massive extinctions." (Guest editorial, *St. Louis Post-Dispatch,* August 14, 1978)
The Medical War on the Unborn	"An essential and humane medical service." (Dr. Alan Guttmacher's view of legalized abortion, *Reader's Digest,* November 1973) "These operations . . . rational abortion . . . an act." (*New York Times,* February 19, 1975) "Freedom of choice . . . exercising her choice . . . freedom to decide." (*Washington Post,* July 2, 1980) "Terminate a pregnancy . . . vacuum aspiration procedure . . . right to choose." (*Life,* November 1981)

opted for a compromise: to publish it, but not in a conspicuous place."[42]

Do any segments of the media today transmit information on what is actually happening to unborn children in abortion chambers?

In those rare instances when members of the media establishment bother to even touch upon the truth of unborn baby killing, they do so only half-heartedly at best. For instance, on February 6, 1982 the *Torrance Daily Breeze,* a small California newspaper, gave major coverage to the discovery of more than 16,000 aborted bodies by workmen in a huge storage container in Wilmington, California. The *New York Times,* like its response to the mass killing of Jews at the end of June 1942, did not consider this revelation important enough to merit much attention. Thus a story containing all the earmarks of front page treatment—after all, it is not every day that the grisly proof of mass extermination of human lives in the womb is so compellingly demonstrated—was relegated instead to the obscurity of a very brief item appearing on page 14.[43] The *New York Times* and other like-minded agents of propaganda in the service of destruction are afflicted with a pronounced aversion to highlighting a reality they have expended so much energy trying to deny or conceal.

The most accurate and candid details concerning the harsh realities of unborn baby killing are disseminated by the newsletters, pamphlets, and newspapers created primarily by groups and organizations associated with the right-to-life movement. They continually try to inform the public about the slaughter of millions taking place inside hospitals and abortion clinics, as well as attempt to get the mainstream media to report the truth regarding what is occurring. The pro-life channels of information transmission occupy a position very similar to the underground press of Poland which made such valiant efforts to get the media of the free world to cooperate in telling the truth about the massacre of Jews in the Eastern territories and death camps.

The contemporary mainline media deny the harsh realities of mass destruction in the womb even more vociferously than the Western media during World War II disbelieved the alarming facts of massive annihilation in the gas chambers. In an exhibition of tragic irony surpassing the media coverup during the Nazi era, the current gatekeepers of public opinion are far more prone to communicate the innocuous versions designed to conceal the killing than the objective accounts intended to bring knowledge of horrendous atrocities to the forefront of public awareness. Incredibly, the distorted linguistics of those who are destroying the unborn are granted the utmost respectability, while the stark, but factual reports of unborn baby killing brought to light by those who oppose the destruction are being dismissed as mere propaganda.

Why, then, have the past and present media been so reluctant to tell the truth about prior and current holocausts?

Up to the time of the "final solution" directed against the Jews, the systematic destruction of millions was considered unthinkable, something preposterous on both the psychological and technical levels. The assembly-line killing of human beings in gas chambers seemed too inherently monstrous, a phenomenon completely beyond the boundaries of human capabilities. The Allied media, as a consequence, found it difficult, if not impossible, to attribute any validity to the stories of mass exterminations.

The media of contemporary America seem to experience a similar problem accepting the authenticity of reports on mass annihilation in the womb. The utter brutality of dismembering huge numbers of human bodies before birth on an assembly-line basis is too horrible a nightmare for human confrontation. The image of doctors as healers selflessly dedicated to caring for and curing the sickest and most vulnerable members of society is still powerful enough, apparently, to offset the radical departures from humane medicine which consitute the very essence of the abortion clinic.

Laqueur's study in the steady flow of incontrovertible evidence pertaining to the destruction of European Jews and its nonacceptance by the media and officials of Allied and neutral countries has direct bearing on a more basic phenomenon: "the denial of reality, the psychological rejection of information . . . the inclination among otherwise normal, sometimes even highly intelligent, human beings to deny reality, however glaring."[44] An identical spectacle dominates the media and therefore populace of today's American society: the widespread tendency among many normal, intelligent people to deny the harsh but incontrovertible reality of planned, systematic extermination directed against human beings in utero by respectable, credentialed medical executioners.

Atrocity Propaganda

How else, in addition to denial, have members of the media, today and in the past, responded to the realities of mass killing?

In ancient times, a common response to the messenger of bad news was destruction of the messenger. Today, the reaction to the bad news of unborn baby killing is either mass denial or the discrediting of those who dare transmit such distasteful revelations. Radical feminist editor Gloria Steinem, a well-entrenched member of the media establishment, specializes in diverting attention away from the striking connections between the killing of Jews and the destruction of the unborn by trying to undermine the credibility of individuals or groups that have the audacity to highlight such associations. Steinem characterizes statements linking contemporary abortion with the Nazi holocaust as "bizarre" and part of "an increasingly vicious campaign" created by a "media world of right-wing newletters, pamphlets, and books distributed through churches."[45] The impression intended is all too obvious: how can anyone believe information emanating from communications networks so completely dominated by vicious, sinister political forces.

What Steinem is doing contains historical precedents. Many individuals in the Allied countries during World War II resorted to similar tactics in an effort to discredit the news about the Nazi holocaust. A British Foreign Service official's use of the phrase "wild story" was intended to generate serious doubt about the veracity of stories from Polish sources pertaining to the slaughter of Jews in the Eastern territories. An American ambassador, Leland Harrison, regarded a report concerning Hitler's plans for the annihilation of European Jewry as a "wild rumour inspired by Jewish fears."[46]

During World War I some of the Allied nations were guilty of spreading false stories concerning German atrocities, including the torture of children, the dismembering of bodies, and the employment of asphyxiating gas against hundred of thousands of victims. Many of these allegations were accepted as fact and published in leading newspapers. When reports of mass murder and the use of poison gas first began circulating in the early 1940s, the Western press was inclined to view them as simply "atrocity propaganda," closely akin to the "atrocity stories" which dominated the war of words in World War I.[47]

The American press, likewise, exhibits a tenacious habit of dismissing as sheer "atrocity propaganda" the unvarnished accounts of dismemberment in the womb and the prolonged death agonies of unborn children subjected to corrosive salt poisoning, even when generated from such an impeccable source as pro-abortion psychologist Dr. Magda Denes in her study of an abortion hospital.[48] According to the *New York Times Book Review,* Dr. Denes' book is just a "highly emotional anti-abortion tract" replete with "horror story after horror story about abortions."[49] The purpose of this characterization is to neutralize the starkness of her portrayals: she calls abortion what it is (the killing of human beings before birth), likens the abortion hospital to a death factory, and furnishes unadorned details of the killing procedures and their effects on the unborn victims. To the *New York Times* and a vast majority of public opinion molders in the media, such disclosures are not facts, but merely "horror stories" concocted by irrational zealots.

An Outrage on the Truth

Was there really a holocaust against the Jews? Dr. Butz said that the number of Jews who expired in the concentration camps was greatly exaggerated, nobody was gassed, and most of the deaths were due to such conditions as overcrowding, diseases, and malnutrition.

Dr. Arthur R. Butz, an associate professor of electrical engineering and computer sciences at Northwestern University, has written a book called *The Hoax of the Twentieth Century,* in which he claims that the murder of six million Jews never happened. The holocaust, he contends further, was a myth fabricated by the Zionists to obtain support for the state of Israel.[50] Dr. Butz's book itself is a monumental hoax. His research is exceedingly shallow, and his conclusions an outrage on the truth.

One of the major reasons Dr. Butz refers to the holocaust as a legend is that he could find no references to the words "kill" or "extermination" in the Nazi documents.[51] Here alone he commits the incredible blunder of taking the Nazi language at face value.

How are Dr. Butz's preposterous conclusions related to the contemporary media coverage of abortion?

Many members of today's media establishment are repeating this same basic error. They accept at face value the sanitized semantics churned out by the abortionists and their most ardent defenders. The media's blind acceptance of the distortions fashioned by those who are destroying human beings in the womb is as much an outrage on the truth as Dr. Butz's mindless incorporation of the fabrications contrived by the killers of the Third Reich!

On the whole, what importance can be attributed to the media in furthering past and current holocausts?

A wise man said long ago that when war comes the first casualty is the truth. Make no mistake, what occurred during the Nazi period was a full-scale war against the Jews and other discards. What exists today also constitutes a full-fledged war against unborn children and increasing hostilities against postnatal discards. The media of both eras—through the severe distortion of facts and the gross manipulation of public perceptions and thoughts—have played absolutely indispensable roles in promoting, spreading, and sustaining wars on the unwanted, both before and after birth. The capitulation of vast numbers of individuals in the field of mass communications to the semantic duplicity manufactured by the killers and their supporters stands in stark contradiction to the media's obligation to convey the facts, no matter how distasteful, and the public's right to know. It also represents an utter mockery of journalism's claim to crusading reform, independence, and objectivity in reporting!

Chart 17
Mass Destruction and Media Complicity

The Third Reich	Contemporary America
Manipulation of the Media	
When Hitler came to power the world's leading and most independent press was reduced to an agent of the Ministry of Propaganda. (Oron J. Hale, *The Captive Press in the Third Reich, 1973)*	"We fed a line of deceit, of dishonesty, of fabrication of statistics and figures. We coddled and caressed and stroked the press." (Former abortion clinic director Dr. Bernard N. Nathanson, 1980)
Question	
The German press should deal with "the Jewish question" without letup. (Instructions of Reich Press Chief, April 29, 1943)	"The unresolvable question." (Portrayal of when human life begins, *Time*, April 6, 1981)
Parasite	
"An entire race of parasites." (Portrayal of Gypsies by two newspapers, *Lemberger Zeitung* and *Krakower Zeitung,* 1942)	Not a "human body" but "more like a parasite." (Description of the unborn on a television program, January 25, 1981)
Cosmetizing the Killing Centers	
A highly positive article on Auschwitz featuring pictures showing a Jewish coffee shop, a group of smiling nurses, and well-nourished young men. (Fritz Fiala, *Pariser Zeitung,* December 23, 1942)	A highly positive article on a St. Louis abortion chamber featuring pictures showing a counseling session, smiling staff members, and a procedure room. (Paul Berg, *St. Louis Post-Dispatch,* May 1973)
Atrocity Stories	
Merely "atrocity propaganda" similar to the "atrocity stories" disseminated during World War I. (Western press reaction to reports on the mass murder of Jews, early 1940s)	"A highly emotional anti-abortion tract" saturated with "horror story after horror story about abortions." (Review of Magda Denes' study of an abortion hospital, *New York Times Book Review,* January 1977)
Half-Hearted Coverage	
The *New York Times* responded to a report on the extermination of one million Jews by publishing a very brief account on page 14. (June 30, 1942)	The *New York Times* responded to a report on a huge number of aborted bodies found in California by publishing a very brief account on page 14. (February 8, 1982)

Chapter 14

Media Responses to Pictures of the Victims

Photos of individuals killed in the Nazi holocaust and today's abortion holocaust have posed a serious threat to those in the media responsible for glossing over horrendous barbarities with semantic camouflage. Pictures of the victims contain a visual dimension capable of cutting through all the linguistic mumbo-jumbo designed to hide the killing of millions. The media elite has exercised extra vigilance to ensure that such powerful evidence of mass destruction never reaches the large bulk of media consumers.

The Suppression and Discrediting of Pictorial Violence

Were orders actually given forbidding the media from taking photographs of past and current atrocities?

The Nazis issued special communiques to prevent soldiers, the media, or anyone from taking and distributing pictures of the exterminated victims. "To every normal person," read one such order, "it is a matter of course that he does not take photographs of such disgusting excesses."[1]

In February 1982 officials from the Los Angeles Coroner's Office and the Department of Health Services told press photographers and television crews that "no photographs" could be taken of aborted bodies found in a huge cargo container in Wilmington, California. "A lot are partially dismembered," explained coroner office representative Mason Johnson. "You wouldn't want to photograph that."[2]

What has been the official justification put forth for not permitting the taking or publishing of pictures of destroyed Jews and aborted babies?

The dissemination of such photographs for public consumption, according to the Nazis and their media cohorts, was considered not only a mark of poor taste, but also highly offensive to the sensitivities of the Germany of Goethe and Kant. The directive issued for the confiscation of pictures taken at the killing sites emphasized that the distribution of photographs "will be regarded as a subversion of decency and discipline" and "beneath the dignity of the German soldier."[3]

A considerable number of media opinion molders in modern-day society possess a strikingly similar attitude toward pictures depicting the victims of today's medical holocaust against the unwanted unborn. To such enlightened observers of the human condition as newspaper columnist Nicholas von Hoffman, the photographic display of aborted babies is downright tasteless, repulsive, and an odious form of yellow journalism, beneath the dignity of upstanding reporters. In one of his syndicated columns, he bemoaned the "tasteless," "shocking and disturbing," and "sick-making business" of showing "revolting photographs" of "mutilated fetuses."[4]

One wonders if von Hoffman would find it in comparably bad taste to show those "revolting" pictures of the Nazi holocaust, the massacre of Vietnamese villagers, the genocide in Cambodia, or the annual slaughter of baby seals? Would he be willing to call for a media moratorium on all visual evidence of mass destruction and accept instead every killer's sophisticated, euphemistic, and benevolent portrayal of what he or she did? Such versions are sure to be saturated with all kinds of tasteful and inoffensive expressions!

What is revolting are not the accurate photographs of extermination, but what is done to the victims portrayed in them. What is repulsive and shocking are not the pictorial reproductions of undisguised violence, but the fact that members of the media elite such as von Hoffman remain so oblivious to the undeniable proof of the most blatant atrocities even when it stares them in the face!

Give some more examples to show how photos of exterminated victims have been discredited.

There is an insidious movement afoot today, initiated and supported by neo-Nazi groups in America and abroad, which contends that six million Jews were never killed in the death camps during the Nazi era. Through books, articles published in magazines and periodicals, reviews in scholarly journals, newspapers, and other media outlets, this outrage on the truth has gained an alarming amount of respectability. Even the most compelling proof of mass killing—pictures of dead and rotted corpses—is dismissed as simply "fake atrocity photographs."[5]

An equally insidious outrage on the truth is being perpetrated by a large segment of the American media. Today's guardians of public information either ignore or deny the existence of a full-scale and ever-escalating medical war on the unborn. Whenever anyone attempts to challenge this extensive coverup with actual pictures of the casualties—dismembered or salt-poisoned bodies—members of the media establishment respond by questioning their authenticity is much the same manner as contemporary anti-Semitic groups try to discredit the pictorial evidence of the Nazi holocaust. A reporter for *Ms* magazine, for example, referred to a picture of aborted bodies crammed into a trash bag as only "supposedly" the result of one day's work at a teaching hospital.[6]

When some photos of 43 of over 16,000 aborted bodies found in a metal shipping container in Wilmington, California were shown at a press conference in the Los Angeles Press Club on May 30, 1982, they were met with intense hostility. The most outspoken reporters tried to undermine the validity of the pictures by implying that they had been obtained illicitly. Even after being reassured that the pictures had been taken by photographers approved by the coroner's office, the reporters persisted in their efforts to brand them illegal.[7]

If members of the Nazi press had been confronted with a photographic display of concentration camp victims, it is highly likely that they too would have become preoccupied with the legality of showing *unauthorized* pictures instead of focusing on the stark, undeniable visual proof of *authorized* mass extermination.

Cinematic Treatment of Abortion: Concealing and Obscuring the Existence of Perceptible Victims

Aren't there segments of the media which do not cosmetize abortion? Films of actual abortions, for example, have even appeared on the Donahue television talk show as well as in television dramas and documentaries.

This so-called exhibition of openness is far more apparent than real. The only types of abortions shown on American television programs are those performed during the early stages of pregnancy when the technology is capable of easily destroying and erasing all traces of victims. The sophistication of the technology together with the small size of the victims guarantee that any visible evidence of destruction is entirely blotted out. No one sees the suction machine tearing apart, dismembering, and obliterating the tiny bodies of living, growing human beings. The lethal acts take place out of sight, inside the uterine walls. All that the perpetrators, nurses, attendants, and viewing audience can detect are indistinguishable, miniscule fragments zipping through a transparent tube.

Along with the obscure visual dimensions, abortion films commonly feature an impressive-sounding voice describing such niceties as dilating the cervix (mouth of the womb), turning on the suction machine, inserting a cannula (attached to the machine by long flexible tubing) into the uterus, and "evacuating" the "debris" into a collecting bottle. As the narrator calmly and precisely provides the scientific details, the viewers are treated to a flawless technical performance. The whole scenario amounts to a slick piece of impression management intended to lend credence to abortion as nothing more significant than the "removal" of mere "products" or "contents" from the womb.

The typical television presentation of abortion would be very similar to creating a film on the Nazi holocaust *minus the victims.* Such a movie would highlight doctors and various technicians busily preoccupied with assessing equipment, operating switches, checking gauges, and making sure the chamber doors are closed tight. Unavailable to the viewing audience, of course, would be scenes of what really happens inside the chamber walls: men, women, and children gasping for breath and life and being trampled to death in their desperate attempts to escape the lethal fumes.

A film on the Nazi holocaust, produced along lines similar to a typical television rendition of abortion, would probably also include the voice of a narrator reassuring the viewers that what they are observing is not the operation of a gas chamber, but simply that of a "disinfection room" or a "bathhouse." The narrator would explain that what is taking place behind the walls of these facilities involves nothing more sinister than either the process of fumigating lice-infested clothes or the taking of showers by "resettled" people.

If the contemporary television networks were really interested in getting at the truth about abortion, they might try showing films of later abortions where the victims are too large and well-developed for the technology to entirely obliterate them. The television cameras might focus on the crushed heads and dismembered body parts being yanked out with curettes and forceps in a D & E abortion, or the acid-soaked corpses being expelled in salt-poisoning abortion labor, or the intact bodies of dead babies being cut out of the womb in the hysterotomy abortion procedure. Television producers might also choose to capture on film for their audiences other aspects of the later abortion-disposal process: doctors assembling the dismembered body parts to make sure that rib cages, heads, legs, or arm fragments have not been inadvertently left inside the mother's body; the final gasps of a saline survivor left unattended in a hospital utility room; nurses dropping aborted bodies into plastic trash bags; and attendants tossing the human "garbage" into the hospital incinerator. The film might appropriately end with close-up shots showing the bodies going up in flames inside the incinerator.

By the same token, if the Nazi media had been allowed and motivated to tell the German public the truth about what happened to the inmates of concentration camps, they would have focused their cameras on such aspects of the victim-disposal process as: body-removal squads dragging compressed and entangled corpses out of the chambers with hook-tipped poles; the carting of bodies and dismembered body parts in litters from the gas chambers to large ditches; prisoners being forced to dump thousands of bodies into huge pits for mass burials; dentists prying gold teeth out of the mouths of the destroyed victims; screaming children being thrown into crematorium furnaces during a period when gas chambers were being overworked. The grand finale might consist of showing how efficiently the crematoriums reduce human flesh to ashes.

Rationale for Media Suppression of Graphic Films and Photos

Why won't today's television networks feature the various phases of later abortions?

For the same reason the media of the Third Reich did not release for public scrutiny truthful movies on the carnage against the Jews: the visual evidence of destroyed humanity is just too compelling, explicit, and prominent to be denied. Projecting films depicting the grim realities of unborn baby killing before audiences would directly contradict the steady diet of benevolent portrayals of abortion so frequently fed to media consumers. Such cinematic candor would not only pose a serious challenge to the very credibility of the medical profession but, even more to the point, expose the complicity of the media in perpetuating a monstrous fraud!

Detailed and frank reports on the horrors of the Vietnam War taught the networks an indispensable lesson about the enormous power of televised violence to arouse an apathetic public and galvanize people into demanding an end to the war and its barbarities.

The 1973 Pulitzer Prize winning news photograph showing terrified Vietnamese children fleeing an aerial napalm bomb attack epitomized the type of coverage provided. "This photo shows how terrible war is," said Associated Press photographer Nuynh Cong Ut of his award-winning picture. "Some people don't know, but I think this picture showed them." The *St. Louis Post-Dispatch* highlighted both his remarks and photograph under the heading: "Photo Shows War is Terrible."[8]

Such unadorned portrayals, in sharp contrast to the abstract, euphemistic versions disseminated by the military, resulted in a powerful and unremitting upsurge of public outrage directed against

American involvement in the hostilities.

In conjunction with this coverage, some basic questions need to be addressed. What has happened to all those gruesome types of photographs and films which, thanks to the efforts of vigilant reporters and editors, used to dominate the daily news during the height of the Vietnam War in the late 1960s and early 1970s? How come newspeople are reluctant to take, let alone display, pictures of the dismembered bodies of mass abortion? Why are they unwilling to publish photos of aborted babies whose outer skin has been burned off or stripped away by the corrosive effect of a concentrated poisonous salt solution? Could it be because they so closely resemble innocent war victims scorched by napalm assaults? Surely the dearth of pictorial evidence of medical violence against the unborn is not due to a shortage of victims! During the war in Vietnam 58,655 Americans lost their lives.[9] Today's medical war against the unwanted unborn of America consumes at least one and one-half million human lives annually, and the numbers continue to increase each year.[10]

The media establishment is not about to duplicate its extensive, non-euphemistic pictorial coverage of the Vietnam War by extending equivalent coverage to today's medical war on the unwanted unborn. It has played too large a role in creating, communicating, and sustaining the linguistic distortions which have proven so instrumental in establishing killing at the level of a holocaust as such a commonplace phenomenon in contemporary American society.

Photographic Evidence of Destruction: Beyond the Rhetoric of Benevolence

Why is it important to show actual pictures of past and current atrocities?

That old adage—*a picture is worth a thousand words*—possesses a considerable amount of wisdom. This is especially the case when it comes to the matter of grasping the terrible truth of large-scale destruction. Pictures contain an unerring capacity to break through the thickest clouds of semantic distortions and reveal the sheer unadorned horror of mass extermination. Photos have a tremendous potential for laying bare the blatant deceit, hypocrisy, and lingusitic corruption deployed to conceal the wholesale slaughter of human lives before and after birth.

The utter brutality of assembly-line killing is nowhere more starkly uncovered than in photographs taken of the victims. As one gazes in horrified shock at the pictures of past and present holocausts—entangled corpses, mangled and dismembered bodies, clenched fists, the agonized and terror-stricken facial expressions—the charade of abstract and beneficient terminology devised to mask the extermination of millions finally becomes evident to all but the most desensitized viewer.

Little wonder, then, that the killers and their most ardent promoters have been so intent on suppressing and discrediting the visual proof of mass annihilation!

Did films and pictures of the Nazi holocaust constitute an influential part of the testimony presented at the Nuremberg war crimes trials?

Even after voluminous printed testimony documenting the Nazi atrocities was presented at Nuremberg, some people still remained skeptical about their authenticity or enormity. The most telling part of the proceedings consisted of movies and photos of the killings. There before the horrified eyes of the court were actual pictures of the massive extermination and its horrendous aftermath: hills of destroyed humanity, bodies thrown into huge pits, victims stuffed in railway wagons like so much trash, expressions of excruciating pain on the faces of severely emaciated corpses, the charred remains of human beings in enormous ovens.

The impact upon the participants was profound. Any semblance of doubt about the commission of heinous atrocities was conclusively dispelled by the pictorial gallery of horrors unveiled at Nuremberg.

Show some photos of Nazi victims and today's aborted victims.

The pictures of past and current holocausts on pages 172-177 were obtained from the following sources:

Photos of the Nazi victims were taken by members of the American military forces upon liberation of the concentration camps in 1945. Many of the destroyed inmates portrayed were deliberately starved to death. U.S. Signal Corps photographers were responsible for compiling this ghastly pictorial evidence of mass annihilation.

Most of the contemporary abortion pictures were taken in March 1982 by photographers in the Los Angeles Coroner's Office of 43 of over 16,000 aborted bodies found in a huge metal shipping container. The autopsy reports revealed that some of the bodies were as old as 30 weeks. Dismemberment and salt poisoning were identified as the major methods of destruction employed. The Center for Documentation of the American Holocaust, a group committed to revealing the horrors of unborn baby killing, furnished this grisly photographic record of mass extermination American style.[11]

Figure 2, which shows aborted babies jammed into a trash bag, was originally published in *Handbook on Abortion* by Dr. and Mrs. J.C. Willke.[12]

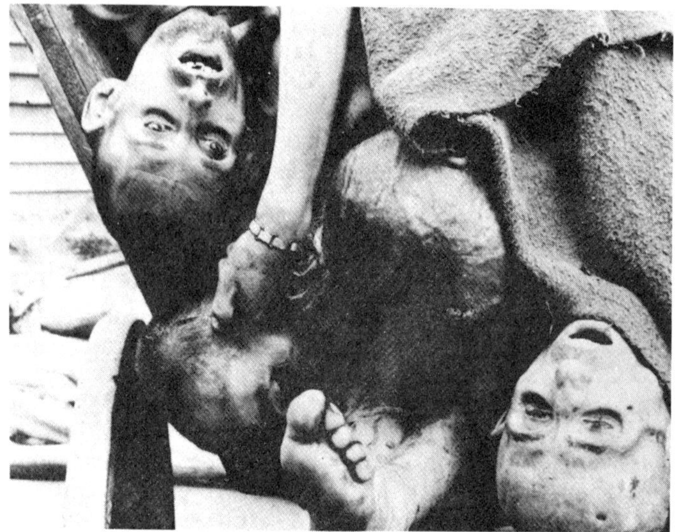

Figure 1: Inmate bodies piled into a cart, Gusen concentration camp (Austria, 1945)

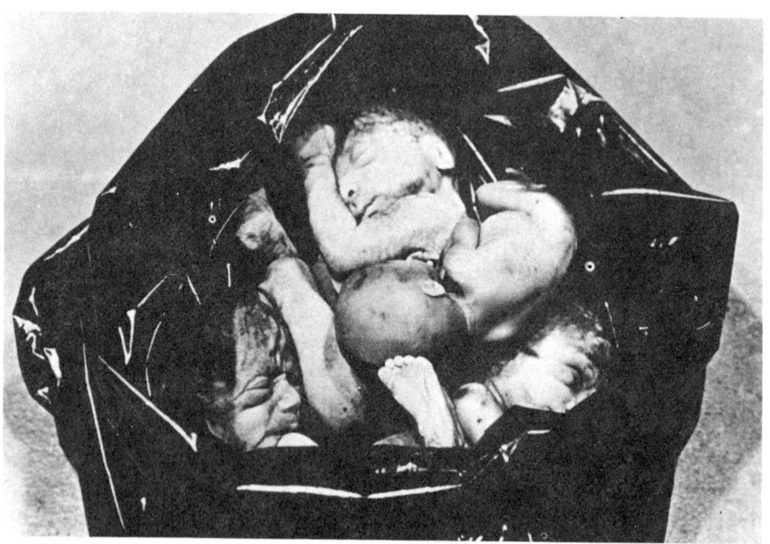

Figure 2: Trash can full of aborted bodies (Canadian teaching hospital, early 1970s)

Figure 3: Truckload of inmate bodies, Buchenwald concentration camp (Germany, 1945)

Figure 4: Aborted bodies stuffed into plastic containers (Los Angeles, 1982)

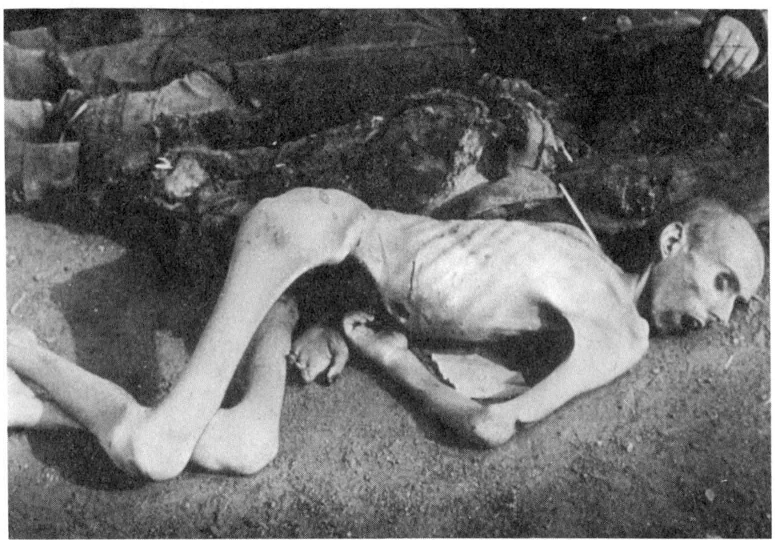

Figure 5: Body of starved slave laborer, Nordhausen concentration camp (Germany, 1945)

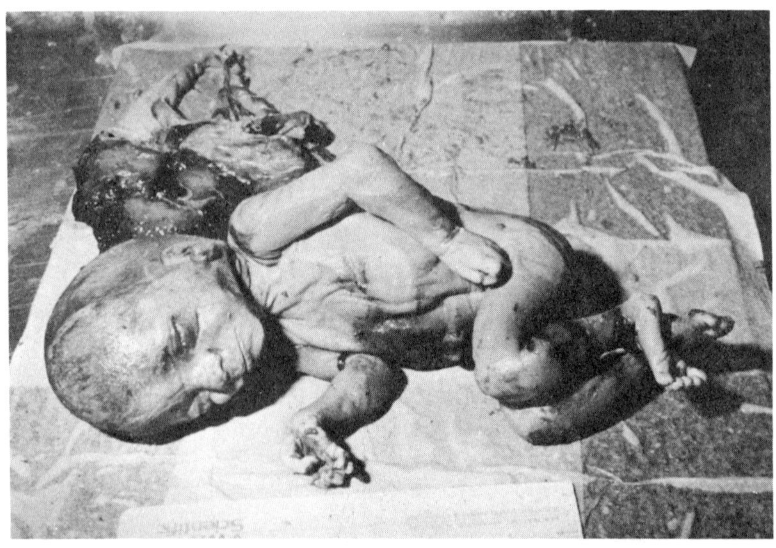

Figure 6: Body of aborted baby, age 22-23 weeks, killed by salt poisoning (Los Angeles, 1982)

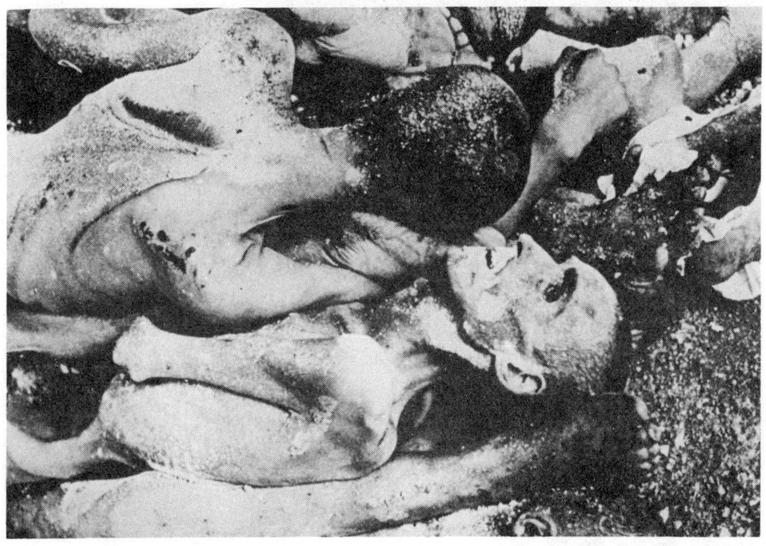

Figure 7: Bodies stacked up like cord wood, Ohrdruf concentration camp (Germany, 1945)

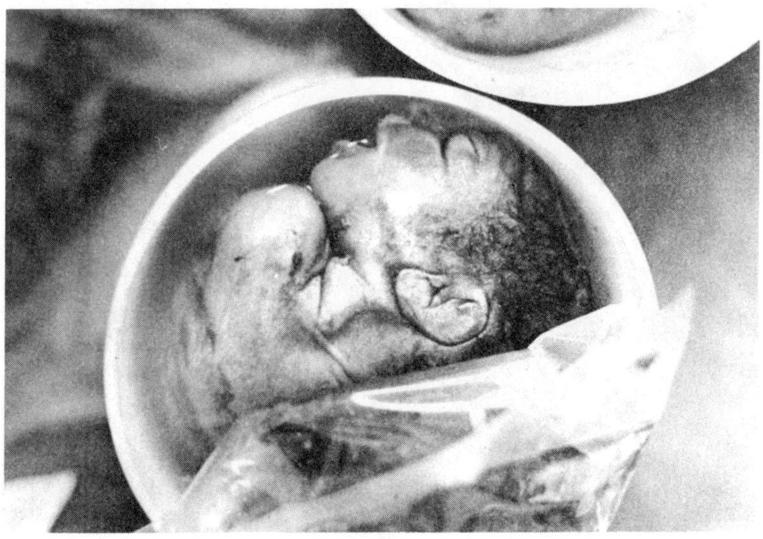

Figure 8: Body of aborted baby, age 25-28 weeks, killed by salt poisoning (Los Angeles, 1982)

Figure 9: Bodies of starved inmates, Landsberg concentration camp (Germany, 1945)

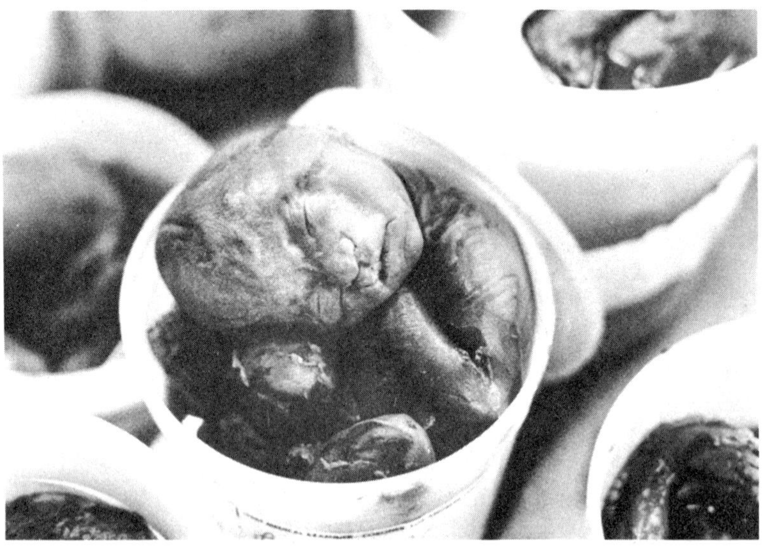

Figure 10: Aborted bodies crammed into containers (Los Angeles, 1982)

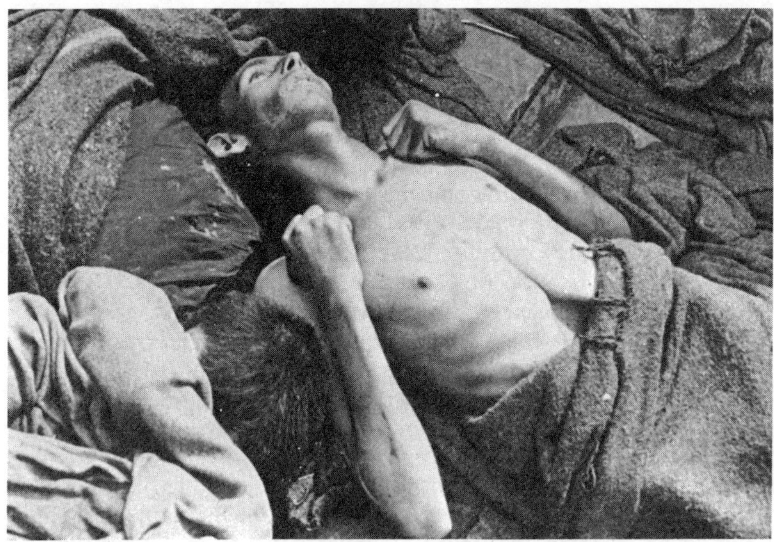

Figure 11: Starved bodies of Jews found in freight car being transported to Dachau concentration camp (Germany, 1945)

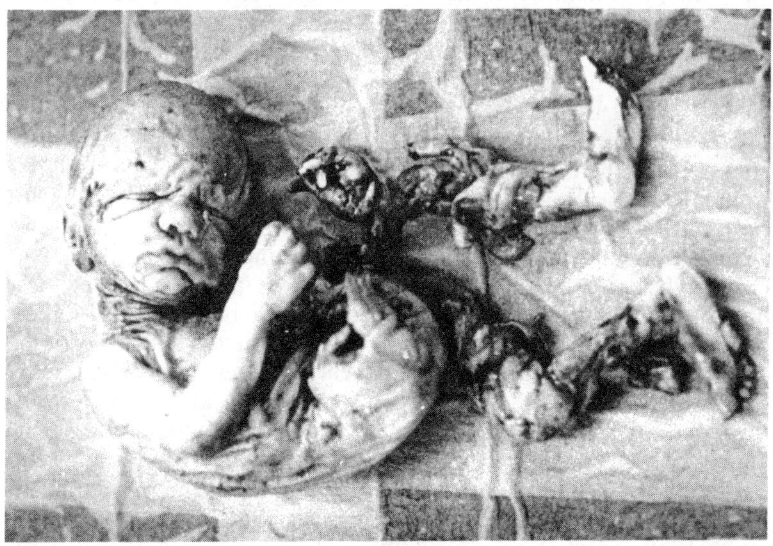

Figure 12: Body of aborted child, age 27-29 weeks, killed by dismemberment (Los Angeles, 1982)

Offensive To Our Readership: A Case of Press-Imposed Censorship

In December 1982 a pro-life medical organization, Missouri Doctors for Life, submitted a two-page ad against abortion for publication in the January 23, 1983 issue of two major daily newspapers: the *St. Louis Post-Dispatch* and the *St. Louis Globe-Democrat.* The ad, aptly entitled "A Decade of Killing," featured the names of close to 1,000 physicians committed to the ethics of Hippocrates contained in the Declaration of Geneva and a fully-documented picture of an aborted baby killed by dismemberment.

Resident censors in the *Post-Dispatch* and *Globe-Democrat* decided to reject the proposed ad. According to a memorandum of December 15, 1982 originating from a *Globe-Democrat* staff member: "Because of our long-standing policy, which does not allow for *gruesome, revolting pictures* to run in our news or advertising columns, we will not accept the photo with this ad" (italics added).[13]

The Nazis, like the thought controllers in today's mainline media, it should be repeated, employed a similar designation—*"disgusting"* —as the official rationale for their policy of confiscating and refusing to publish pictures of the death camp victims.[14]

In another statement starkly reminiscent of censorship during the darkest days of the Third Reich, the molders of public perception at the *Post* and *Globe* concluded: "We have determined that the photo submitted would be *offensive to our readership"* (italics added).[15] What is really offensive is not what such photos so graphically reveal, but what has been permitted to happen to the victims portrayed in them! Equally offensive are the heavy-handed tactics employed by newspaper editors to squelch visual documentation so clearly at odds with the relentless flow of benign images of abortion which the media elite specializes in transmitting to the public.

Today's gatekeepers of what the public is allowed to view are not so much concerned about protecting their readers' sensitivities as they are with propagating their own set of myths and distortions. Just as members of the Nazi government and press corps knew fully well how dangerous the pictures of death camp atrocities were to the cause of National Socialism, so too the contemporary self-appointed watchdogs in the press are acutely aware of how damaging the photos of abortion chamber barbarities are to the pro-abortion cause. They realize that such irrefutable evidence of mass killing not only threatens the respectability and legitimacy of the abortion establishment, but also calls into question the very credibility of a press establishment so fully implicated in perpetuating the annihilation of millions of unwanted human lives before birth!

Chapter 15

Counteracting the Repetition of Historical Atrocities

As today's abortion culture becomes more deeply rooted, and the number of unborn human lives slaughtered by credentialed medical executioners escalates, it becomes increasingly urgent that the parallels in this book be communicated to a vast audience. Every possible opportunity must be taken to show that contemporary abortion constitutes nothing less than a horrendous holocaust containing many alarming resemblances to the barbarities perpetrated against the born and unborn expendables of the Third Reich. Knowledge of these shocking parallels needs to penetrate every facet of society through newsletters, the press, magazines, television, professional journals, books, conferences, and any other vehicle responsible for the dissemination of information to the public.

At the most general level, it must be pointed out how much mass extermination is dependent upon the operation of an array of interrelated forces. Among some of the most significant are the perversion of law, the development of sophisticated destructive techniques, the distortion of language, the transformation of physicians from healers into killers, and the complicity of a large corps of extremely compliant public opinion molders. It is the *interdependence* of these factors, operating in concert, which has spelled doom for millions of victims.

On another level, the striking similarities between past and current atrocities within some key areas need to be identified and spelled out, accompanied by appropriate documentation, and then communicated. The following are some indications of how this might be carried out in several of the key areas:

Legality

When today's abortion proponents invoke the law to justify the destruction of the unborn, it should be indicated that abortion, euthanasia, and genocide also constituted the law of the land during the time of the Third Reich.

When American abortionists justify the extermination of human beings in the womb by citing the 1973 U.S. Supreme Court decision which declared them to be *legal nonpersons*, they should be made aware of a 1936 German Supreme Court decision which defined Jews as *nonpersons* in the *legal sense.* Modern-day medical killers of the unborn should also be told about Hannah Arendt's book, *The Origins of Totalitarianism,* in which she concludes that a major characteristic of totalitarian governments—whether communist, fascist, or whatever—is the treatment of those deemed stateless and expendable as *legal nonpersons.*

"What is legal is moral" is a frightening slogan employed to justify all kinds of violence down through history, including the ownership of slaves, the extermination of Jews, and the massacre of the unborn.

The utter legality of the Nazi war against the European Jews is most starkly revealed in the statistics: some four hundred laws and decrees were enacted leading up to the "final solution" to the Jewish question![1] Today's medical war on the unborn of America, it should be pointed out, enjoys an even greater degree of legal respectability in all fifty states of the union!

It also needs to be emphasized that both wars represent the ultimate in the perversion of the law.

Technology

When contemporary medical abortionists conceal their destructive procedures under the guise of "surgical operations," they should be told that former concentration camp doctors referred to their destructive activities as "medical operations."

When an emphasis is placed on the "cleanliness" of America's abortion chambers, reports on the "spotlessly clean" gas chambers of Auschwitz ought to be brought to the fore.

When today's killers of the unborn brag about how *quickly* and *efficiently* abortion chambers carry out their destructive tasks, they should be informed that *speed* and *efficiency* were also the hallmarks of Nazi gas chamber operations.

When today's abortionists deny responsibility for killing unborn children by claiming they are simply technicians operating suction machines and wielding curettes, they should be told that the Nazi gas chamber operators employed a similar rationalization to justify their involvement in the bureaucratic genocide of the Jews.

In both instances, the effects are identical: the reduction of mass, assembly-line extermination to the trivial level of a technical procedure divested of any feelings of revulsion or psychological discomfort. This "technicalization of destruction" is limitless because, according to psychoanalyst Erich Fromm, "nobody *destroys*; one only serves the machine for programmed—hence, apparently rational—purposes."[2]

The technology of death and destruction directed against prenatal discards must be replaced by a technology of life and living. Dramatic progress in fetal surgery, ultrasound, and the growing capacity to improve fetal viability represents a powerful technological challenge to the destructive procedures developed by the medical abortionists. The technology of curing human beings in utero poses an especially serious threat because its healing thrust is so starkly at odds with the destructive emphasis inherent in abortion methodology. The development of this life-sustaining technology presents another danger to the pro-abortion cause by highlighting what the abortionists are trying to conceal, by making visible what is being obscured: the existence of real, living human beings who look and act amazingly baby-like from a very early stage of growth and development.

At a National Abortion Federation meeting in May 1982, Alfred Moran, executive vice-president of Planned Parenthood of New York, warned his cohorts that "we are going to find ourselves isolated someplace" unless "we are prepared to begin to recognize that technology and medical sciences and perceptions of fetal viability are radically changing in our society." He was particularly horrified by the consequences of the new life-enhancing fetal technology—"we begin to see the fetus as a patient, which tends to personalize it"—for jeopardizing the right to abort. He even went so far as to rate technological changes designed to aid the unborn as "more powerful" than legislative attempts to outlaw abortion "because they are human personifications."[3]

The new technology, based on a perception of unborn children as legitimate patients, has an enormous potential for *personalizing* the plight of those victims whom the abortionists have so effectively *depersonalized*. Greater effort, therefore, must be expended to bring the details of these life-saving procedures and their recipients to larger numbers of people. It is extremely ironic that technology, which has played such a vital role in making killing at the level of a holocaust possible, may well prove to be an essential ingredient in exposing and undoing the entire abortion industry of America!

Continuing advances in the treatment of unborn children promise to accentuate ever more compellingly the sheer absurdity and perversity of today's killing centers for the unborn. Another way to show how utterly foreign the destruction of unborn children is to the profession of medicine is to repeat an alarming but profound historical perspective provided by Dr. Leo Alexander regarding the science of annihilation as practiced in the euthanasia hospitals and death camps of the Third Reich. "The killing center," he concluded, "is the *reductio ad absurdum* of all health care planning."[4]

Language

It cannot be reiterated enough that those bent on genocide have commonly subjected their victims to an orgy of name-calling as a preparatory step to their extermination. The *war of words* against the victims usually *precedes* the *actual war* by decades. The killing phase represents the translation of noxious attitudes into practice. Unfortunately, this is as true today as it was during the darkest days of the Third Reich.

When today's defenders of abortion dispute the humanity of the unborn, they should be told about how the Nazis disputed the humanity of the Jews.

When contemporary perpetrators characterize the unborn as just a "form of subhumanity," it should be made known to them that the Nazi researcher Dr. August Hirt called death camp inmates "a repulsive yet characteristic subhumanity."

When radical feminists refer to the unwanted unborn as a *parasite* within the mother's body, they should hear about Adolf Hitler's portrayal of Jews as a *parasite* in the body of other peoples.

When doctors liken abortion to "operating on an appendix or removing gangrenous bowel" from the mother's body, it should be revealed that Auschwitz physician Dr. Fritz Klein compared the killing of Jews to removing "a pus-filled appendix in the body of Europe."

While the images created of the victims are essentially derogatory in nature, the approach toward portraying what happens to them requires an entirely different semantic tactic. The emphasis shifts to a reliance on pleasant-sounding and highly inoffensive language.

When abortion advocates claim they are just making *choices*, they should be reminded that the death camp doctors maintained they were only making *selections.* Just as contemporary victims are *chosen to perish* in abortion chambers, the Nazi victims were *selected* to *expire* in gas chambers!

When physician abortionists contend they are only "interrupting pregnancies," they should be informed that "pregnancy interruption" was the prime euphemism devised to conceal the killing of unborn children at Auschwitz.

When today's medical executioners say they are simply *evacuating products* from the womb, it should be disclosed that the Nazis stated they were merely *evacuating Jews* from the ghettoes.

When American medical bureaucrats portray abortion as "treatment for the venereal disease of unwanted pregnancy," they should be apprised of the fact that the Hadamar euthanasia hospital staff called the administration of lethal injections to patients "treatment for their lung disease."

The Medical Profession

An exceedingly formidable obstacle to preventing the repulsive but truthful aspects of unborn baby killing from reaching the public is organized medicine itself. The extent of medical duplicity on the topic of abortion is nowhere more blatantly illustrated than in a legal brief submitted to the U.S. Supreme Court on August 30, 1982, by four medical groups to have the Akron, Ohio abortion ordinance declared unconstitutional.[5] One of the most reprehensible features of this ordinance, according to these medical elites, is its insistence that doctors provide women with *some basic facts* about abortion, including the possible negative effects, before they make a decision on abortion.

The brief filed before the Court contains a pack of lies, distortions, and misleading statements intended to discredit the informed consent principle embodied in the Akron regulations. Among the many provisions which the illustrious medical groups found fault with was a requirement that the doctor inform the woman that abortion "can result in serious complications, including hemorrhage, perforated uterus, infection, menstrual disturbances, sterility and miscarriage and prematurity in subsequent pregnancies; and that abortion may leave essentially unaffected or may worsen any existing psychological problems she may have, and can result in severe emotional disturbances."[6] The four medical organizations asserted that "most physicians" believe this information "to be demonstrably false," and indicated "there is little or no evidence that a properly performed abortion increases the risk of any such complications."[7]

Despite what "most physicians" may believe or choose to believe, it needs to be brought to public attention that the physical complications resulting from abortion, even when performed flawlessly early in pregnancy, have been extensively substantiated in the medical literature. Writing in the *American Journal of Obstretrics and Gynecology* (December 1, 1981), Vanderbilt University medical researchers listed the following complications associated with abortions induced in the first trimester of pregnancy: *increased risk of miscarriage and premature delivery, bleeding during pregnancy, retained placenta after delivery,* and *placenta previa* (attachment of the placenta near the entrance to the womb), a complication related to a greater frequency of *stillbirth, prematurity, hemorrhage in the mother,* and *death of the newborn.*[8]

The public should also be made aware that a number of studies have confirmed the existence of *serious psychological disturbances* resulting from abortion. According to an article published in the *British Columbia Medical Journal* in 1978, 30 women undergoing psychotherapy identified abortion as *the major precipitating factor* in their problem, and as a continuing factor in its prolongation.[9] Psychiatrists Myre Sim and Robert Neisser uncovered 114 cases of severe mental illness (psychoses) following abortion.[10]

Another Akron measure considered quite irksome to the eminent medical groups was the regulation that the physician inform his patient about the unborn child's *sensitivity to pain.*[11] The groups' brief declared that there is "no medical foundation" for the provision of such information and emphasized "the medical profession's complete ignorance" on the subject of fetal pain.[12]

When the above type of medical ignorance is claimed, the conclusions of pediatrician Dr. H.M.I. Liley should be repeated: "When doctors first began invading the sanctuary of the womb, they did not know that the unborn baby would react to pain" just as "violently as would a baby lying in a crib" by "flaying out his tiny arms, wriggling has entire body, and crying."[13] Furthermore, it is a well-established scientific fact that intrauterine blood transfusions cannot be accomplished unless the unborn child is heavily sedated. The child experiences pain from the needle puncture and will move away from the needle until the proper amount of pain-relieving medication is administered.[14] Loud sounds also produce fetal distress. Many women have given up concert-going during pregnancy because the music caused such violent kicking in their unborn offspring.[15] A dramatic example of how early the unborn baby responds to a painful stimulus was revealed in the television special *The Miracle Months,* which features films of fetal development taken inside the womb. One particular sequence shows an unborn child of only *nine weeks gestation* trying to shield himself from the camera lights by placing his hands over his eyes.[16]

One cannot help but get the impression that it is *not ignorance but duplicity* which motivates prestigious medical associations to keep the public ignorant about the negative consequences of extermination in the womb for both the mother and her unborn child. The American medical establishment, apparently, will resort to any tactic, including the most outlandish falsehoods, to defend unborn baby killing as a legitimate component of mainstream medical practice!

When today's physicians try to relieve the medical profession of responsibility for the wholesale killing of the unborn by indicating that only a minority of doctors actually perform abortions, it should be pointed out that only a minority of German doctors also actually participated in destructive activities during the Nazi era. It should be added, however, that it takes no more than a minority of physicians to carry out an enormous amount of destruction.

It must be kept uppermost in mind that the large-scale killing of human beings by a relatively small number of physicians is not possible unless the rest of the medical profession expresses either approval or apathy toward what is happening. The lack of opposition from organized medicine to the involvement of doctors in the Nazi holocaust rated the severest indictment by the prosecution at the Nuremberg Doctors' Trial. The complicity or deafening silence manifested by the American medical establishment regarding the medical holocaust perpetrated against the unborn merits equivalent condemnation.

It should be recalled that when the Nazi government inaugurated the final solution to the Jewish question in 1941, doctors had already become the most experienced killers in Germany. Hitler was well aware of how efficiently physicians did away with Germany's unwanted through abortion and euthanasia.

American medical science consultant to the Nuremberg Doctors' Trial, Dr. Andrew C. Ivy, considered the role played by German doctors in the euthanasia program so significant that he was prompted to conclude: "Had the profession taken a strong stand against the mass killing of sick Germans before the war, it is conceivable that the entire idea and technique of death factories for genocide would not have materialized. From all the evidence available, it is necessary to conclude that, far from opposing the Nazi state militantly, part of the German medical profession cooperated consciously and even willingly, while the remainder acquiesced in silence."[17]

It should also be emphasized, in a parallel manner, that in 1973 when the U.S. Supreme Court was confronted with the question of what to do with unwanted unborn children, doctors had long since become the most experienced killers of the unborn in America. The Court had before it an extensive history of medical killing and medical agitation for legal destruction of the unwanted before birth upon which to draw. Paraphrasing Dr. Ivy, if the American Medical Association and other illustrious medical groups had taken strong stands against killing unborn humans during the 1960s and early 1970s, the Supreme Court would never have allowed their legal extermination. And since 1973, again paraphrasing Dr. Ivy's conclusions about medicine in the Third Reich: a considerable portion of American doctors *cooperate consciously* and even *willingly* in the killing, while the remainder, for the most part, *acquiesces in silence.*

Doctors must be more than just personally opposed to unborn baby killing. There is an urgent need for them to band together and mount a vigorous campaign against any colleague or medical facility actively pursuing or even tolerating a policy favoring the intentional destruction of human beings in the womb. Physicians need to become highly visible defenders of the unborn child's right to life. This means joining public demonstrations against abortion, and even sitting in at abortion clinics. Greater involvement of doctors in such activities could not help but have a profound impact on many other physicians and the rest of society.

Medical Models for Action

How can members of the medical profession get involved in the above mentioned activities without being branded as religious fanatics bent on imposing a narrow sectarian morality onto the whole of society?

Doctors need not venture beyond the boundaries of the medical profession to find solid support for forceful actions in defense of innocent human lives. There are several exquisite models which provide excellent guidelines for physicians in their efforts to restore the profession to its only rightful role as guardians and healers of human life at all stages of development.

The Hippocratic Oath

The first and most fundamental model, the very foundation of medicine as a learned and ethical profession, is the Oath of Hippocrates. It is within the contents of this statement that the moral roots of the medical profession are lodged. The sanctity-of-life ethic incorporated in the Hippocratic Oath and its modern counterpart, The Declaration of Geneva, must once again occupy a prominent spot in the mores, values, and practices of every person who becomes a medical doctor. The Oath must once again become a required part of the graduation ceremonies of every medical school in America. As a beginning step in this direction, students in every medical school in America should be encouraged to insist that all doctors upon graduation be given an opportunity to make a public commitment to the principles embodied in the uncensored, uncut version of the Geneva Code adopted by the World Medical Association in 1948. Even if only a few students in each graduating class are willing to confront the hypocrisy of the medical school establishment, such a compelling example of dedication to the do-no-harm legacy of Hippocrates cannot help but eventually exert a profound influence on the rest of the medical community.

It cannot be emphasized enough that the Oath does not reflect a rigid, dogmatic position, but a broad *universal ethic* which transscends the boundaries of race, religion, and creed.

For those medical abortionists who maintain that the Hippocratic Oath is no longer relevant, it should be recalled that the German doctors on trial at Nuremberg invoked the exact same rationalization to justify their participation in crimes against humanity.

Ironically, on July 22, 1980, the 279-member House of Delegates of the American Medical Association recognized the relevance of the Oath as *the* ethical standard for enacting a formal prohibition against medical involvement in administering lethal injections for state-ordered executions. "A physician as a member of a profession dedicated to preserving life," the report accompanying the prohibition stated, "should not be a participant in a legally authorized execution."[18] In another reference to Hippocrates' Oath, Dr. James R. Kircher of Burley, Idaho, one of the four states with death-by-injection capital punishment laws, expressed his opposition to this type of medical involvement in the deliberate taking of human life because it "would destroy one of the most important principles in the history of healing."[19]

An influential article, which appeared in the *New England Journal of Medicine* six months before the above AMA policy, laid the historical and ethical groundwork for opposition to medical participation in capital punishment by drug injection. "This new method of capital punishment," declared the authors, "presents the most serious and intimate challenge in modern American history to active medical participation in state-ordered killing of human beings . . . this procedure requires the direct application of biomedical knowledge and skills in a corruption and exploitation of the healing profession's role in society."[20]

The authors are crystal clear on the ethical basis for their stance: "The Hippocratic Oath itself is the foundation of this position. Its essential purpose was to identify the Greek group of physicians as healers who would never kill or harm their patients." The appropriate passages from the Oath are even cited: "I will use treatment to help the sick according to my ability and judgment, but never with a view to injury and wrong-doing. Neither will I administer a poison to anyone when asked to do so nor will I suggest such a course." A quotation from the modern reaffirmation of the Hippocratic Oath—The Declaration of Geneva—is also highlighted: "Even under threat, I will not use my medical knowledge contrary to the laws of humanity."[21]

If the writers of the above article had also included the passage from the Hippocratic Oath which states "Similarly, I will not give to a woman a pessary to cause abortion," and the passage from the Declaration of Geneva which reads "I will maintain the utmost respect for human life from the time of its conception," they would have made an equally compelling case against permitting physicians to serve as legal executioners of the unborn.

How come the AMA considers the Hippocratic Oath and the Declaration of Geneva appropriate ethical standards for support of its prohibition against medical participation in legally authorized executions and yet remains blind to their relevance as a basis for opposition to the medical execution of millions before birth? The glaring *inconsistencies* between the AMA positions on *capital punishment* (repudiation of physicians as legal executioners of condemned criminals) and *abortion* (approval of physicians as legal executioners of the condemned unborn) must be exposed and remedied!

Selective application of the Hippocratic Oath and its modern version to castigate one type of medical atrocity and not another constitutes a severe prostitution of the very essence of these statements. They were both intended to *permanently remove* the physician from involvement in *all forms of killing,* both inside and outside the womb.

The AMA Abortion Policy Statements of 1859 and 1871

Another excellent model of action worthy of emulation by contemporary doctors in their efforts to return the physician to the role of healer should include the policy statements against abortion enacted by the House of Delegates of the American Medical Association in 1859 and 1871. During those two periods the AMA developed a comprehensive plan for passing strong laws protective of unborn human life at all stages of pregnancy. This "physicians' crusade against abortion," which took place between the latter 1850s and 1880s, was so successful that it produced what historian James C. Mohr called "the most important burst of anti-abortion legislation in the nation's history. At least 40 anti-abortion statutes of various kinds were placed upon state and territorial lawbooks during that period." Furthermore, he concluded, "the anti-abortion policies sustained in the United States through the first two-thirds of the twentieth century had their formal legislative origins, for the most part, in the wave of tough laws passed in the wake of the doctors' crusade and the public response their campaign evoked."[22]

A summary of the main points emphasized by the AMA in 1859 and 1871[23] include the following:

1) The establishment of conception as the scientifically-documented beginning of human life.

In 1859 the AMA characterized the contention that "the foetus is not alive until after the period of quickening" as an error "based, and only based, upon mistaken and exploded medical dogmas."

In 1871 the AMA asserted: "Physiology considers the foetus as much a living being immediately after conception as at any other time before delivery, and its future progress but as the development and increase of those constituent principles which it then received . . . Indeed, no other doctrine appears to be consonant with reason or physiology but that which admits the embryo to possess vitality from the very moment of conception."

2) A candid, non-euphemistic portrayal of the true nature of abortion.

In 1859 the AMA called abortion the "slaughter of countless children" and "such unwarrantable destruction of human life."

In 1871 the AMA referred to abortion as "the work of destruction," "the wholesale destruction of unborn infants" and "a foul, unprovoked murder."

3) A strong condemnation of physician-abortionists.

The AMA of 1871 described medical abortionists as "men who cling to a noble profession only to dishonor it," "a disgusting caudal appendage," "false brethern," "educated assassin," "an enemy to the human family," "modern Herods," "monsters of iniquity" and "the executioners."

4) Harsh treatment of physician-abortionists, including their expulsion from the medical profession.

In 1871 the AMA recommended dealing with medical abortionists in the following manner: "These men should be marked as Cain was marked; they should be made the outcasts of society . . . respectable men should cease to consult with them, should cease to speak to them, should cease to notice them except with contempt . . . Resolved, That we repudiate and denounce the conduct of abortionists, and that we will hold no intercourse with them professionally or otherwise, and that we will, whenever an opportunity presents, guard and protect the public against the machinations of these characters by pointing out the physical and moral ruin which follows in their wake."

5) The establishment of abortion as a serious crime.

In 1859 the AMA entered "an earnest and solemn protest against such unwarrantable destruction of human life" and recommended that "the Association present this subject to the attention of the several legislative assemblies of the Union" for the purpose of revising the permissive abortion laws then in effect.

In 1871 the AMA passed a resolution that "it will be unlawful and unprofessional for any physician to induce abortion or premature labor, without the concurrent opinion of at least one respectable consulting physician, and then always with a view to the safety of the child—if that be possible."

6) Employment of the commandment against killing as *the* ethical foundation for opposition to abortion.

In 1871 the AMA declared: "Thou shalt not kill. This commandment is given to all, and applies to all without exception . . . it matters not at what stage of development his victim may have arrived—it matters not how small or how apparently insignificant it may be."

7) Enlistment of the clergy in the movement to halt the destruction of human lives before birth.

One of the resolutions passed by the AMA in 1871 reads: "We respectfully call the attention of the clergy of all denominations to the perverted views of morality [approval of destruction in the womb] . . . on this important question, and the ruin which has resulted and continues to result daily to the human family from such views."

The Association went a step further and recommended that state and local medical societies "send delegates to the clergymen in their respective districts to request their aid in so important an undertaking."

Significantly, physicians, not the clergy, led the moral crusade against killing in the womb. It was doctors who were responsible for getting the clergy involved, and not the other way around. The nature and thrust of medical leadership is understandable when one considers the fact that by the 1850s doctors at last had solid scientific evidence that the entity in the womb was human from conception onward[24] and abortion constituted nothing less than the destruction of a bona fide human being.

The medical profession thus felt compelled to communicate these facts to the clergy so that the Judeo-Christian prohibition against killing could be extended to a class of individuals which up to that time had not been recognized as legitimate members of the human race. Exposure to the new scientific-based findings prompted the members of the clergy to join the physicians in a highly successful campaign directed toward updating the law to reflect the most recent scientific knowledge about life before birth and the concomitant need for legal protection of individuals at all the prenatal phases of development.

Desperately needed today is *another physicians' crusade against unborn baby killing* much like the one so successfully waged by the AMA from the latter 1850s through 1880! Familiarity with the preceding information on how it was accomplished provides indispensable insights as to what contemporary doctors can do to stem the tidal wave of medical extermination in which the destruction of unborn children is now the most frequently performed surgical procedure in America, outstripping even tonsillectomy.[25]

An integral part of this crusade should include an awareness of the astonishing *incompatibilities* between *AMA oppostion* to legalized abortion in 1859 and 1871, and *AMA approval* of legalized abortion in 1967 and 1970. It is tragically ironic that the current

AMA positions highly supportive of abortion (1967 and 1970)[26] helped facilitate the literal demolition of the strong wall of legal protection erected on behalf of the unborn, a legal structure which the AMA of 1859 and 1871 played such a vital role in constructing and sustaining. The current AMA stance on abortion represents not only a complete repudiation of the courageous leadership exercised by the AMA of the past in defense of the silenced minority, but also constitutes a spineless and deplorable regression back to the dark age of pre-Hippocratic medicine when the physician functioned in the schizophrenic role of killer-healer!

Chart 18

The American Medical Association on Abortion: An Anatomy of Contrasting Policy Statements

When Does Human Life Begin?	
1871—"No other doctrine appears to be consonant with reason or physiology but that which admits the embryo to possess vitality from the very moment of conception."	The AMA abortion policy statements of 1967 and 1970 include no references to the scientific fact that human life begins at conception.
What Is Abortion?	
1859—"The slaughter of countless children; such unwarrantable destruction of human life." **1871**—"The work of destruction; the wholesale destruction of unborn infants."	**1967**—"The interruption of pregnancy; the induced termination of pregnancy." **1970**—"A medical procedure."
What Should the Ethics of Abortion Be?	
1871—"Thou shalt not kill. This commandment is given to all without exception...it matters not at what stage of development his victim may have arrived."	**1967**—"This is a personal and moral consideration which in all cases must be faced according to the dictates of the conscience of the patient and her physician."
Who Should Perform Abortions?	
1871—"It will be unlawful and unprofessional for any physician to induce abortion."	**1970**—"Abortion should be performed only by a duly licensed physician."
Who Are Physician-Abortionists?	
1871—"Men who cling to a noble profession only to dishonor it; false brethern; educated assassin; modern Herods; the executioners."	**1967**—"Conscientious practitioners; conscientious physicians."
What Should Be Done to Physician-Abortionists?	
1871—"These men should be marked as Cain was marked; they should be made the outcasts of society."	**1970**—They should be permitted to perform abortions as long as they take place "in an accredited hospital."

The Dutch Physicians' Statement

Of all the medical associations in countries under Nazi domination, only the Dutch physicians as a national medical body stood up against the Nazi attempt to transform medical doctors into instruments of the state for malevolent purposes. When the Dutch doctors learned about the Nazi plan to impose draconic regulations which radically compromised their personal and professional integrity, they resigned from the Dutch Medical Society. They also issued a formal protest which invoked the sanctity-of-life and physician-as-healer philosophy encoded in the Hippocratic Oath as the basis for their refusal to abide by the anti-life, utilitarian philosophy inherent in the directives of National Socialism (see Chart 19).[27]

Medical scholar Dr. Herbert Ratner's observations on the statement of the Dutch physicians against Nazi oppression, made in 1972, contain a remarkably prophetic quality, and are as relevant today as when they were first presented:

> This protest underscores the *raison d'etre* of the Hippocratic Oath and the timelessness of that inspired document that today is undergoing attack from brave new crops of medical students, professors of obstetrics turned sociologists, social ethicist reformers, population engineers, less than thoughtful segments of the women's liberation movement, crusading lawyer-simplifiers of criminal codes, and abortionists and 'mercy' killers.
>
> Today, more than three decades after the above protest was made to the Nazi overture to alter the traditional concept of the medical profession, we have yet to learn the lesson the Dutch physicians proffered. Instead, we now have American physicians, newly captured by the promise of power within the Nazi overture, chorusing the discordant tune of the conquered—that the physician's obligation to society transcends his obligation to the individual—as they march headlong down the infamous road to live fetal and handicapped child experimentation, the dispatching of defective or unwanted children, unborn and born, and extensive so-called mercy killing.[28]

The Dutch physicians who signed the statement of opposition to the intrusion of Nazi values paid dearly. Many of them were dispatched to concentration camps where they died in gas chambers and crematoriums. Their act of collective resistance stands as a superb model of courage and conviction in the face of the most adverse circumstances.

Physicians today who are horrified by, or at least uneasy about the medical holocaust against the unwanted unborn and the growing

Chart 19

Dutch Physicians' Protest Against Nazi Regulations

The undersigned Dutch physicians, having heard of your intention to issue a directive to us for the purpose of instituting a "Physician's Bureau," take the liberty of bringing the following to your attention:

When we discontinued our membership in our Dutch Medical Society last September it was our intention, as you are undoubtedly aware, to express our conviction that the function of the physician is born of his own high moral and spiritual norms, and therefore should be free from political control.

No matter how much the ideas and constitutions of nations may have changed in the course of time, the physician has always remained the undisputed protector of two holy and precious values: the respect for life, and charity toward the sick human being. From time immemorial until the present the vocation of the physician has been a vocation of confidence, indeed a priestly vocation. The physician as a person who realizes the smallness of his knowledge in the face of the magnitude of the mystery of life, suffering and death, can retain the necessary spiritual power for his responsible work only as long as he experiences his profession as a calling from God, and his duties as dictated by eternal, supernatural laws.

We are gravely concerned about your forthcoming directive for physicians. We know that you represent a very special philosophy of life. Our knowledge of the German "physicians' ordinance" concerning the task of the physician in which the care for race and nation take precedence over that of the individual, makes it only too clear to what extent the national-socialistic conception of the medical profession differs from ours.

Although we do not deny that the care of the community and the participation in social hygiene measures constitute part of the task of the physician, we can recognize this duty only insofar as it proceeds from and is not in conflict with the first and holiest precept of the physician, namely, the respect for life and for the physical well-being of the individual who entrusts himself to his care.

If you now put us, physicians, under the discipline of a civil service body endowed with authoritarian power, we have every reason to fear that its officials to whom our ideas and sensibilities are utterly foreign, will meddle with the treatment of our sick, and will demand our direct or indirect cooperation in the taking of measures which are in conflict with our conscience as well as our professional views.

We are convinced that we speak according to the wishes of the people of the Netherlands, when, in appealing to the most holy human rights, we request you most urgently to spare us the conflict of conscience which threatens to engage us as the result of your forthcoming directive for physicians.

Knowing ourselves bound by the oath or solem vow of acceptance of our task as physicians, we consider it our duty to inform you that we shall remain faithful to the high standards which have been the foundation of our profession since time immemorial, and that in the exercise of our profession we shall only be motivated by considerations which are justified by our conscience, our sense of duty and our medical science.

assaults against postnatal expendables, and yet remain silent or do little to alter the appalling state of affairs, might seriously reconsider their apathy in light of the magnificent legacy of activism bequeathed to medicine and society by the Dutch doctors.

The World Federation of Doctors Who Respect Human Life

At a European Conference on Respect for Life on May 12, 1974, doctors from Austria, Belgium, Canada, France, Germany, the Netherlands, Norway, Spain, Switzerland, and the United States established a new organization of physicians, the World Federation of Doctors Who Respect Human Life, in response to the monolithic abortion-on-demand juggernaut which threatened to engulf every country on the face of the earth. Drawing upon the most important documents relating to the ethical foundation of humane medicine from Hippocrates to the present, the conference participants developed a set of invaluable resolutions and guidelines to counter the world-wide, anti-life movement.

The declaration enacted furnishes an essential framework for upholding the physician in the role of healer and repudiating the role of medical executioner. The exact wording of the declaration can be found in Chart 20.[29]

Doctors For Life

In 1978 a national organization of American physicians, Doctors for Life, was established as a vehicle for coordinating the various activities and educational endeavors of pro-life doctors and medical groups throughout the United States. One of its primary goals is to counterbalance the pro-abortion stances of the AMA and other medical associations which claim to speak for the Amercian medical community on human life issues.

Along with commitment to the ethical principles embodied in the Hippocratic Oath and the Declaration of Geneva, and the characterization of each individual human life beginning at conception/fertilization as "a basic fact of science," Doctors for Life subscribes to the following propositions:

> The zygote, embryo, fetus, toddler, teenager, young adult, middle-aged and older adult all represent stages in the human life continuum. All are human life and all are equally worthy of our respect and medical assistance.
>
> There can be no compromise with those factions, both within and outside of organized medicine, which would make physicians medical executioners. We will not kill, whether at

Chart 20

Declaration of the World Federation of Doctors Who Respect Human Life

(May 12, 1974)

1) This federation adheres to the Declaration of Geneva of 1948 [The Geneva Statement of the Hippocratic Oath], and reiterates that its members will maintain the utmost respect for human life from the time of fertilization until natural death.

2) This federation, furthermore, upholds the fundamental, unconditional, individual right to life, regardless of its stage of development or mental, physical, or material circumstance, and notwithstanding any changes that may occur within society.

3) Doctors should not kill or harm their patients; doctors cannot therefore take part in selective killing in order to solve a psychological, socio-economic, or demographic problem.

4) Experience has shown that legalized abortion fails to reduce the number of illegal abortions significantly, although it does lead to an escalation of the total number of abortions. There is good medical evidence that a permissive abortion policy induces younger women to accept abortion as a birth-control method of choice.

5) This federation also adheres to the United Nations Declaration of Rights of the Child, which states that "the child, by reason of his physical and mental immaturity, needs special safeguards and care, including appropriate legal protection, before as well as after birth."

6) There is no medical evidence to suggest that handicapped children would, themselves, prefer not to have been born; neither is there evidence to show a causal relationship between the unwanted pregnancy and the rejected child.

7) The specialties of obstetrics and gynecology, which honor and revere womanhood and procreation, find that abortion degrades and humiliates women, and that abortion creates more moral, psychological, and physical problems among patients than it solves in the way of improved "quality of life."

8) This federation agrees that in countries in which abortion is legalized under whatever safeguards, the clinical freedom of doctors has been subjected to inevitable and unacceptable pressures.

In the interest of the dignity of human life, of the health of our patients and in the integrity of the medical profession, therefore, we appeal for the withdrawal of proposed or existing [permissive] abortion laws.

We urge governments to take positive steps to help women with unintentional pregnancies and children whose conception was unintentional by adopting adequate social and economic measures.

the behest of the pregnant woman, the terminally ill, those satiated, saddened, or only bored by life, or the State desiring the physician to ". . . give a deadly drug . . ." to condemned criminals.

> The biggest battles are yet to come. It is essential that we face these battles together against our common foe—all those who would make a mockery of this noble profession by turning healers into killers.[30]

The Media

When today's gatekeepers of public information conceal the harsh realities of unborn baby killing under a thick cloud of *abstract, benign,* or so-called *neutral terminology,* they should be told that the Nazi press resorted to the same semantic strategy in covering up the distasteful truth of extermination in the death camps.

When the contemporary molders of public perception accept *at face value* the euphemistic versions concocted by those who are destroying human lives in the womb, they should be made aware that they are repeating the same astonishing blunder committed by Professor Arthur R. Butz of Northwestern University who relies on the benevolent images manufactured by the Nazis as a basis for declaring that the holocaust against the Jews never happened.

When modern-day reporters utilize the most *horrifying language* to characterize the destruction of convicted criminals, war victims, dolphins, seals, birds, or snail darters, they should be taken to task for failing to exercise equivalent zeal in covering the medical war on the unborn.

When the members of the media elite suppress or discredit *photographs* of aborted babies, it should be asked: Why don't they stifle or undermine pictures of other victims with comparable fervor? Those watchdogs in the field of mass communications entrusted with the task of controlling what the public is allowed to view are in dire need of exposure to the photographic evidence which so vividly and objectively reveals the striking similarities between violence against Jews of the Third Reich and unborn children of contemporary America.

Members of the media should refrain from serving as puppets and parrots for anti-life rhetoric. These agents of destruction-inducing propaganda must be challenged to stop treating the killers as heroes and start opposing their right to destroy the most vulnerable and least visible members of the human race. A media so renowned for a history of fearless independence and crusading reform might try living up to this reputation by *exposing* the severe *corruption* of *language* and *thought* that masks the medical execution of millions!

The Public

It is hoped that once those lawyers, doctors, journalists, and others who defend abortion become aware of the striking similarities between their participation in the contemporary carnage visited upon the unborn and the involvement of attorneys, physicians, reporters, and others in the extermination of human lives during the Nazi regime, they will change their attitudes and get active in the movement to put an end to today's bloodbath. The task of getting the necessary information into their hands remains a formidable one indeed. Few individuals implicated in the current massive slaughter of the unborn are especially receptive to facts which present such a serious challenge to the very credibility of what they are doing.

Even if some abortion apologists displayed a willingness to examine the disturbing comparisons between past and present holocausts and the ample documentation which backs them up, this would not guarantee an end to the killing. Many professionals possess too great a vested interest—whether monetary, ideological, or otherwise—to oppose the monstrosity they have helped create and continue to perpetuate. Tragically, too many members of the medical profession, in particular, are so blindly wedded to exterminative technology, astronomical profits, mind-boggling terminology, and misplaced idealism that they may have lost the capability to seriously pause and reflect on how radically they have departed from their time-honored tradition as guardians and healers of human life.

In a society such as contemporary America, where the law serves injustice, medicine perpetrates destruction, and journalism transmits falsehoods, the public-at-large may well be the only group with sufficient autonomy to call to task each profession for failing grievously to live up to its most fundamental ethical and professional standards. The issue is one of *professional responsibility* and *public accountability.* No profession is an island unto itself. Even medicine, probably the most powerful of the lot, still owes its position of preeminence to public support and confidence.

The existence of a truly civilized society depends upon the presence of 1) a public which insists that the most basic role of an attorney or judge or law maker is the impartial *extension* of *legal protection* to all human beings, however small or insignificant; 2) a public which demands that the only legitimate role for a physician is to *heal* or *care for human life* despite its status, condition, or stage of development; and 3) a public which requires of journalists nothing less than *complete* and *consistent coverage* of all atrocities perpetrated, whether the victims be born or unborn.

Many years ago India's great spiritual leader and foremost proponent of nonviolent resistance, Mahatma Gandhi, was asked about the greatest sorrow of his life. Significantly, he pointed to "the hardness of heart of the educated.''[31]

Psychiatrist Fredric Wertham, in his study of the psychiatric holocaust against Germany's handicapped, reached a similar conclusion: ''Violence does not usually come from the uncontrolled instincts of the undereducated, but frequently is a rationalized policy from above.''[32]

The unwanted expendables of the Third Reich and contemporary American society have had much more to fear from *educated ideologues* than from either *mobs in the streets* or *backalley butchers!*

In the final analysis, then, much of the impetus for placing a permanent ban on violence in the womb is far more likely to come from an aroused public rather than from professional elites. A truly heartening sign of public awareness and involvement is the phenomenal growth of that segment of the population which speaks out against the destruction of unborn children and postnatal discards, and takes direct personal and political action in opposition to the abortionists and ''mercy'' killers of America. Right-to-life organizations from every geographical area comprise the largest and most rapidly expanding civil rights movement in contemporary society.

If unborn babies could riot in the streets, there would be very few abortions! Since they cannot, they constitute the most *absolutely oppressed minority* in history, a group in desperate need of advocates. The pro-life movement thus serves as an increasingly potent voice on behalf of those who cannot defend themselves from the onslaughts of legal, medical, and media perpetrators.

If members of the professions implicated in the massacre, and those who stand by and do nothing, choose to remain oblivious to how the horrendous events of the past continue in the present, it is incumbent upon the public to replace ignorance with knowledge. It is imperative that members of the great grassroots movement for life become thoroughly familiar with the whole history of medical, legal, linguistic, and media violence perpetrated in the Third Reich and be prepared to demonstrate how this appalling history is being repeated today on a massive scale.

Truth-In-Telling

Along with the current efforts to restore protection of the law to the unborn and others at risk under the banner of an amoral, elitist, utilitarian medical ethic, a campaign of truth-in-telling is long overdue.

An essential part of this campaign might well include citing the rationale employed by the American Medical Association of 1871 which called abortion ''the wholesale destruction of unborn infants'' and severely castigated physicians who performed abortions as "monsters of iniquity" and "the executioners":

> If in the foregoing report our language has appeared to some strong and severe, or even intemperate, let the gentlemen pause for a moment and reflect on the importance and gravity of our subject . . . We had to deal with human life. In a matter of less importance we could entertain no compromise. An honest judge on the bench would call things by their proper names. We could do no less.[33]

The task of getting people to face the horrifying realities of the present-day abortion holocaust still remains an arduous one indeed. Anyone who attempts to tell the terrible truth about the massive slaughter of unborn children in abortion chambers is immediately branded a dangerous fanatic, a crackpot, or a deranged monger of unabashed sensationalism. Many people, like the proverbial ostrich with its head buried in the sand, prefer not to believe the horrendous atrocities hidden behind the slick veneer of today's killing centers for the unborn.

When the American people first heard the truth about the Nazi death camps, they too responded with disbelief. In 1944, a Nazi S.S. officer related the following to Nazi hunter Simon Wiesenthal:

> You could tell the truth about the death camps to the people in America—and you know what would happen? They wouldn't believe you. They'd say you were crazy. They might even put you in a madhouse.[34]

Today, pro-abortion zealots such as Bill Baird, owner and operator of several abortion chambers on the east coast, wage a vicious verbal campaign against those who dare to expose the flagrant lies which make the destruction of unborn children such a widespread reality. Baird, a pugnacious fanatic with considerable financial interests at stake, calls Catholics United for Life a "bunch of crazies."[35] This highly dedicated group of Christians (many of them are former Jews and some of them have had abortions) constitutes a grave threat to Baird because its members are committed to telling the truth about what really happens to unborn children in abortion chambers, and actively opposes the slaughter of the unborn at the killing sites with prayers, sidewalk counseling, and sit-ins.

One could easily envision the Nazi death camp commanders exercising zeal comparable to Baird's in attempting to discredit the integrity and mental stability of any critic who might dare try to expose and challenge what went on inside the gas chambers.

The modern version of Hitler's *big-lie philosophy*—the entity in the womb is subhuman at best and abortion is merely the evacuation of tissue fragments from the womb—has become deeply embedded in the public mindset. A longstanding and relentless barrage of derogatory stereotypes and slogans, or as Professor Henry Friedlander said of the Nazi holocaust, "transforming cliches into reality by repetition,"[36] has taken its toll.

If the truth is ever to overcome the current well-entrenched fabrications, it must be conveyed with comparable persistence and backed up with compelling documentation. Unless the stark parallels between past and present horrors are honestly confronted, contemporary society will continue to plunge ever more deeply into an abyss of anarchy with survival of the fittest irreversibly established as the prevailing norm. The findings in this book, although alarming, are offered in the spirit of that search for truth and subsequent hope expressed by one philosopher: "Only when we draw conclusions from the past, can there be hope for the future."

NOTES

Citations listed in the notes beginning with one or several letters followed by a series of numbers are the actual initials and page numbers of court transcripts circulated during the war crimes trials held at Nuremberg. Among the abbreviations used, "EC" refers to the "Economic Case," a group of documents processed by the Economic Section of the Office of the United States Chief Counsel (OCC) at Frankfurt. The letter "L" stands for documents processed by the London office of the OCC. "PS," short for "Paris-Storey," indicates material processed by OCC offices in Paris and Nuremberg. Documents translated by Lt. Walter Rothschild are designated by the letter "R" and those processed by the British prosecuting staff are covered by the letter "D." The initials "NO" refer to Nazi organizational documents and "NG" to documents issued by agencies and ministries of the German government.

Complete photostats of the original court testimony are available at major depository libraries such as the Library of Congress and the Columbia Law Library. Where printed collections of Nuremberg documents are available, they are employed as text sources. Some of the major collections can be found in the following publications: International Military Tribunal, *Trial of the Major War Criminals* (Nuremberg, 1947-1949), 42 vols.; Office of United States Counsel for Prosecution of Axis Criminality, *Nazi Conspiracy and Aggression* (Washington D.C., 1946-1948), 11 vols.; Nuernberg Military Tribunals, *Trials of War Criminals* (Washington D.C., 1947-1950), 15 vols.

Chapter 1
The Abortion-Holocaust Connection

1. Willard Gaylin and Marc Lappe, "Fetal Politics: The Debate on Experimenting with the Unborn," *Atlantic*, May 1975, p. 66.

2. "Opinion and Judgment: Methods of Execution," *Trials of War Criminals Before the Nuernberg Military Tribunals,* 15 vols. (Washington D.C.: U.S. Government Printing Office, 1950), 4: 443-445.

3. John F. McDermott and Walter F. Char, "Abortion Repeal in Hawaii: An Unexpected Crisis in Patient Care," *American Journal of Orthopsychiatry* 41 (July 1971): 621.

4. Olga Lengyel, *Five Chimneys: The Story of Auschwitz* (Chicago and New York: Ziff-Davis, 1947), p. 75.

5. Warren M. Hern and Billie Corrigan, "What About Us? Staff Reactions to the D & E Procedure," Paper presented at the Annual Meeting of the Association of Planned Parenthood Physicians, San Diego, California, October 26, 1978, p. 9.

6. Ota Kraus and Erich Kulka, *The Death Factory: Document on Auschwitz* trans, Stephen Jolly (New York: Pergamon Press, 1966), p. 114.

7. Dr. & Mrs. J.C. Willke, *Handbook on Abortion,* rev. ed. (Cincinnati: Hayes Publishing Company, 1975), pp. 30-31; Burritt W. Newton, "The Art of Abortion," *Postgraduate Medicine* 50 (September 1971): 215.

8. Robert S. Galen et al., "Fetal Pathology and Mechanism of Fetal Death in Saline-Induced Abortion: A Study of 143 Gestations and Critical Review of the Literature," *American Journal of Obstetrics and Gynecology* 120 (October 1, 1974): 353-354.

9. The People of the State of California vs. William Baxter Waddill, Jr., Transcript of Preliminary Examination, In the Municipal Court of the West Orange County Judicial District, State of California, Case No. 77W2085, April 18, 1977, p. 40.

Chapter 2
The Campaign to Legalize Abortion In Pre-Nazi Germany and Pre-Roe v. Wade America

1. "The Question of Legalized Abortion," *Journal of the American Medical Association* 93 (September 21, 1929): 934.
2. "Interruption of Pregnancy from Eugenic Indications," *Journal of the American Medical Association* 86 (February 27, 1926): 639.
3. James C. Mohr, *Abortion in America: The Origins and Evolution of National Policy, 1800-1900* (New York: Oxford University Press, 1978), p. 200.
4. Eugene Quay, "Justifiable Abortion—Medical and Legal Foundations," *Georgetown Law Journal* 49 (Spring 1961): 516.
5. John T. Noonan, *A Private Choice: Abortion in America in the Seventies* (New York: Free Press, 1979), pp. 33-34.
6. "The Problem of Abortion," *Journal of the American Medical Association* 95 (July 19, 1930): 216.
7. Bernard N. Nathanson with Richard N. Ostling, *Aborting America* (Garden City, New York: Doubleday, 1979), p. 61.
8. "The Session of the League of German Medical Societies," *Journal of the American Medical Association* 85 (October 17, 1925): 1237.
9. "Induced Interruption of Pregnancy," *Journal of the American Medical Association* 86 (March 20, 1926): 888.
10. "Modification of Punishment for Abortion," *Journal of the American Medical Association* 88 (January 22, 1927): 259.
11. "Birth Control," *Journal of the American Medical Association* 92 (January 26, 1929): 330.
12. "Attack on the Law Concerning Abortion," *Journal of the American Medical Association* 96 (February 14, 1931): 541.
13. "Abortion and Race Hygiene," *Journal of the American Medical Association* 105 (July 20, 1935): 212.
14. Frederick J. Taussig, *Abortion Spontaneous and Induced: Medical and Social Aspects* (St. Louis: C.V. Mosby, 1936), pp. 28, 402, 404, and 444.
15. Cited by Lawrence Lader, *Abortion* (Boston: Beacon Press, 1966), p. 4.
16. Mary S. Calderone, ed., *Abortion in the United States* (New York: Hoeber-Harper, 1958), pp. 162-167.
17. Jerome M. Kummer and Zad Leavy, "Criminal Abortion: A Consideration of Ways to Reduce Incidence," *California Medicine* 95 (September 1961): 170, 173.
18. Jerome E. Bates and Edward S. Zawadzki, *Criminal Abortion: A Study in Medical Sociology* (Springfield, Ill.: Charles C. Thomas, 1964), pp. 3-4.
19. Lader, *Abortion,* p. 66.
20. California Committee on Therapeutic Abortion, "The Truth About Abortion: Must 10,000 Women Die This Year?" Brochure, 1966.
21. Abraham Flexner, *Medical Education: A Comparative Study* (New York: Macmillan, 1925), p. 38.

22. Mary S. Caiderone, "Illegal Abortion as a Public Health Problem," *American Journal of Public Health* 50 (July 1960): 948-954.
23. Herbert Ratner, "A Public Health Physician Views Abortion," *Child and Family* 7 (Winter 1968): 3.
24. Nathanson with Ostling, *Aborting America,* p. 193.
25. "Session of the League of Medical Societies," p. 1237.
26. Taussig, *Abortion Spontaneous and Induced,* p. 394.
27. Abraham J. Rongy, *Abortion: Legal or Illegal?* (New York: Vanguard Press, 1933), p. 130.
28. Taussig, *Abortion Spontaneous and Induced,* p. 449.
29. Proceedings of a Conference of the National Committee on Maternal Health, *The Abortion Problem* (Baltimore: Williams and Wilkins, 1944), p. viii.
30. Alan F. Guttmacher, "Therapeutic Abortion in a Large General Hospital," *Surgical Clinics of North America* 37 (April 1957): 468.
31. Alan F. Guttmacher, "The Law That Doctors Often Break," *Redbook Magazine,* August 1959, p. 96.
32. William B. Walker and J.F. Hulka, "Attitudes and Practices of North Carolina Obstetricians: The Impact of the North Carolina Abortion Act of 1967," *Southern Medical Journal* 64 (April 1971): 441-445.

Chapter 3
The Expansion of Abortion in the Third Reich And Roe v. Wade America

1. Henry Friedlander, "Toward a Methodology of Teaching about the Holocaust," *Teachers College Record* 80 (February 1979): 522.
2. Malcolm Potts, "Abortion in Europe," *Newsweek,* January 28, 1980, p. 6.
3. Ellen Willis, "Abortion Rights: Overruling Neo-Fascists," *Village Voice,* February 4, 1980, p. 8.
4. Gloria Steinem, "The Nazi Connection: If Hitler Were Alive, Whose Side Would He Be On?" *Ms*, October 1980, p. 89.
5. "Physicians and the New Penal Code," *Journal of the American Medical Association* 89 (October 8, 1927): 1265; "The Question of Legalized Abortion," *Journal of the American Medical Association* 93 (September 21, 1929): 935; "Indications for Abortion and the Law," *Journal of the American Medical Association* 96 (May 23, 1931): 1810.
6. John T. Noonan, *A Private Choice: Abortion in America in the Seventies* (New York: Free Press, 1979), pp. 33-34.
7. Frederick J. Taussig, *Abortion Spontaneous and Induced: Medical and Social Aspects* (St. Louis: C.V. Mosby, 1936), p. 424; "Criteria for the Interruption of Pregnancy," *Journal of the American Medical Association* 102 (January 13, 1934): 144.
8. Roe v. Wade, 410 U.S. 163-165 (1973).
9. "Indications for Abortion and the Law," p. 1810.
10. "The Question of Legalized Abortion," p. 935.
11. American College of Obstetricians and Gynecologists, "Statement on Therapeutic Abortion," May 1968.
12. Doe v. Bolton, 410 U.S. 192 (1973).
13. "The Question of Legalized Abortion," p. 935.

14. Ernst Haeckel, *The Wonders of Life: A Popular Study of Biological Philosophy,* trans. Joseph McCabe (London: Watts and Company, 1904), p. 122; Daniel Gasman, *The Scientific Origins of National Socialism in Ernst Haeckel and the German Monist League* (New York: Elsevier, 1971), p. 93.

15. Frederick Ausubel, Jon Beckwith, and Kaaren Janssen, "The Politics of Genetic Engineering: Who Decides Who's Defective?" *Psychology Today,* June 1974, p. 40.

16. "Protection to Posterity in Relation to Social Politics," *Journal of the American Medical Association* 78 (February 11, 1922): 448.

17. T. Ferguson Rodger, "Attitudes Toward Abortion," *American Journal of Psychiatry* 125 (December 1968): 808.

18. "Indications for Abortion and the Law," p. 1810.

19. Mary S. Calderone, ed. *Abortion in the United States* (New York: Hoeber-Harper, 1958), pp. 183-184.

20. "Abortion and Race Hygiene," *Journal of the American Medical Association* 105 (July 20, 1935): 213.

21. "Extract from the Testimony of Prosecution Witness Brieder," *Trials of War Criminals Before the Nuernberg Military Tribunals,* 15 vols. (Washington D.C.: U.S. Government Printing Office, 1950), 4: 1088.

22. "Interruption of Pregnancy from Eugenic Indications," *Journal of the American Medical Association* 86 (February 27, 1926): 639; "Birth Control," *Journal of the American Medical Association* 92 (January 26, 1929): 330.

23. "Circular, Signed by Kaltenbrunner, 9 June 1943, Concerning Interruption of Pregnancy of Female Eastern Workers," *Trials of War Criminals,* 4: 1078.

24. Renata Laxova, "Prenatal Diagnosis of Genetic Diseases," *Comprehensive Therapy* 6 (December 1980): 66-76.

25. Ibid., p. 74.

26. Ibid.

27. "Abortion and Race Hygiene," p. 212.

28. Clarissa Henry and Marc Hillel, *Of Pure Blood,* trans. Eric Mossbacher (New York: McGraw-Hill, 1976), p. 177.

29. "Account of an Interministerial Conference held May 27, 1941, at the Ministry of the Interior of the Reich," NG-844.

30. Leon Poliakov, *Harvest of Hate: The Nazi Program for the Destruction of the Jews of Europe,* rev. and exp. ed. (New York: Schocken Books, 1979), p. 273.

31. "Letter from Bormann to Rosenberg, Führer's Headquarters, July 23, 1942," NO-1878.

32. "Abortions on Eastern Workers," *Trials of War Criminals,* 5: 109.

33. "Circular, Signed by Kaltenbrunner," *Trials of War Criminals,* 4: 1077-1079.

34. "Circular Letter from Kaltenbrunner to the Higher SS and Police Leaders, Gestapo Directorates and Criminal Police Directorates, 1 August 1943, Concerning Interruption of Pregnancy of Female Eastern Workers and Polish Women," *Trials of War Criminals,* 4: 1079-1080.

35. "Memorandum from the Labor Office, Katowice, to the RKFDV Branch Office, Katowice, 1 August 1944, Concerning Interruption of Pregnancy of Female Eastern Workers," *Trials of War Criminals,* 4: 1084-1085.

36. "Meeting of the Prussian Council on Health," *Journal of the American Medical Association* 99 (August 20, 1932): 666.

37. "Letter of 30 October 1943, Enclosing Report from the Bayreuth Branch Office of the SD to Dr. Hessler, District Officer for Public Health," *Trials of War Criminals,* 4: 1081-1084.

38. "Letter from the Higher SS and Police Leader Southeast to the RKFDV, Katowice, 29 September 1944, Concerning a Pregnancy Interruption," *Trials of War Criminals,* 4: 1085-1086.

39. E.B. Linton and Robert G. Brame, "Abortion: Should the Physician Be the Conscience of Society?" *Obstetrics and Gynecology* 35 (March 1970): 465.

40. Dr. Paul R. Ehrlich, *The Population Bomb,* rev. ed. (New York: Ballantine Books, 1971), p. 84.

41. Clare Howard, "Probing the Population Problem," *Scholastic Teacher,* April 1973, p. 13.

42. "Abortions on Eastern Workers," *Trials of War Criminals,* 5: 112.

43. Mary Meehan and Elizabeth Moore, "Forced Abortion Suggested at Clinic Owners' Conference," *National Right to Life News,* June 2, 1980, p. 13.

44. Willis, "Abortion Rights: Overruling Neo-Fascists," p. 8.

45. Taussig, *Abortion Spontaneous and Induced,* p. 424.

Chapter 4
Hitler on Abortion

1. "Criteria for the Interruption of Pregnancy," *Journal of the Amercian Medical Association* 102 (January 13, 1934): 144.

2. "Abortion and Race Hygiene," *Journal of the American Medical Association* 105 (July 20, 1935): 212.

3. American College of Obstetricians and Gynecologists, "Statement on Therapeutic Abortion," May 1968; "Therapeutic Abortion," *Proceedings of the American Medical Association House of Delegates* (June 1967): 40-51; "Therapeutic Abortion," *Proceedings of the American Medical Association House of Delegates* (June 1970): 221.

4. Leon Poliakov, *Harvest of Hate: The Nazi Program for the Destruction of the Jews of Europe,* rev. and exp. ed. (New York: Schocken Books, 1979), p. 273.

5. Ibid.

6. Clarissa Henry and Marc Hillel, *Of Pure Blood,* trans. Eric Mossbacher (New York: McGraw-Hill, 1976), p. 148.

7. "Letter from Bormann to Rosenberg, Führer's Headquarters, July 23, 1942," NO-1878.

Chapter 5
Bureaucratic Extermination

1. Henry Friedlander, "Toward a Methodology of Teaching about the Holocaust," *Teachers College Record* 80 (February 1979): 530-531.

2. G.M. Gilbert, *The Psychology of Dictatorship* (New York: The Ronald Press, 1950), p. 246.

3. Miklos Nyiszli, *Auschwitz: A Doctor's Eyewitness Account,* trans. Tibere Kremer and Richard Seaver (New York: Frederick Fell, 1960), pp. 50-52.

4. "Stacy's Day at the Abortion Clinic," *Time*, April 10, 1978, p. 26.

5. Dorothea Kerslake and Donn Casey, "Abortion Induced by Means of the Uterine Aspirator," *Obstetrics and Gynecology* 30 (July 1967): 35.

6. Bernd Naumann, *Auschwitz: A Report on the Proceedings Against Robert Karl Ludwig Mulka and Others Before the Court at Frankfurt,* trans. Jean Steinberg (New York: Frederick A. Praeger Publishers, 1966), pp. 151, 295.

7. Pamela Zekman and Pamela Warrick, "Dr. Ming Kow Hah: Physician of Pain," *Chicago Sun-Times,* November 15, 1978, pp. 1, 4-5.

8. Raul Hilberg, *The Destruction of the European Jews* (Chicago: Quadrangle Books, 1967), p. 555.

9. Olga Lengyel, *Five Chimneys: The Story of Auschwitz* (Chicago and New York: Ziff-Davis, 1947), pp. 68-69.

10. Charles Remsberg and Bonnie Remsberg, "Second Thoughts on Abortion from the Doctor Who Led the Crusade for It," *Good Housekeeping,* March 1976, p. 130.

11. Jean-Francois Steiner, *Treblinka,* trans. Helen Weaver (New York: Simon and Schuster, 1967), pp. 208-209.

12. Herbert McLaughlin, "Clinic Design Emphasizes Restraint to Minimize Patients' Tension," *Modern Hospital,* September 1973, pp. 74-75.

13. Gitta Sereny, *Into That Darkness: From Mercy Killing to Mass Murder* (London: Andre Deutsch, 1974), p. 200.

14. Barbara Grizzutti Harrison, "Now that Abortion is Legal," *McCall's,* November 1973, p. 64.

15. Evelyn Waugh, *The Loved One* (Boston: Little, Brown and Company, 1948).

16. Henri Rosencher, "Medicine in Dachau," *British Medical Journal* 2 (December 21, 1946): 953.

17. Elie A. Cohen, *Human Behaviour in the Concentration Camp,* trans. M.H. Braaksma (London: Jonathan Cape, 1954), p. 261.

18. Pamela Dillett, "Inside an Abortion Clinic," *National Observer,* February 15, 1975, p. 18.

19. Naumann, *Auschwitz,* p. 175.

20. McLaughlin, "Clinic Design Emphasizes Restraint," pp. 74-75.

21. Hilberg, *Destruction of European Jews,* p. 29.

22. Lengyel, *Five Chimneys,* p. 71.

23. "Stacy's Day at the Abortion Clinic," p. 26.

24. "Personal Experience at a Legal Abortion Center," *American Journal of Nursing* 72 (January 1972): 111.

25. Hannah Arendt, *Eichmann in Jerusalem: A Report on the Banality of Evil* (New York: Viking Press, 1963), pp. 22-23.

26. Bruno Bettelheim, Forward to *Auschwitz,* by Miklos Nyiszli, pp. xvi-xvii.

27. Naumann, *Auschwitz,* pp. 78, 138.

28. Ibid., p. 154.

29. Harold M. Schmeck, "Twin Found Defective in Womb Reported Destroyed in Operation," *New York Times,* June 18, 1981, pp. 1, A19.

30. Thomas D. Kerenyi and Usha Chitkara, "Selective Birth in Twin Pregnancy with Discordancy for Down's Syndrome," *New England Journal of Medicine* 304 (June 18, 1981): 1527.

31. Robert E. Petres and Fay Redivine, "Selective Birth in Twin Pregnancy," Correspondence, *New England Journal of Medicine* 35 (November 12, 1981): 1218.

32. "Doctors of the Death Camps," *Time,* June 25, 1979, p. 68.

33. Robert E. Hall, ed., *Abortion in a Changing World,* 2 vols. (New York and London: Columbia University Press, 1970), 2: 109.

34. Max Weber, *From Max Weber: Essays in Sociology,* trans. and ed. Hans H. Gerth and C. Wright Mills (New York: Oxford University Press, 1958), pp. 196-244.

35. "Extract from the Testimony of Walter E. Schmidt," *The Medical Case: Trials of War Criminals Before the Nuernberg Military Tribunals,* 2 vols. (Washington D.C.: U.S. Government Printing Office, 1949), 1: 890.

36. Thomas G. Gulick, "Even Abortionists Having Second Thoughts," *Human Events,* April 12, 1980, pp. 20-21.
37. Earl W. Kinter, ed., *The Hadamar Trial: Trial of Alfons Klein and Others* (London: William Hodge and Company, 1949), pp. 22, 234.
38. "Doctor Convicted in Death of Fetus," *St. Louis Post-Dispatch,* February 16, 1975, p. 14A.
39. Richard L. Rubenstein, *The Cunning of History: Mass Death and the American Future* (New York: Harper & Row, 1975), p. 87.
40. Erich Fromm, *The Anatomy of Human Destructiveness* (New York: Holt, Rinehart and Winston, 1973), pp. 346-347.
41. *Confluence,* January 25, 1981.
42. Erich Fromm, "Man Would as Soon Flee as Fight," *Psychology Today,* August 1973, pp. 39, 41.
43. Robert Jay Lifton, *Death in Life: Survivors of Hiroshima* (New York: Random House, 1967), p. 509.
44. Alexander Mitscherlich and Fred Mielke, *Doctors of Infamy: The Story of the Nazi Medical Crimes,* trans. Heinz Norden (New York: Henry Schuman, 1949), p. 86.
45. Magda Denes, *In Necessity and Sorrow: Life and Death in an Abortion Hospital* (New York: Basic Books, 1976), p. 141.
46. Robert Jay Lifton, "Victims and Executioners," in *Crimes of War,* ed. Richard A. Falk, Gabriel Kolko, and Robert Jay Lifton (New York: Random House, 1971), p. 423.
47. "MDs Shun 16th Week D & E as Reminder of Destroyed Fetus," *Medical Tribune,* January 25, 1978, p. 9.
48. Ibid.
49. Warren M. Hern and Billie Corrigan, "What About Us? Staff Reactions to the D & E Procedure," Paper presented at the Annual Meeting of the Association of Planned Parenthood Physicians, San Diego, California, October 26, 1978, p. 9.
50. Sadja Goldsmith, Nancy B. Kaltreider, and Alan J. Margolis, "Second Trimester Abortion by Dilation and Extraction (D & E): Surgical Techniques and Psychological Reactions," Paper presented at the Annual Meeting of the Association of Planned Parenthood Physicians, Atlanta, Georgia, October 13-14, 1977, p. 6.

Chapter 6
Experimental Barbarities

1. "Letter from Sievers to Rudolf Brandt, 9 February 1942, and Report by Hirt Concerning the Acquisition of Skulls of Jewish-Bolshevik Commissars," *The Medical Case: Trials of War Criminals Before the Nuernberg Military Tribunals,* 2 vols. (Washington D.C.: U.S. Government Printing Office, 1949), 1: 749.
2. "Letter from Goering's Office to Himmler, 8 October 1942, with attached invitation to the Conference on 'Medical Problems Arising from Hardships of Sea and Winter,'" *The Medical Case,* 1: 223-225; "Extracts from Report on the Third Conference East of Consulting Specialists on 24 to 26 May 1943 at the Miliary Academy, Berlin," *The Medical Case,* 1: 378-380; "Extract from 'Clinic and Practice,' Weekly Journal for the Practicing Physician, Regarding Bone Transplantation," *The Medical Case,* 1: 405-407; "Minutes of Conference at the Reich Ministry of Aviation, 20 May 1944, Concerning Methods for Making Sea Water Potable," *The Medical Case,* 1: 448-451.

3. John A. Morris et al., "Measurement of Fetoplacental Blood Volume in the Human Previable Fetus," *American Journal of Obstetrics and Gynecology* 118 (April 1, 1974): 927.

4. Anne Bannon, "'Use of the Fetus' Symposium," *Missouri Citizens for Life Newspaper,* November 1980, p. 3.

5. *Cumulated Index Medicus,* Subject Index, vols. 21 (1980) and 22 (1981) (Washington D.C.: U.S. Government Printing Office, 1980 and 1981).

6. Stanley Henshaw et al., "Abortion in the United States, 1978-1979," *Family Planning Perspectives* 13 (January/February 1981): 17.

7. National Commission for the Protection of Human Subjects of Biomedical and Behavioral Research, *Research on the Human Fetus: Report and Recommendations* (Washington D.C.: Department of Health, Education, and Welfare, 1975), pp. 6, 74.

8. "Letter from Rascher to Himmler, 15 May 1941, Concerning High-Altitude Experiments on Human Beings," *The Medical Case,* 1: 142; "Letter from Rascher to Himmler, 5 April 1942, and Report, undated, on High-Altitude Experiments," *The Medical Case,* 1: 145.

9. "Minutes of Conference at the Reich Ministry of Aviation, 20 May 1944, Concerning Methods for Making Sea Water Potable," *The Medical Case,* 1: 450; "Letter from Schroeder to Himmler and Grawitz, 7 June 1944, Requesting Subjects for Sea-Water Experiments," *The Medical Case,* 1: 452; "Extract from the Final Plea for Defendant Schroeder," *The Medical Case,* 1: 435.

10. "Extract from the Closing Brief Against Defendant Gebhardt," *The Medical Case,* 1: 360-361.

11. "Letter from Rascher to Himmler, 11 May 1942, and Secret Report Concerning High-Altitude Experiments," *The Medical Case,* 1: 152-154.

12. E. Holzloehner, S. Rascher, and E. Finke, "Report of 10 October 1942, On Cooling Experiments on Human Beings," *The Medical Case,* 1: 226-242.

13. Bjorn Westin, Rune Nyberg, and Goran Enhorning, "A Technique for Perfusion of the Previable Fetus," *Acta Paediatrica* 47 (July 1958): 339-349.

14. Geoffrey Chamberlain, "An Artificial Placenta: The Development of an Extracorporeal System for Maintenance of Immature Infants with Respiratory Problems," *American Journal of Obstetrics and Gynecology* 100 (March 1, 1968): 624.

15. "Extracts from the Review of the Proceedings of the General Military Court in the Case of the United States vs. Weiss, Ruppert, et al., held at Dachau, Germany," *The Medical Case,* 1: 291-294.

16. Timothy Harper, "Is Fetal Research Inhibited by Fight Over Abortion?" *St. Louis Post-Dispatch,* November 15, 1981, p. 31.

17. "United States vs. Carl Krauch et al.," *The Farben Case: Trials of War Criminals Before the Nuernberg Military Tribunals,* vols. 7 and 8 (Washington D.C.: U.S. Government Printing Office, 1952), 7: 113.

18. Harper, "Is Fetal Research Inhibited by Fight Over Abortion?" p. 31.

19. "Particulars of Defendants' Participation in Slavery and Mass Murder," *The Farben Case,* 7: 54-55.

20. Niels H. Lauersen and Kathleen H. Wilson, "Midtrimester Abortion Induced with a Single Intra-Amniotic Instillation of Prostaglandin F2a," *American Journal of Obstetrics and Gynecology* 118 (January 15, 1974): 210-217.

21. Holzloehner, Rascher, and Finke, "On Cooling Experiments on Human Beings," pp. 228-230, 236.

22. Goran Enhorning and Bjorn Westin, "Experimental Studies of the Human Fetus in Prolonged Asphyxia," *Acta Physiologica Scandinavica* 31 (1954): 361-372.

23. Sigmund Rascher, "First Interim Report on the Low-Pressure Chamber Experiments in the Concentration Camp of Dachau," *The Medical Case,* 1: 146.

24. Chamberlain, "An Artificial Placenta," p. 624.

25. Miklos Nyiszli, *Auschwitz: A Doctor's Eyewitness Account,* trans. Tibere Kremer and Richard Seaver (New York: Frederick Fell, 1960), p. 175.

26. Robert S. Galen et al., "Fetal Pathology and Mechanism of Fetal Death in Saline Induced Abortion: A Study of 143 Gestations and Critical Review of the Literature," *American Journal of Obstetrics and Gynecology* 120 (October 1, 1974): 347-355.

27. Rascher, "First Interim Report on Low-Pressure Experiments," pp. 146-147.

28. Robert C. Goodlin, "Cutaneous Respiration in a Fetal Incubator," *American Journal of Obstetrics and Gynecology* 86 (July 1, 1963): 574.

29. Holzloehner, Rascher, and Finke, "On Cooling Experiments on Human Beings," pp. 229, 239.

30. Bela A. Resch et al., "Comparison of Spontaneous Contraction Rates of In Situ and Isolated Fetal Hearts in Early Pregnancy," *American Journal of Obstetrics and Gynecology* 118 (January 1, 1974): 73-74.

31. "Letter from Sievers to Brandt and Report by Hirt Concerning Acquisition of Skulls," *The Medical Case,* 1: 749.

32. Peter A.J. Adam et al., "Oxidation of Glucose and D-B-Oh-Butyrate by the Early Human Fetal Brain," *Acta Paediatrica Scandinavica* 64 (January 1975): 18.

33. Bernhard Schreiber, *The Men Behind Hitler: A German Warning to the World,* trans. H.R. Martindale (Les Mureaux: La Haye-Mureaux, n.d.), p. 56.

34. Naomi Wade, "Aborted Babies Kept Alive for Bizarre Experiments," *National Examiner,* August 19, 1980, pp. 20-21.

35. "Letter from Rascher to Himmler and Secret Report Concerning High-Altitude Experiments," *The Medical Case,* 1: 154.

36. J. Fishman et al., "Catechol Estrogen Formation by the Human Fetal Brain and Pituitary," *Journal of Clinical Endocrinology and Metabolism* 42 (1976): 177-180.

37. "Extract from the Closing Brief Against Defendant Rudolf Brandt," *The Medical Case,* 1: 702; "Covering Letter from Brack to Himmler, 28 March 1941, with Report on Experiments Concerning Sterilization and Castration by X-Rays," *The Medical Case,* 1: 720.

38. F.I. Reyes, J.S.D. Winter, and C. Faiman, "Studies on Human Sexual Development. I. Fetal Gonadol and Adrenal Sex Steroids," *Journal of Clinical Endocrinology and Metabolism* 37 (July 1973): 74-78.

39. "Affidavit of Mrs. Zdenka Nedvedova-Nejedla," *The Medical Case,* 1: 401.

40. "A Thymus for Maggie," *Time,* February 28, 1972, p. 54.

41. Mary Anne Warren, Commentary on "Can the Fetus be an Organ Farm?" *Hastings Center Report,* October 1978, p. 23.

42. Schreiber, *The Men Behind Hitler,* p. 56.

43. Wade, "Aborted Babies Kept Alive for Bizarre Experiments," p. 20.

44. Aziz, *Doctors of Death,* 3: 205.

45. Ouoted in Dr. and Mrs. J.C. Willke, *Handbook on Abortion,* rev. ed. (Cincinnatti, Ohio: Hayes Publishing Company, 1975), p. 131.

46. "Extracts from the Testimony of Defendant Rose," *The Medical Case,* 2: 70.

47. Willard Gaylin and Marc Lappe, "Fetal Politics: The Debate on Experimenting with the Unborn," *Atlantic,* May 1975, pp. 69-70.

48. Gisella Pearl, *I Was a Doctor in Auschwitz* (New York: International Universities Press, 1948), p. 74.

49. Joseph Wechsberg, ed., *The Murderers Among Us: The Wiesenthal Memoirs* (New York: McGraw-Hill, 1967), p. 315.

50. David H. Sherman, "Salting Out: Experience in 9,000 Cases," *Journal of Reproductive Medicine* 14 (June 1975): 241.
51. Wechsberg, *The Murderers Among Us,* p. 315.
52. Helen I. Glueck et al., "Hypertonic Saline-Induced Abortion: Correlation of Fetal Death with Disseminated Intravascular Coagulation," *Journal of the American Medical Association* 225 (July 2, 1973): 28; Sherman, "Salting Out," p. 241.
53. Wechsberg, *The Murderers Among Us,* p. 315.
54. "Extract from a Sworn Statement by Dr. Erwin Schuler (Ding), 20 July 1945, Concerning Euthanasia with Phenol Injection," *The Medical Case,* 1: 687.
55. Galen et al., "Fetal Pathology and Mechanism of Fetal Death," pp. 353-354.
56. "Extract from Statement by Dr. Erwin Schuler (Ding) Concerning Euthanasia with Phenol," *The Medical Case,* 1: 687.
57. Galen et al., "Fetal Pathology and Mechanism of Fetal Death," p. 352.
58. "Extract from the Field Interrogation of Kurt Gerstein, 26 April 1945, Describing the Mass Gassing of Jews and Other Undesirables," *The Medical Case,* 1: 868-869.
59. G.M. Gilbert, *The Psychology of Dictatorship* (New York: The Ronald Press, 1950), p. 246.
60. "Avoiding Tough Abortion Complication: A Live Baby," *Medical World News,* November 14, 1977, p. 83.
61. George Stroh and Alan R. Hinman, "Reported Live Births Following Induced Abortion: Two and One-Half Years' Experience in Upstate New York," *American Journal of Obstetrics and Gynecology* 126 (September 1, 1976): 83-90.
62. Liz Jeffries and Rick Edmonds, "Abortion: The Dreaded Complication," *Philadelphia Inquirer,* August 2, 1981, p. 16.
63. Ibid., p. 17.
64. "Extract from the Closing Brief Against Defendant Sievers: Freezing Experiments," *The Medical Case,* 1: 203.
65. "Post-Abortion Fetal Study Stirs Storm," *Medical World News,* June 8, 1973, p. 21.
66. "Affidavit of Mrs. Zdenka Nedvedova-Nejedla, M.D., of Prague, Concerning Experimental Operations Conducted on Fellow Inmates at Ravensbrueck Concentration Camp," *The Medical Case,* 1: 401-402.
67. Wade, "Aborted Babies Kept Alive for Bizarre Experiments," p. 20.
68. H.M.I. Liley with Beth Day, *Modern Motherhood: Pregnancy, Childbirth and the Newborn Baby,* rev. ed. (New York: Random House, 1969), p. 50.
69. For an excellent discussion of the latest scientific findings on the capacity of unborn children to feel pain, see John T. Noonan, "The Experience of Pain by the Unborn," in *New Perspectives on Human Abortion,* ed. Thomas W. Hilgers, Dennis J. Horan and David Mall (Frederick, Maryland: University Publications of America: Aletheia Books, 1981), pp. 205-216.
70. Wade, "Aborted Babies Kept Alive for Bizarre Experiments," p. 20.
71. "Extracts from the Testimony of Prosecution Witness Jadwiga Dzido," *The Medical Case,* 1: 382.
72. "The Law Pertaining to the Protection of Animals," *Journal of the American Medical Association* 102 (February 17, 1934): 551-552.
73. "Opening Statement of the Prosection by Brigadier General Telford Taylor, 9 December 1946," *The Medical Case,* 1: 71.
74. "Transportation, Sale, and Handling of Certain Animals," *United States Code,* 12 vols. (Washington D.C.: U.S. Government Printing Office, 1977), 1: 1426.
75. Peter Singer, "Bioethics: The Case of the Fetus," *New York Review of Books,* November 11, 1976, p. 34.
76. "Affidavit of Defendant Fischer, 19 November 1946, Concerning Sulfanilamide Experiments Conducted in the Concentration Camp Ravensbrueck," *The Medical Case,* 1: 375.

77. "Post-Abortion Fetal Study Stirs Storm," p. 21.

78. William L. Shirer, *The Rise and Fall of the Third Reich: A History of Nazi Germany* (New York: Simon and Schuster, 1960), p. 979.

79. Douglas Johnson, "House Votes Funding Ban on Fetal Experimentation," *National Right to Life News,* October 14, 1982, pp. 1, 10; Paul A. Fisher, "House Bans Fetal Experimentation," *The Wanderer,* October 14, 1982, pp. 1, 7.

Chapter 7
The Commercialization of Killing

1. Karl Binding and Alfred Hoche, *The Release of the Destruction of Life Devoid of Value* (Leipzig, Germany: Felix Meiner, 1920), compiled by Robert L. Sassone (Santa Ana, Calif.: A Life Quality Paperback, 1975), pp. 35-36.

2. Ibid., p. 36.

3. "Legalized Abortion and the Public Health," Report of a Study by a Committee of the Institute of Medicine, National Academy of Sciences, May 1975, p. 107.

4. Ibid.

5. Philippe Aziz, *Doctors of Death,* trans. Edourd Bizub and Philip Haentzler, 4 vols. (Geneva, Switzerland: Ferni Publishers, 1976), 4: 133.

6. "Genetic Testing Could Curb Handicaps, Doctors Say," *St. Louis Globe-Democrat,* February 14, 1978, p. 6A.

7. Hanns Lohr, "The Physician Must Come to Terms with the Irrational," in *Nazi Culture: Intellectual, Cultural and Social Life in the Third Reich,* ed. George L. Mosse, trans. Salvator Attanasio et al. (New York: Grosset & Dunlap, 1966), p. 233.

8. Ann Landers, "More of Doctor's Views on 'Human Life,'" *St. Louis Post-Dispatch,* September 9, 1981, p. 2F.

9. "Extracts from the Closing Brief for Defendant Sievers," *The Medical Case: Trials of War Criminals Before the Nuernberg Military Tribunals,* 2 vols. (Washington D.C.: U.S. Government Printing Office, 1949), 1: 209.

10. Mark Julienne, "Suddenly I'm a Legal Abortionist," *Medical Economics* 47 (November 23, 1970): 168.

11. Pamela Zekman and Pamela Warrick, "Meet the Profiteers: Men Who Profit From Women's Pain," *Chicago Sun-Times,* November 13, 1978, p. 4.

12. Pamela Zekman and Karen Koshner, "Job Funds Withheld From Abortion Clinic," *Chicago Sun-Times,* November 14, 1978, p. 3.

13. Lorraine Bennett, "Abortion Clinic Doctor: 'Applying Principles of Good Business,'" *Los Angeles Times* (Orange County Edition), October 16, 1977, p. 1.

14. Raul Hilberg, *The Destruction of the European Jews* (Chicago: Quadrangle Books, 1967), pp. 567-568.

15. "The Abortion Play," *Business Week,* February 3, 1973, p. 53.

16. Joseph Borkin, *The Crime and Punishment of I.G. Farben* (New York: The Free Press, 1978), p. 123.

17. The following are just some of the medical journal articles which acknowledge indebtedness to the Upjohn Company for financial and/or other support in carrying out prostaglandin-induced killing and its experimental dividends: W.E. Brenner et al., "Coagulation Changes During Abortion Induced by Prostaglandin F2a," *American Journal of Obstetrics and Gynecology* 117 (December 15, 1973): 1080-1087; Niels H. Lauersen and Kathleen H. Wilson, "Midtrimester Abortion Induced with a Single Intra-Amniotic Instillation of Prostaglandin F2a," *American Journal of Obstetrics and Gynecology* 118 (January 15, 1974): 210-217; Arthur G. Shapiro, "Extraovular Prostaglandin F2a for Early Midtrimester Abortion," *American Journal of Obstetrics and Gynecology* 121 (February 1, 1975): 333-336.

18. Charles W. Theisen, "Upjohn Prices Soar with Publicity of New 'Abortion Kit,'" *Detroit News,* September 10, 1978, p. 2E.
19. Filip Friedman, *This Was Oswiecim: The Story of a Murder Camp,* trans. Joseph Leftwich (London: The United Jewish Relief Appeal, 1946), p. 64.
20. Michael Litchfield and Susan Kentish, *Babies for Burning: The Abortion Business in Britain* (London: Serpentine Press, 1974), p. 146.
21. Nick Thimmesch, "Bizarre Cases of Abortions Gone Awry," *St. Louis Globe-Democrat,* June 19-20, 1982, p. 5B.
22. The Jewish Black Book Committee, *The Black Book: The Nazi Crime Against the Jewish People* (New York: Duell, Sloan and Pearce, 1946), p. 285.
23. John Boland, "Chicago Firm Offers Embryos, Human Organ 'Paper Weights,'" *The Wanderer,* June 10, 1976, p. 1.
24. Miklos Nyiszli, *Auschwitz: A Doctor's Eyewitness Account,* trans. Tibere Kremer and Richard Seaver (New York: Frederick Fell, 1960), p. 54.
25. Willard Cates, "For a Graduated Scale of Fees for Legal Abortion," *Family Planning Perspectives* 12 (July/August 1980): 219-221.
26. "Affidavit of Franz Blaha, November 25, 1945," *Nazi Conspiracy and Aggression,* 11 vols. (Washington D.C.: U.S. Government Printing Office, 1946), 5: 952.
27. "PW Intelligence Bulletin No. 2/20, December 19, 1944," *Nazi Conspiracy and Agression,* 6: 122-123.
28. B.D. Colen, "Hospital Got Cash for Fetuses," *Washington Post,* February 29, 1976, pp. B1, B11.
29. Walter C. Alvarez, "Death with Dignity," *The Humanist,* September/October 1971, p. 12.
30. "Florida Legislator Says People Favor Bill to Let Mongoloids and Terminal Patients Die," *The Sun,* January 11, 1973, p. A3.
31. Memorandum on Additional Cost-Saving Initiatives, to Secretary Joseph A. Califano from Robert A. Derzon, Health Care Financing Administration, Department of Health, Education and Welfare, June 4, 1977, pp. 8-9.

Chapter 8
From Abortion to Infanticide

1. Leo Alexander, "Medical Science Under Dictatorship," *New England Journal of Medicine* 241 (July 14, 1949): 44.
2. Joseph Fletcher, "Ethics and Euthanasia," in *To Live and To Die: When, Why, and How,* ed. Robert H. Williams (New York: Springer-Verlag, 1973), p. 116; Joseph Fletcher, "Infanticide and the Ethics of Loving Concern," in *Infanticide and the Value of Life,* ed. Marvin Kohl (Buffalo, New York; Prometheus Books, 1978), p. 17.
3. Joseph Fletcher, "The Right to Die: A Theologian Comments," *Atlantic Monthly,* April 1968, pp. 63-64.
4. Michael Tooley, "Abortion and Infanticide," *Philosophy & Public Affairs* 2 (Fall 1972): 37-65.
5. James D. Watson, "Children From The Laboratory," *Prism,* May 1973, p. 13.
6. Ibid.
7. Cited by Francis A. Schaeffer and C. Everett Koop, *Whatever Happened to the Human Race?* (Old Tappan, New Jersey: Fleming H. Revell, 1979), p. 73.
8. Kenneth Vaux, "Danville's Siamese Twins Test Society's Deepest Beliefs," *Chicago Tribune,* June 28, 1981, Section 2, p. 1.
9. Norman Podhoretz, "Beyond ZPG," *Commentary,* May 1972, pp. 6-8.

10. "The Right of Putting Incurable Patients Out of the Way" and "Demand of the Independent Social Democrats that the Penalties for Abortion Be Removed," *Journal of the American Medical Association* 75 (November 6, 1920): 1283.

11. "The Question of Legalized Abortion," *Journal of the American Medical Association* 93 (September 21, 1929): 935; "Indications for Abortion and the Law," *Journal of the American Medical Association* 96 (May 23, 1931): 1810; "Criteria for the Interruption of Pregnancy," *Journal of the American Medical Association* 102 (January 13, 1934): 144.

12. "Letter from Hitler to Karl Brandt and Bouhler, 1 September 1939, Charging Them with the Execution of Euthanasia," *The Medical Case: Trials of War Criminals Before the Nuernberg Military Tribunals,* 2 vols. (Washington D.C.: U.S. Government Printing Office, 1949), 1: 848.

13. Roe v. Wade, 410 U.S. 163-165 (1973); Doe v. Bolton, 410 U.S. 192 (1973).

14. Eugene F. Diamond, *This Curette for Hire* (Chicago: ACTA Foundation, 1977), p. 124.

15. Leon Poliakov, *Harvest of Hate: The Nazi Program for the Destruction of the Jews of Europe,* rev. and exp. ed. (New York: Schocken Books, 1979), p. 274.

16. James F. Gustafson, "Mongolism, Parental Desires and the Right to Life," *Perspectives in Biology and Medicine* 16 (Summer 1973): 531.

17. Alexander Mitscherlich and Fred Mielke, *Doctors of Infamy: The Story of the Nazi Medical Crimes,* trans. Heinz Norden (New York: Henry Schuman, 1949), p. 101.

18. James Bopp, "The Death of Infant Doe," *National Right to Life News,* May 20, 1982, pp. 1, 8.

19. Claudia MacLachlan and Roger Signor, "Baby Starvation Illegal Here, Rothman Says," *St. Louis Post-Dispatch,* May 21, 1982, p. 6A.

20. Earl W. Kinter, ed., *The Hadamar Trial: Trial of Alfons Klein and Others* (London: William Hodge, 1949), p. 102.

21. "Extracts from the Closing Brief for Defendant Karl Brandt," *The Medical Case,* 1: 834.

22. James Lachs, "Humane Treatment and the Treatment of Humans," *New England Journal of Medicine* 294 (April 8, 1976): 838-840.

23. Nancy Koster, "An Open Letter to Abortion Advocates," *National Right to Life News,* April 22, 1982, p. 2.

24. Ernst Haeckel, *The Wonders of Life: A Popular Study of Biological Philosophy,* trans. Joseph McCabe (London: Watts and Company, 1904), pp. 118-124.

25. "Severely Disabled Newborn Like Horse with Broken Leg, Philosopher Says," *National Right to Life News,* March 11, 1982, p. 4.

26. Kinter, *Hadamar Trial,* p. 177.

27. Diane Brozek, "Infant Euthanasia: Crime or Compassion?" *Milwaukee Journal,* June 15, 1981, p. 1.

28. Anne Bannon, "The Case of the Bloomington Baby," *Human Life Review* 8 (Fall 1982): 64.

29. Ibid., p. 68.

Chapter 9
Racist Foundations of Violence Against Jews and the Unborn

1. George L. Mosse, *Toward the Final Solution: A History of European Racism* (New York: Howard Fertig, 1978), p. 3.

2. Comte Arthur de Gobineau, *The Inequality of Human Races,* trans. Adrian Collins (New York: Howard Fertig, 1967).

3. Donauzeitung (Belgrade), July 3, 1943, p. 3, cited by Raul Hilberg, *The Destruction of the European Jews* (Chicago: Quadrangle Books, 1967), p. 47.

4. Arnold Beichman, "Holocaust: Why Did it Happen in Germany?" *Boston Globe,* December 30, 1979.

5. Alfred D. Low, *Jews in the Eyes of the Germans: From the Enlightenment to Imperial Germany* (Philadelphia: Institute for the Study of Human Issues, 1979); Jacob Katz, *From Prejudice to Destruction: Anti-Semitism, 1700-1933* (Cambridge, Mass.: Harvard University Press, 1980).

6. "The Battle Over Abortion," *Time,* April 6, 1981, p. 23.

7. Bernard Weinraub, "Senator Agrees to Extend Hearings on Abortion Bill," *New York Times,* April 25, 1981, p. 7.

8. Hannah Arendt, *The Origins of Totalitarianism* (New York: A Harvest/HBJ Book, 1973), p. 290.

9. Ernst Fraenkel, *The Dual State: A Contribution to the Theory of Dictatorship,* trans. E.A. Shils with Edith Lowenstein and Klaus Knorr (New York: Oxford University Press, 1941), p. 95.

10. Roe v. Wade, 410 U.S. 158 (1973).

11. Mosse, *Toward the Final Solution,* p. 210.

12. Sierra Club v. Morton, 405 U.S. 741-752 (1971); also cited by Dennis J. Horan, John D. Gorby and Thomas W. Hilgers, "Abortion and the Supreme Court: Death Becomes a Way of Life," in *Abortion and Social Justice,* ed. Thomas W. Hilgers and Dennis J. Horan (New York: Sheed & Ward, 1972), pp. 302-303.

13. Mosse, *Toward the Final Solution,* p. 109.

14. Mary Anne Warren, Commentary on "Can the Fetus Be an Organ Farm?" *Hastings Center Report,* October 1978, p. 23.

15. Paul W. Massing, *Rehearsal for Destruction: A Study of Political Anti-Semitism in Imperial Germany* (New York: Harper & Brothers, 1949), p. 84.

16. C.C. Aronsfeld, "The Nazi Design Was Extermination, Not Emigration," *Patterns of Prejudice* 9 (May-June 1975): 22.

17. "Letter from Sievers to Rudolf Brandt, 9 February 1942, and Report by Hirt Concerning the Acquisition of Skulls of Jewish-Bolshevik Commissars," *The Medical Case: Trials of War Criminals Before the Nuernberg Military Tribunals,* 2 vols. (Washington D.C.: U.S. Government Printing Office, 1949), 1: 749.

18. Amitai Etzioni, "A Review of *The Ethics of Fetal Research,*" *Society,* March/April 1976, p. 72.

19. Joseph Fletcher, "Ethics and Euthanasia," in *To Live and To Die: When, Why, and How,* ed. Robert H. Williams (New York: Springer-Verlag, 1973), p. 116.

20. Benjamin Thamrong and North Jersey Women's Health Organization v. James Duggan, Transcript of Deposition of Benjamin Thamrong, Superior Court of New Jersey Law Division, Passaic County Docket No. L 13357-77, October 10, 1978, p. 126.

21. Clarissa Henry and Marc Hillel, *Of Pure Blood,* trans. Eric Mossbacher (New York: McGraw-Hill, 1976), p. 32.

22. Norma Rosen, "Between Guilt and Gratification: Abortion Doctors Reveal Their Feelings," *New York Times Magazine,* April 17, 1977, p. 75.

23. Warren, Commentary on "Can the Fetus Be an Organ Farm?" pp. 23-24.

24. Mosse, *Toward the Final Solution,* p. 22.

25. Ibid., p. 68.

26. Arendt, *Origins of Totalitarianism,* p. 194.

27. "Hermann Ahlwardt on the Semitic Versus the Teutonic Race," in *Rehearsal for Destruction* by Paul W. Massing, pp. 300-305.

28. Karl Binding and Alfred Hoche, *The Release of the Destruction of Life Devoid of Value* (Leipzig, Germany: Felix Meiner, 1920), compiled by Robert L. Sassone (Santa Ana, Calif.: A Life Quality Paperback, 1975), p. 38.

29. Gitta Sereny, *Into That Darkness: From Mercy Killing to Mass Murder* (London: Andre Deutsch, 1974), p. 201.

30. Leon Poliakov, *Harvest of Hate: The Nazi Program for the Destruction of the Jews of Europe,* rev. and exp. ed. (New York: Schocken Books, 1979), p. 129.

31. Philippe Aziz, *Doctors of Death,* trans. Edouard Bizub and Philip Haentzler, 4 vols. (Geneva, Switzerland: Ferni Publishers, 1976), 1: 232.

32. David Granfield, *The Abortion Decision* (Garden City, New York: Doubleday/Image, 1971), pp. 32-33.

33. Howard D. Kibel, "Staff Reactions to Abortion: A Psychiatrist's View," *Obstetrics and Gynecology* 39 (January 1972): 131.

34. Rosen, "Between Guilt and Gratification," p. 75.

35. Warren, Commentary on "Can the Fetus Be an Organ Farm?" pp. 23-24.

36. Mosse, *Toward the Final Solution,* p. 117.

37. George L. Mosse, *The Crisis of German Ideology: Intellectual Origins of the Third Reich* (New York: Grosset & Dunlap, 1964), p. 143.

38. Havelock Ellis, *Studies in the Psychology of Sex,* vol. 6, *Sex in Relation to Society* (Philadelphia: F.A. Davis, 1910), p. 605.

39. Katz, *From Prejudice to Destruction,* p. 60.

40. The Freeman Report, Cable News Network, Washington D.C., September 9, 1981.

41. Katz, *From Prejudice to Destruction,* pp. 149-150.

42. Robert E. Hall, ed., *Abortion in a Changing World,* 2 vols. (New York and London: Columbia University Press, 1970), 1: 175.

43. "Hermann Ahlwardt on the Semitic Versus the Teutonic Race," in *Rehearsal for Destruction* by Paul W. Massing, pp. 300-305.

44. John F. McDermott and Walter F. Char, "Abortion Repeal in Hawaii: An Unexpected Crisis in Patient Care," *American Journal of Orthopsychiatry* 41 (July 1971): 623.

45. Adolf Hitler, *Mein Kampf* (Boston: Houghton Mifflin, 1939), p. 419.

46. Boston Women's Health Book Collective, *Our Bodies, Ourselves: A Book By and For Women* (New York: Simon and Schuster, 1973), p. 144.

47. "Report prepared by Alfred Wetzel, November 25, 1939, in collabortion with Hecht, Director of the Section for Ethnic Germans and Minorities," PS-560.

48. Sereny, *Into That Darkness,* p. 201.

49. William J. Sweeny with Barbara Lang Stern, *Woman's Doctor: A Year in the Life of an Obstetrician-Gynecologist* (New York: William Morrow, 1973), p. 207.

50. McDermott and Char, "Abortion Repeal in Hawaii," p. 623; Walter F. Char and John F. McDermott, "Abortions and Acute Identity Crisis in Nurses," *American Journal of Psychiatry* 128 (February 1972): 956.

51. "'Donahue' Show Confirms Nuns' Pro-Abortion Stand," *The Wanderer,* July 8, 1982, p. 8.

52. Poliakov, *Harvest of Hate,* p. 112.

53. Mosse, *Toward the Final Solution,* p. 196.

54. Poliakov, *Harvest of Hate,* p. 128.

55. Ibid., p. 115.

56. Sereny, *Into That Darkness,* p. 201.

57. Dorothea Kerslake and Donn Casey, "Abortion Induced by Means of the Uterine Aspirator," *Obstetrics and Gynecology* 30 (July 1967): 37, 43.

58. Garrett Hardin, "Abortion—Or Compulsory Pregnancy?" *Journal of Marriage and the Family* 30 (May 1968): 251.

59. Cited by Dr. and Mrs. J.C. Willke, *Handbook on Abortion,* rev. ed. (Cincinnati, Ohio: Hayes Publishing Company, 1975), p. 131.

60. Naomi Wade, "Aborted Babies Kept Alive for Bizarre Experiments," *National Examiner,* August 19, 1980, pp. 20-21.

61. Nick Thimmesch, "Bizarre Cases of Abortions Gone Awry," *St. Louis Globe-Democrat,* June 19-20, 1982, p. 5B; Nick Thimmesch, "Investigation Underway into Storage of 1,000 Aborted Fetuses," *National Right to Life News,* February 22, 1982, pp. 1, 8.

62. "Opening Statement of the Prosecution: Nazi Doctrine of Superior and Inferior Races," *Trials of War Criminals Before the Nuernberg Military Tribunals,* 15 vols. (Washington D.C.: U.S. Government Printing Office, 1950), 4: 35.

63. Hilberg, *Destruction of European Jews,* p. 8.

64. Helen Fein, *Accounting for Genocide: National Responses and Jewish Victimization During the Holocaust* (New York: The Free Press, 1979), p. 8.

65. Hardin, "Abortion—Or Compulsory Pregnancy?" pp. 250-251.

66. Hilberg, *Destruction of European Jews,* p. 669.

67. Anthony Lewis, "After Auschwitz," *New York Times,* October 2, 1980, p. A23.

68. "Pittsburgh Talk Show Host Backs Prolife Cause," *National Right to Life News,* June 1, 1981, p. 9.

Chapter 10
The Semantics of Mass Destruction

1. Robert K. Merton, "The Self-Fulfilling Prophecy," *Social Theory and Social Structure,* rev. and enl. ed. (Glencoe, Ill.: The Free Press, 1957), pp. 421-436.

2. "A New Ethic for Medicine and Society," *California Medicine* 113 (September 1970): 67-68.

3. Ibid.

4. Leo Alexander, "The Molding of Personality Under Dictatorship: The Importance of the Destructive Drives in the Social-Psychological Structure of Nazism," *Journal of Criminal Law and Criminology* 40 (May-June 1948-1949): 11.

5. Raul Hilberg, *The Destruction of the European Jews* (Chicago: Quadrangle Books, 1967), p. 216.

6. Germaine Tillion, *Ravensbrück: An Eyewitness Account of a Woman's Concentration Camp,* trans. Gerald Satterwhite (Garden City, New York: Anchor Press/Doubleday, 1975), p. 116.

7. Raul Hilberg, "Confronting the Moral Implications of the Holocaust," *Social Education* 42 (April 1978): 275.

8. Leonide M. Tanner, ed., "Developing Professional Parameters: Nursing and Social Work Roles in the Care of the Induced Abortion Patient," *Clinical Obstetrics and Gynecology* 14 (December 1971): 1271.

9. Paul Marx, *The Death Peddlers: War on the Unborn* (Collegeville, Minn.: St. John's University Press, 1971), p. 21.

10. Raymond Phillips, ed., *The Belsen Trial: Trial of Josef Kramer Defendant and Forty-Four Others* (London: William Hodge & Company, 1949), p. 717.

11. Ibid., pp. 184, 717.

12. Lester R. Brown and Kathleen Newland, "Abortion Liberalization: A Worldwide Trend," A Worldwatch Institute Paper, 1976, pp. 1-7.

13. Phillips, *The Belsen Trial,* p. 73.

14. Thomas D. Kerenyi and Usha Chitkara, "Selective Birth in Twin Pregnancy with Discordancy for Down's Syndrome," *New England Journal of Medicine* 304 (June 18, 1981): 1525-1527.

15. "A Choice in the Womb," *Newsweek,* June 29, 1981, p. 86.

16. Hilberg, *Destruction of European Jews,* p. 441.

17. David A. Edelman, William E. Brenner and Gary S. Berger, "The Effectiveness and Complications of Abortion by Dilatation and Vacuum Aspiration Versus Dilatation and Rigid Metal Curettage," *American Journal of Obstetrics and Gyencology* 119 (June 15, 1974): 474-475.

18. Jewish Black Book Committee, *The Black Book: The Nazi Crime Against the Jewish People* (New York: Duell, Sloan and Pearce, 1946), p. 329.

19. *Assignment Life,* New Liberty Films, Burbank, California, 1980.

20. Hilberg, *Destruction of European Jews,* p. 333.

21. "Abortion: Questions and Answers," Brochure, National Abortion Rights Action League, New York City.

22. Hilberg, *Destruction of European Jews,* p. 445.

23. Thomas D. Kerenyi, Nathan Mendelman and David H. Sherman, "Five Thousand Consecutive Saline Inductions," *American Journal of Obstetrics and Gynecology* 116 (July 1, 1973): 595.

24. *Krakauer Zeitung,* December 31, 1940/January 1, 1941, GG page, cited by Hilberg, *Destruction of European Jews,* p. 140.

25. A. Peretz et al., "Evacuation of the Gravid Uterus by Negative Pressure (Suction Evacuation)," *American Journal of Obstetrics and Gynecology* 98 (May 1, 1967), p. 18.

26. Summary of *Generalgouvernement* Health Conference, July 9, 1943, *Frank Diary,* PS-2233.

27. Thomas F. Dillion et al., "The Efficacy of Prostaglandin F2a in Second-trimester Abortion: Coagulation and Hormonal Aspects," *American Journal of Obstetrics and Gynecology* 118 (May 1, 1974): 690.

28. "A Total Cleanup": Himmler's Order, July 19, 1942, cited by Lucy S. Dawidowicz, ed., *A Holocaust Reader* (New York: Behrman House, 1976), p. 97.

29. Planned Parenthood of New York City, *Abortion: A Woman's Guide* (New York: Abelard-Schuman, 1973), p. 22.

30. Meister der Gendarmerie Fritz Jacob to OGruf. Rudolf Querner, May 5, 1942, NO-5654.

31. Cathy Yarbrough, "Abortion Big Business in Atlanta," *Atlanta Constitution,* July 18, 1973, p. 3-B.

32. Hilberg, *Destruction of European Jews,* p. 658.

33. "Abortion: Questions and Answers."

34. "Birth Control," *Journal of the American Medical Association* 92 (January 26, 1929): 330.

35. Harold Rosen, "Psychiatric Implications of Abortion: A Case Study in Social Hypocrisy," *Western Reserve Law Review* 17 (1965): 435-464.

36. "Memorandum from the Labor Office, Katowice, to the RKFDV Branch Office, Katowice, 1 August 1944, Concerning Interruption of Pregnancy of Female Eastern Workers," *Trials of War Criminals Before the Nuernberg Military Tribunals,* 15 vols. (Washington D.C.: U.S. Government Printing Office, 1950), 4: 1084-1085.

37. Kerenyi, Mendelman and Sherman, "Five Thousand Consecutive Saline Inductions," pp. 593-600.

38. "Extracts from the Testimony of Defendant Brack," *The Medical Case: Trials of War Criminals Before the Nuernberg Military Tribunals,* 2 vols. (Washington D.C.: U.S. Government Printing Office, 1949), 1: 877-878.

39. Walter F. Char and John F. McDermott, "Abortions and Acute Identity Crisis in Nurses," *American Journal of Psychiatry* 128 (February 1972): 957.

40. Hilberg, *Destruction of European Jews,* p. 218.

41. Zigmond M. Lebensohn, "Abortion, Psychiatry, and the Quality of Life," *American Journal of Psychiatry* 128 (February 1972): 950.

42. "Extract from the Field Interrogation of Kurt Gerstein, 26 April 1945, Describing the Mass Gassing of Jews and Other Undesirables," *The Medical Case,* 1: 870.

43. Michael S. Burnhill, "Humane Abortion Services: A Revolution in Human Rights and the Delivery of a Medical Service," *Mount Sinai Journal of Medicine* 42 (September-October 1975): 438.

44. Hilberg, *Destruction of European Jews,* p. 648.

Chapter 11
The Medicalization of Annihilation

1. Howard Wolinsky, "War and Holocaust are Focus of His Work," *American Medical News,* June 13, 1980, p. 15; "Doctors of the Death Camps," *Time,* June 25, 1979, p. 68.

2. Ellen Sullivan, Christopher Tietze, and Joy G. Dryfoos, "Legal Abortion in the United States, 1975-1976," *Family Planning Perspectives* 9 (May/June 1977): 116.

3. Henry Friedlander, "The Manipulation of Language," in *The Holocaust: Ideology, Bureaucracy, and Genocide,* ed. Henry Friedlander and Sybil Milton (Milwood, New York: Kraus International Publications, 1980), pp. 109-110.

4. "Doctors of the Death Camps," p. 68.

5. Carl O. Rice, "Operation on Demand?" *Minnesota Medicine* 36 (May 1973): 412.

6. Bernd Naumann, *Auschwitz: A Report of the Proceedings Against Robert Karl Ludwig Mulka and Others Before the Court at Frankfurt,* trans. Jean Steinberg (New York: Frederick A. Praeger, 1966), p. 94.

7. Thomas D. Kerenyi and Usha Chitkara, "Selective Birth in Twin Pregnancy with Discordancy for Down's Syndrome," *New England Journal of Medicine* 304 (June 18, 1981): 1525-1527.

8. Speech by Himmler at *Gruppenfuhrer* meeting in Poznan, October 4, 1943, PS-1919.

9. Natalie Shainess, "Abortion Is No Man's Business," *Psychology Today,* May 1970, p. 20.

10. Philippe Aziz, *Doctors of Death,* trans. Edouard Bizub and Philip Haentzler, 4 vols. (Geneva, Switzerland: Ferni Publishers, 1976), 2: 114.

11. Shainess, "Abortion Is No Man's Business," p. 20.

12. *Krakauer Zeitung,* March 24, 1941, p. 5; April 23, 1941, p. 5, cited by Raul Hilberg, *The Destruction of the European Jews* (Chicago: Quadrangle Books, 1967), p. 151.

13. Summary of *Generalgouvernement* Health Conference, July 9, 1943, Frank

Diary, PS-2233.

14. *11 Million Teenagers: What Can Be Done About the Epidemic of Adolescent Pregnancies in the United States,* Booklet, New York: Planned Parenthood Federation of America, 1976.

15. Mary Meehan and Elizabeth Moore, "Forced Abortion Suggested at Clinic Owners' Conference," *National Right to Life News,* June 2, 1980, p. 13.

16. Aziz, *Doctors of Death,* 1: 46.

17. Robert E. Hall, ed., *Abortion in a Changing World,* 2 vols. (New York and London: Columbia University Press, 1970), 1: 46.

18. Richard A. Knox, "Holocaust—The Healer as Killer," *Los Angeles Times,* Part V, February 11, 1982, p. 23.

19. Mary S. Calderone, ed., *Abortion in the United States* (New York: Hoeber-Harper, 1958), p. 164.

20. "Doctors of the Death Camps," p. 68.

21. Hall, *Abortion in a Changing World,* p. 99.

22. "Circular, 5 April 1943, Containing the Decree of Reich Health Leader Dr. Conti, Concerning the Interruption of Pregnancy of Female Eastern Workers," *Trials of War Criminals Before the Nuernberg Military Tribunals,* 15 vols. (Washington D.C.: U.S. Government Printing Office, 1950), 4: 1094-1095.

23. Warren M. Hern, "Is Pregnancy Really Normal?" *Family Planning Perspectives* 3 (January 1971): 5-10.

24. Alice Platen-Hallermund, *The Killing of Mental Patients in Germany* (Frankfurt au Main: Verlag Der Frankfurter Hefte, 1948), pp. 46-47.

25. Ibid., pp. 49-50.

26. Planned Parenthood of New York City, *Abortion: A Woman's Guide* (New York: Abelard-Schuman, 1973), p. 26.

27. Alice Lake, "For Teenagers Only: Confidential Birth Control Clinics," *Good Housekeeping,* June 1976, p. 153.

28. Earl W. Kinter, ed., *The Hadamar Trial: Trial of Alfons Klein and Others* (London: William Hodge and Company, 1949), p. 176.

29. Willard Cates, David A. Grimes and Jack C. Smith, "Abortion as a Treatment for Unwanted Pregnancy: The Number Two Sexually Transmitted 'Disease,'" Paper presented at the 14th Annual Meeting of the Association of Planned Parenthood Physicians, Miami Beach, Florida, November 11, 1976, pp. 5-6.

30. Jack A. Pritchard and Paul C. MacDonald, *Williams Obstetrics,* 15th ed. (New York: Appleton-Century-Crofts, 1976), p. 842.

31. "Letter from Greiser to Himmler, 1 May 1942, Concerning the Plan for Mass Extermination of Tubercular Poles," and "Letter from Himmler (Signed by Rudolf Brandt) to Greiser, 27 June 1942, Concerning the Extermination of Tubercular Poles," *The Medical Case: Trials of War Criminals Before the Nuernberg Military Tribunals,* 2 vols. (Washington D.C.: U.S. Government Printing Office, 1949), 1: 770, 776.

32. Brief *Amici Curiae* of the American College of Obstetricians and Gynecologists, the American Medical Association, the American Academy of Pediatrics, and the Nurses Association of the American College of Obstetricians and Gynecologists in Support of Akron Center for Reproductive Health, Inc., et al., City of Akron v. Akron Center for Reproductive Health, Inc., et al., In the Supreme Court of the United States, October Term, 1982, pp. 2-3.

33. Ibid., p. 19.
34. Naumann, *Auschwitz,* p. 78.
35. Planned Parenthood of New York City, *Abortion: A Woman's Guide,* p. 58.
36. Leo Alexander, "Medical Science Under Dictatorship," *New England Journal of Medicine* 241 (July 14, 1949): 39-40.
37. Ibid., p. 40.
38. "IRS Grants 'Non-Profit' Status to Abortion Clinics," *National Right to Life News,* March 1979, p. 4A.
39. Hilberg, *Destruction of European Jews,* p. 189.
40. Fred M. Hechinger, "Educators Seek To Teach Context of the Holocaust," *New York Times,* May 15, 1979, p. C5.
41. Stanley K. Henshaw et al., "Abortion Services in the United States, 1979 and 1980," *Family Planning Perspectives* 14 (January/February 1982): 5-15.

Chapter 12
Subversion of Hippocrates and His Oath

1. Roberto Margotta, *An Illustrated History of Medicine* (Feltham, Middlesex, England: The Hamlyn Publishing Group, 1968), pp. 15-16.
2. Quoted in Maurice Levine, *Psychiatry and Ethics* (New York: George Braziller, 1972), pp. 324-325.
3. W.H.S. Jones, trans., *Hippocrates,* 4 vols. (Cambridge, Mass.: Harvard University Press, The Loeb Classical Library, 1923), 2: 127-183.
4. Arturo Castiglioni, *A History of Medicine,* trans. E.B. Krumbhaar, 2nd ed., rev. and enl. (New York: Alfred A. Knopf, 1958), p. 148.
5. Jones, *Hippocrates,* 1: 299-301.
6. Levine, *Psychiatry and Ethics,* p. 324.
7. Ibid., p. 325.
8. Ibid.
9. "Extracts from the Testimony of Prosecution Expert Witness Dr. Andrew C. Ivy," *The Medical Case: Trials of War Criminals Before the Nuernberg Military Tribunals,* 2 vols. (Washington D.C.: U.S. Government Printing Office, 1949), 2: 85-86.
10. Herbert Ratner, "The Hippocratic Oath," *Child and Family* 11, No. 2 (1972): 99.
11. Herbert Ratner, "The Oath—III. Why?" *Child and Family* 10, No. 2 (1971): 100.
12. Karl Binding and Alfred Hoche, *The Release of the Destruction of Life Devoid of Value* (Leipzig, Germany: Felix Meiner, 1920), compiled by Robert L. Sassone (Santa Ana, Calif.: A Life Quality Paperback, 1975), p. 30.
13. Henry V. Dicks, *Licensed Mass Murder: A Socio-Psychological Study of Some SS Killers* (New York: Basic Books, 1972), p. 146.
14. "Opening Statement of the Prosecution by Brigadier General Telford Taylor, 9 December 1946," *The Medical Case,* 1: 68.
15. "Extracts from the Testimony of Dr. Andrew Ivy," *The Medical Case,* 2: 86.
16. "Final Statement of Defendant Poppendick," *The Medical Case,* 2: 156.
17. Albert Deutsch, "A Note on Medical Ethics (Including the New Hippocratic Oath of the World Medical Association)," in Alexander Mitscherlich and Fred Mielke, *Doctors of Infamy: The Story of the Nazi Medical Crimes,* trans. Heinz Norden (New York: Henry Schuman, 1949), p. xxxviii.
18. Ibid., p. xxxvii.

19. Ibid., p. xxxviii.
20. Ibid., pp. xxxviii-xxxix.
21. Oral Arguments in the Supreme Court Abortion Decisions, Jane Roe, et al., v. Henry Wade, No. 70-18, October 11, 1972; also in Robert E. Ratermann, ed. *Oral Arguments in the Supreme Court Abortion Decisions* (St. Louis: Sanctity of Life Publications, 1976), pp. 56-57.
22. Bolivar M. Escobedo, "More on When Life Begins," *St. Louis Post-Dispatch,* January 17, 1979, p. 4C.
23. Thomas G. Gulick, "Even Abortionists Having Second Thoughts," *Human Events,* April 12, 1980, p. 18.
24. Roe v. Wade, 410 U.S. 131 (1973).
25. Ibid., p. 132.
26. Ibid., pp. 131-132.
27. Ludwig Edelstein, *The Hippocratic Oath: Text, Translation and Interpretation* (Baltimore: Johns Hopkins University Press, 1943).
28. Carolyn F. Gerster, "What Happened to Medical Ethics?" *National Right to Life New,* April 1979, p. 13.
29. Ibid.
30. Joseph T. Gill, "A Modest, But Powerful Protest," *The Wanderer,* July 8, 1982, p. 4.
31. Ibid.
32. "A Statement on Abortion by One Hundred Professors of Obstetrics," *American Journal of Obstetrics and Gynecology* 112 (April 1, 1972): 992-998.
33. Herbert Ratner, "Editor's Comments," *Child and Family* 12, No. 3 (1973): 286.

Chapter 13
The Media as Agents of Destructive Propaganda

1. Oron J. Hale, *The Captive Press in the Third Reich* (Princeton, New Jersey: Princeton University Press, 1973), pp. 1-14.
2. George L. Mosse, ed., *Nazi Culture: Intellectual, Cultural and Social Life in the Third Reich,* trans. Salvator Attanasio et al. (New York: Grosset & Dunlap, 1968).
3. Bernard N. Nathanson, "Aborting America," Keynote Address, National Right to Life Convention '80, Anaheim, California, June 26, 1980.
4. Bernard N. Nathanson, Featured Address, Missouri Citizens for Life Convention '81, Columbia, Missouri, May 2, 1981.
5. S. Robert Lichter and Stanley Rothman, "Media and Business Elites," *Public Opinion,* October/November 1981, pp. 42-46, 59-60.
6. Cited by George L. Mosse, *Toward the Final Solution: A History of European Racism* (New York: Howard Fertig, 1978), p. 165.
7. "Instructions by Reich Press Chief, April 29, 1943," NG-4705.
8. *Donauzeitung* (Belgrade), July 3, 1943, p. 3, cited by Raul Hilberg, *The Destruction of the European Jews* (Chicago: Quadrangle Books, 1967), p. 471.
9. Irving Louis Horowitz, "Book Review of *Judenrat: The Jewish Councils in Eastern Europe Under Nazi Occupation,*" *Commonweal,* April 13, 1973, p. 139.
10. "The Battle Over Abortion," *Time,* April 6, 1981, p. 23.
11. Bernard Weinraub, "Senator Agrees to Extend Hearings on Abortion Bill," *New York Times,* April 25, 1981, p. 7.
12. Donald Kenrick and Grattan Puxon, *The Destiny of Europe's Gypsies* (New York: Basic Books, 1972), p. 140.
13. *Confluence,* January 25, 1981.

14. *Pariser Zeitung,* December 23, 1942, p. 353.

15. Paul Berg, "Battle Lines in a Moral and Legal Dispute," *Sunday Pictures—St. Louis Post-Dispatch,* May 20, 1973, pp. 1-15.

16. Leon Poliakov, *Harvest of Hate: The Nazi Program for the Destruction of the Jews of Europe,* rev. and exp. ed. (New York: Schocken Books, 1979), p. 175.

17. Helen Dudar, "Abortion for the Asking," *Saturday Review: The Society*, April 1973, p. 31.

18. Hilberg, *Destruction of European Jews,* p. 16.

19. Ibid., p. 203.

20. Robert Levey, "The Code Words in the Battle over Abortion, *Boston Globe,* November 21, 1980, p. 3.

21. Francis Baudry and Alfred Wiener, "The Pregnant Patient in Conflict About Abortion: A Challenge for the Obstetrician," *American Journal of Obstetrics and Gynecology* 119 (July 1, 1974): 710.

22. "Plan East," prepared for the SS Reichsfuhrer by Professor Wetzel, Berlin, April 27, 1942, NG-2325.

23. "Those Missing Babies," *Time,* September 16, 1974, pp. 56, 61.

24. Willard Cates, et al., "Legal Abortion Mortality in the United States: Epidemiologic Surveillance, 1972-1974," *Journal of the American Medical Association* 237 (January 31, 1977): 452-455.

25. Patrick A. Malone, "Defects and Death Possible for Young Mothers, Babies," *St. Louis Post-Dispatch,* June 27, 1975, p. 5H.

26. Stanley Henshaw et al., "Abortion in the United States, 1978-1979," *Family Planning Perspectives* 13 (January/February 1981): 13.

27. Ardis Hyland Danon, "Organizing an Abortion Service," *Nursing Outlook* 21 (July 1973): 460.

28. "AMA Policy on Therapeutic Abortion," *Journal of the American Medical Association* 201 (August 14, 1967): 544.

29. Cited by Walter Laqueur, *The Terrible Secret: Suppression of the Truth About Hitler's 'Final Solution'* (Boston: Little, Brown, 1980), pp. 217-218.

30. Colin Turnbull, "The Barbarism of Execution," *St. Louis Post-Dispatch,* May 2, 1978, p. 2C.

31. "The Killings at Song My," *Newsweek*, December 8, 1969, pp. 33-41.

32. William Claiborne, "Protest to Halt Killing of Seals," *Washington Post,* March 22, 1976, pp. A1, A6.

33. Ronald Yates, "Dolphin Slaughter Turns Sea Red," *Chicago Tribune,* March 16, 1980, pp. 1, 8.

34. Erik Eckholm, "The Importance of Snail Darters," *St. Louis Post-Dispatch,* August 14, 1978, p. 2C.

35. "Abortion Error," *New York Times,* February 19, 1975, p. 34.

36. "Bird Massacre," *New York Times,* February 19, 1975, p. 34.

37. Alan F. Guttmacher, "Why I Favor Liberalized Abortion," *Reader's Digest,* November 1973, p. 143.

38. "Freedom of Choice," *Washington Post,* July 2, 1980, p. A22.

39. "Abortion: Women Speak Out, An Exclusive Poll," *Life,* November 1981, pp. 45-54.

40. Laqueur, *The Terrible Secret,* pp. 3, 106.

41. "1,000,000 Jews Slain by Nazis, Report Says," *New York Times,* June 30, 1942, p. 14.

42. Laqueur, *The Terrible Secret,* pp. 74-75.

43. "500 Fetuses Found By Storage Company in Repossessed Crate," *New York Times*, February 8, 1982, p. A14.
44. Laqueur, *The Terrible Secret*, p. 3.
45. Gloria Steinem, "Feminist Notes: The Nazi Connection," *Ms*, October 1980, p. 88.
46. Laqueur, *The Terrible Secret*, pp. 79-80.
47. Ibid., pp. 8-9.
48. Magda Denes, *In Necessity and Sorrow: Life and Death in an Abortion Hospital* (New York: Basic Books, 1976).
49. Norman E. Zinberg, "Review of *In Necessity and Sorrow*," *New York Times Book Review*, January 9, 1977, pp. 12-13.
50. Arthur R. Butz, *The Hoax of the Twentieth Century* (Torrance, Calif.: Institute for Historical Review, 1976), p. 249.
51. Ibid., pp. 100-132.

Chapter 14
Media Responses to Pictures of the Victims

1. "Order by Otto Wöhler, July 22, 1941," NOKW-2523.
2. Mary Dunn, "500 Fetal Bodies Found," *National Catholic Register*, February 21, 1982, p. 1.
3. "Order by Wöhler."
4. Nicholas von Hoffman, "Abortion Fight Still Is Raging," *Chicago Tribune*, June 21, 1977, section 1, p. 10.
5. Lucy Dawidowicz, "Lies About the Holocaust," *Commentary*, December 1980, p. 35.
6. Louise Farr, "I Was a Spy at a Right-to-Life Convention," *Ms*, February 1976, p. 78.
7. "The American Holocaust," Brochure, Center for the Documentation of the American Holocaust, Palm Springs, California, 1982.
8. "Photo Shows War Is Terrible," *St. Louis Post-Dispatch*, May 8, 1973, p. 1C.
9. "Casualties in Principal Wars of the U.S.," *The World Almanac Book of Facts and Figures* (New York: Newspaper Enterprise Association, 1981), p. 335.
10. Stanley K. Henshaw et al., "Abortion Services in the United States, 1979 and 1980," *Family Planning Perspectives* 14 (January/February 1982): 5-15.
11. "The American Holocaust," Brochure.
12. Dr. and Mrs. J.C. Willke, *Handbook on Abortion*, rev. ed. (Cincinnati, Ohio: Hayes Publishing Company, 1975), p. 34.
13. Correspondence with Dr. Anne Bannon, Chairman of Missouri Doctors for Life, St. Louis, Missouri, December 20, 1982.
14. "Order by Wöhler."
15. Correspondence with Dr. Anne Bannon.

Chapter 15
Counteracting the Repetition of Historical Atrocities

1. Lucy Dawidowicz, *The War Against the Jews, 1933-1945* (New York: Holt, Rinehart and Winston, 1975), p. 58.
2. Erich Fromm, *The Anatomy of Human Destructiveness* (New York: Holt, Rinehart and Winston, 1973), p. 348.

3. "Technological Advances to Make Pro-abortion Position Tougher, Planned Parenthood Official Tells National Abortion Federation," *National Right to Life News,* October 14, 1982, p. 8.

4. Leo Alexander, "Medical Science Under Dictatorship," *New England Journal of Medicine* 241 (July 14, 1949): 46.

5. Brief *Amici Curiae* of the American College of Obstetricians and Gynecologists, the American Medical Association, the American Academy of Pediatrics, and the Nurses Association of the American College of Obstetricians and Gynecologists in Support of Akron Center for Reproductive Health, Inc., et al., City of Akron v. Arkon Center for Reproductive Health, Inc., et al., In the Supreme Court of the United States, October Term, 1982, pp. 1-30.

6. Akron, Ohio, *Codified Ordinances,* Chapter 1870.06 (B5), "Informed Consent," 1978, p. 4.

7. Brief *Amici Curiae,* pp. 10-11.

8. Jeffrey M. Barrett, Frank H. Boehm, and Allen P. Killam, "Induced Abortion: A Risk Factor for Placenta Previa, *American Journal of Obstetrics and Gynecology* 141 (December 1, 1981): 769-772.

9. I. Kent et al., "Emotional Sequelae of Therapeutic Abortion: A Comparative Study," *British Columbia Medical Journal* 20 (1978): 118-119.

10. Myre Sim and Robert Neisser, "Post-Abortive Psychoses: A Report from Two Centers," in *The Psychological Aspects of Abortion,* ed. David Mall and Walter F. Watts (Washington D.C.: University Publications of America, 1979), pp. 1-13.

11. Akron, Ohio, *Codified Ordinances,* Chapter 1870.06 (B3), "Informed Consent," p. 4.

12. Brief *Amici Curiae,* p. 12.

13. H.M.I. Liley with Beth Day, *Modern Motherhood: Pregnancy, Childbirth and the Newborn Baby,* rev. ed. (New York: Random House, 1969), p. 50.

14. H.B. Valman and J.F. Pearson, "What the Fetus Feels," *British Medical Journal* 280 (January 26, 1980): 233-234.

15. Thomas Verney, *The Secret Life of the Unborn Child* (New York: Summit Books, 1981), pp. 39, 84.

16. "Viewing Life Before Birth," *Time,* March 14, 1977, p. 60.

17. "Statement by Andrew C. Ivy," in Alexander Mitscherlich and Fred Mielke, *Doctors of Infamy: The Story of the Nazi Medical Crimes,* trans. Heinz Norden (New York: Henry Schuman, 1949), p. xi.

18. "Lethal Injections at Execution Not Role for Doctor, AMA Says," *St. Louis Review,* August 1, 1980, p. 1.

19. "AMA Revises Its Code, Allowing Doctors' Ads," *St. Louis Post-Dispatch,* July 23, 1980, p. 6A.

20. William J. Curran and Ward Casscells, "The Ethics of Medical Participation in Capital Punishment by Intravenous Drug Injection," *New England Journal of Medicine* 302 (January 24, 1980): 230.

21. Ibid., p. 227.

22. James C. Mohr, *Abortion in America: The Origins and Evolution of National Policy, 1800-1900* (New York: Oxford University Press, 1978), p. 200.

23. Horatio R. Storer et al., "Report on Criminal Abortion," *Transactions of the American Medical Association* 12 (1859): 75-78; D.A. O'Donnell and W.L. Atlee, "Report on Criminal Abortion," *Transactions of the American Medical Association* 22 (1871): 239-258.

24. In 1847 the distinguished histologist Dr. Albert von Kolliker "first demonstrated the true development of the spermatozoa, showing that they are not extraneous

bodies, but originate in the testicular cells and fertilize the ovum.'' Fielding H. Garrison, *An Introduction to the History of Medicine,* 4th ed., reprint (Philadelphia and London: W.B. Saunders, 1929), p. 461.

25. Ellen Sullivan, Christopher Tietze, and Joy F. Dryfoos, ''Legal Abortion in the United States, 1975-1976,'' *Family Planning Perspectives* 9 (May/June 1977): 116.

26. ''Therapeutic Abortion,'' *Proceedings of the American Medical Association House of Delegates* (June 1967): 40-51; ''Therapeutic Abortion,'' *Proceedings of the American Medical Association House of Delegates* (June 1970): 221.

27. ''Dutch Physicians' Protest Against Nazi Regulations,'' *Child and Family,* vol. 11, no. 2 (1972): 171-172.

28. Herbert Ratner, ''Editor's Comment,'' *Child and Family,* vol. 11, no. 2 (1972): 172.

29. ''Declaration of the World Federation,'' *Primum Non Nocere: Newsletter of the World Federation of Doctors Who Respect Human Life,* American Section, September 1980, pp. 3-4.

30. Doctors for Life, Charter Membership Brochure, St. Louis, Missouri.

31. Franklin H. Littell, ''Church Struggle and the Holocaust,'' in *The German Church Struggle and the Holocaust,* ed. Franklin H. Littell and Hubert G. Locke (Detroit: Wayne State University Press, 1974), p. 20.

32. Fredric Wertham, *A Sign for Cain: An Exploration of Human Violence* (New York: Warner Books, 1969), p. 158.

33. O'Donnell and Atlee, ''Report on Criminal Abortion,'' pp. 257-258.

34. Simon Wiesenthal Center for Holocaust Studies, Associate Membership Letter, Los Angeles, California, n.d.

35. Ellen Futterman, '''Holy War' Over Abortion,'' *St. Louis Post-Dispatch,* September 12, 1982, p. 3F.

36. Henry Friedlander, ''The Manipulation of Language,'' in *The Holocaust: Ideology, Bureaucracy, and Genocide,* ed. Henry Friedlander and Sybil Milton (Millwood, New York: Kraus International Publications, 1980), p. 103.

INDEX